# THE UNFOLDING MYSTERY OF THE DIVINE NAME

*The God of Sinai in Our Midst*

MICHAEL P. KNOWLES

IVP Academic
An imprint of InterVarsity Press
Downers Grove, Illinois

*InterVarsity Press*
*P.O. Box 1400, Downers Grove, IL 60515-1426*
*World Wide Web: www.ivpress.com*
*E-mail: email@ivpress.com*



*InterVarsity Press® is the book-publishing division of InterVarsity Christian Fellowship/USA®, a movement of students and faculty active on campus at hundreds of universities, colleges and schools of nursing in the United States of America, and a member movement of the International Fellowship of Evangelical Students. For information about local and regional activities, write Public Relations Dept., InterVarsity Christian Fellowship/USA, 6400 Schroeder Rd., P.O. Box 7895, Madison, WI 53707-7895, or visit the IVCF website at <www.intervarsity.org>.*



*Cover design: Cindy Kiple*
*Interior design: Beth Hagenberg*
*Images: ©Antagain/iStockphoto*

*ISBN 978-0-8308-3985-8*

*Printed in the United States of America* ∞

green press INITIATIVE *InterVarsity Press is committed to protecting the environment and to the responsible use of natural resources. As a member of Green Press Initiative we use recycled paper whenever possible. To learn more about the Green Press Initiative, visit <www.greenpressinitiative.org>.*

**Library of Congress Cataloging-in-Publication Data**

*Knowles, Michael (Michael P.)*
*The unfolding mystery of the divine name : the God of Sinai in our midst /Michael P. Knowles.*
*p. cm.*
*Includes bibliographical references and index.*
*ISBN 978-0-8308-3985-8 (pbk. : alk. paper)*
*1. Bible. O.T. Exodus XXXIV, 5-9—Criticism, interpretation, etc. 2 God (Christianity)—Name—Biblical teaching. I. Title.*
*BS1245.52.K56 2012*
*231—dc23*

*2012027675*

| | | | | | | | | | | | | | | | | | | | | |
|---|---|---|---|---|---|---|---|---|---|---|---|---|---|---|---|---|---|---|---|---|
| **P** | 20 | 19 | 18 | 17 | 16 | 15 | 14 | 13 | 12 | 11 | 10 | 9 | 8 | 7 | 6 | 5 | 4 | 3 | 2 | 1 |
| **Y** | 29 | 28 | 27 | 26 | 25 | 24 | 23 | 22 | 21 | 20 | 19 | 18 | 17 | 16 | 15 | 14 | 13 | 12 | | |

# Contents

# Texts and Translations

Unless otherwise indicated, biblical texts in English are either cited from or based on the New Revised Standard Version (© 1989, by the Division of Christian Education of the National Council of the Churches of Christ in the United States of America). Hebrew and Greek texts are cited from *Biblia Hebraica Stuttgartensia*, edited by Karl Elliger et al., 5th corrected edition, edited by Adrian Schenker (Stuttgart: Deutsche Bibelgesellschaft, 1997); *Septuaginta*, edited by Alfred Rahlfs (Stuttgart: Württembergische Bibelanstalt; Deutsche Bibelgesellschaft, 1935); and *The Greek New Testament*, edited by Kurt Aland et al., 4th revised edition (Stuttgart: Deutsche Bibelgesellschaft, 1994), all accessed via Gramcord for Windows 2.3 (Vancouver, WA: Gramcord Institute, 1998) and its various program components. Unless otherwise indicated, the Babylonian Talmud is cited from *The Babylonian Talmud; Translated into English with Notes, Glossary and Indices*, edited by I. Epstein (18 vols.; London: Soncino, 1935-1952), the Palestinian or Jerusalem Talmud from *The Talmud of the Land of Israel: A Preliminary Translation and Explanation*, translated by Jacob Neusner et al. (35 vols.; Chicago: University of Chicago Press, 1982-1993).

# ABBREVIATIONS

**General**

| | |
|---|---|
| // | parallel text(s) |
| BCE | Before the Common Era |
| ca. | circa |
| CE | Common Era |
| cf. | *confer*, compare |
| d. | died |
| ed. | edition |
| ed(s). | editor(s), edited by |
| e.g. | *exempli gratia*, for example |
| esp. | especially |
| Gk. | Greek |
| i.e. | *id est*, that is |
| lit. | literally |
| mg. | margin |
| n(n.) | note(s) |
| par. | parallel passage(s) |
| pl. | plural |
| p(p). | page(s) |
| repr. | reprint |
| rev. | revised |
| trans. | translator, translated by |
| vol(s.) | volume(s) |

**Ancient Texts, Text Types and Versions**

| | |
|---|---|
| LXX | Septuagint |
| MT | Masoretic Text |
| Tg. | Targum |

**Translations of the Bible**

| | |
|---|---|
| JB | Jerusalem Bible |
| KJV | King James Version |
| NASB | New American Standard Bible |
| NEB | New English Bible |
| NIV | New International Version |
| NJB | New Jerusalem Bible |

| | |
|---|---|
| NJPS | *Tanakh: The Holy Scriptures; The New JPS Translation According to the Traditional Hebrew Text* |
| NRSV | New Revised Standard Version |
| RSV | Revised Standard Version |
| TNIV | Today's New International Version |

**Apocrypha and Septuagint**

| | |
|---|---|
| 1–2 Esd | 1–2 Esdras |
| 1–4 Macc | 1–4 Maccabees |
| Pr Man | Prayer of Manasseh |
| Sir | Sirach |
| Tob | Tobit |

**Old Testament Pseudepigrapha**

| | |
|---|---|
| *2 Bar.* | *2 Baruch (Syriac Apocalypse)* |
| *1 En.* | *1 Enoch (Ethiopic Apocalypse)* |
| *4 Ezra* | *4 Ezra* |
| *Gk. Apoc. Ezra* | *Greek Apocalypse of Ezra* |
| *Jos. Asen.* | *Joseph and Aseneth* |
| *Jub.* | *Jubilees* |
| *L.A.B.* | *Liber antiquitatum biblicarum* (Pseudo-Philo) |
| *Let. Arist.* | *Letter of Aristeas* |
| *Pss. Sol.* | *Psalms of Solomon* |
| *T. Zeb.* | *Testament of Zebulon* |

**Dead Sea Scrolls**

| | |
|---|---|
| CD | *Damascus Document* |
| 1QH[a] | *1QHodayot[a]* |
| 1QS | *1QRule of the Community* |
| 1Q28b (1QSb) | *1QRule of Benedictions* |
| 11Q10 (11QtgJob) | *11QTargum of Job* |
| Targumic Texts | |
| Tg. Neof. | Targum Neofiti |
| Tg. Onq. | Targum Onqelos |
| Tg. Ps.-J. | Targum Pseudo-Jonathan |

**Tractates in the Mishnah, Tosefta, and Talmud**

| | |
|---|---|
| *m.* | Mishnah |
| *t.* | Tosefta |
| *b.* | Babylonian Talmud |

| | |
|---|---|
| *y.* | Jerusalem Talmud |
| *ʾAbot* | *ʾAbot* |
| *B. Meṣiʿa* | *Ḃ Meṣiʿa* |
| *B. Qam.* | *Baba Qamma* |
| *Ber.* | *Berakot* |
| *ʿErub.* | *ʿErubin* |
| *Giṭ.* | *Giṭṭin* |
| *Ketub.* | *Ketubbot* |
| *Meg.* | *Megillah* |
| *Peʾah* | *Peʾah* |
| *Pesaḥ.* | *Pesaḥim* |
| *Qidd.* | *Qiddušin* |
| *Roš. Haš.* | *Roš Haššanah* |
| *Sanh.* | *Sanhedrin* |
| *Šabb.* | *Šabbat* |
| *Šebu.* | *Šebuʿot* |
| *Soṭah* | *Soṭah* |
| *Taʿan.* | *Taʿanit* |
| *Tamid* | *Tamid* |
| *Yoma* | *Yoma* |

**Other Rabbinic Works**

| | |
|---|---|
| *ʾAbot R. Nat.* | *ʾAbot de Rabbi Nathan* |
| *Mek.* | *Mekilta* |
| *Midr.* | *Midrash* |
| *Pesiq. Rab.* | *Pesiqta Rabbati* |
| *Pirqe R. El.* | *Pirqe Rabbi Eliezer* |
| *Rab.* | (biblical book +) *Rabbah* |
| *S. Eli. Rab.* | *Seder Eliyahu Rabbah* |
| *S. Eli. Zut.* | *Seder Eliyahu Zuta* |
| *Sipra* | *Sipra* |
| *Sipre* | *Sipre* |
| *Tanḥ.* | *Tanḥuma* |

**Apostolic Fathers**

| | |
|---|---|
| *1–2 Clem.* | *1–2 Clement* |

**Greek and Latin Works**

Athanasius

| | |
|---|---|
| *Inc.* | *De incarnatione (On the Incarnation)* |

Augustine

| | |
|---|---|
| *Enchir.* | *Enchiridion de fide, spe, et carite (Enchiridion on Faith, Hope, and Love)* |
| *Faust.* | *Contra Faustum Manichaeum (Reply to Faustus the Manichean)* |
| *Grat. Chr.* | *De gratia Christi, et de peccato originali (The Grace of Christ and Original Sin)* |
| *Trin.* | *De Trinitate (The Trinity)* |

Cyprian

| | |
|---|---|
| *Epist.* | *Epistulae (Epistles)* |

Irenaeus

| | |
|---|---|
| *Haer.* | *Adversus haereses (Against Heresies)* |

John Chrysostom

| | |
|---|---|
| *Hom. Phil.* | *Homiliae in epistulam ad Philippenses (Homilies on the Epistle to the Philippians)* |
| *Fr. Ep. Cath.* | *Fragmenta in Epistolas Catholicas* |

Josephus

| | |
|---|---|
| *Ant.* | *Antiquitates judaicae (Jewish Antiquities)* |

Origen

| | |
|---|---|
| *Hom. Ezech.* | *Homiliae in Ezechielem (Sermons on Ezekiel)* |

Tertullian

| | |
|---|---|
| *Pat.* | *De patientia (On Patience)* |

**Periodicals, Reference Works, and Serials**

| | |
|---|---|
| AB | Anchor Bible |
| *ABD* | *Anchor Bible Dictionary*, ed. D. N. Freedman (6 vols.; New York: Doubleday, 1992) |
| ACCS | Ancient Christian Commentary on Scripture |
| ACW | Ancient Christian Writers |
| AGJU | Arbeiten zur Geschichte des antiken Judentums und des Urchristentums |
| AnBib | Analecta biblica |
| *ANF* | *Ante-Nicene Fathers: The Writings of the Fathers Down to A.D. 325*, ed. A. Robertson and J. Donaldson (10 vols.; repr., Grand Rapids: Eerdmans, 1956) |
| ArBib | The Aramaic Bible |
| BJS | Brown Judaic Studies |
| BNTC | Black's New Testament Commentaries |
| BZAW | Beihefte zur Zeitschrift für die alttestamentliche Wissenschaft |
| CBC | Cambridge Bible Commentary |

| | |
|---|---|
| *EncJud* | *Encyclopedia Judaica* (16 vols.; Jerusalem: Encyclopedia Judaica, 1972) |
| FC | Fathers of the Church |
| HSM | Harvard Semitic Monographs |
| IBC | Interpretation: A Bible Commentary for Teaching and Preaching |
| *IDBSup* | *Interpreter's Dictionary of the Bible: Supplementary Volume*, ed. K. Crim (Nashville: Abingdon, 1976) |
| *JBL* | *Journal of Biblical Literature* |
| JPSTC | JPS Torah Commentary |
| JSOTSup | Journal for the Study of the New Testament: Supplement Series |
| NCB | New Century Bible |
| NICOT | New International Commentary on the Old Testament |
| *NIDOTTE* | *New International Dictionary of Old Testament Theology and Exegesis*, ed. W. A. VanGemeren (5 vols.; Grand Rapids: Zondervan, 1997) |
| NovTSup | Novum Testamentum Supplements |
| *NPNF*[1] | *Nicene and Post-Nicene Fathers of the Christian Church*, Series 1 |
| *NPNF*[2] | *Nicene and Post-Nicene Fathers of the Christian Church*, Series 2 |
| NTL | New Testament Library |
| OTL | Old Testament Library |
| *OTP* | *Old Testament Pseudepigrapha*, ed. J. H. Charlesworth (2 vols.; New York: Doubleday, 1983-1985) |
| PG | Patrologia graeca [= Patrologiae cursus completus: Series graeca], ed J.-P. Migne (162 vols.; Paris: Migne, 1857-1886) |
| PNTC | Pelican New Testament Commentaries |
| SB | Sources bibliques |
| SBL | Studies in Biblical Literature |
| SBLEJL | Society of Biblical Literature Early Judaism and Its Literature |
| SJ | Studia judaica |
| SNTSMS | Society for New Testament Studies Monograph Series |
| StP | Studia Pohl |
| TBN | Themes in Biblical Narrative |
| *TDNT* | *Theological Dictionary of the New Testament*, ed. G. Kittel and G. Friedrich, trans. G. W. Bromiley (10 vols.; Grand Rapids: Eerdmans, 1964-1976) |
| WBC | Word Biblical Commentary |
| WS | World Spirituality |
| YJS | Yale Judaica Series |

# Preface

This series of studies on the "name" and character of God has developed slowly over several years, and in a number of different forms. I first encountered the question of the divine name as I wrestled more than thirty years ago—in the course of a first degree in theology—with the meaning of chapters 9 through 11 of Paul's letter to the Romans. What caught my attention in particular was Paul's quotation in Romans 9:15 of God's words to Moses in Exodus 33:19 (often cited to buttress a particular theology of predestination): "I will have mercy on whom I have mercy, and I will have compassion on whom I have compassion" (see, e.g., Augustine, *Enchir.* 98-99; *Grat. Chr.* 1.51). Since then I have preached numerous times on the call and ministry of Moses, and the question of God's "name" has never been far from my thoughts. In August of 1997 I had an opportunity to consolidate some of these reflections in the form of an address to Caribbean and North American InterVarsity Christian Fellowship leaders who were meeting at Ontario Pioneer Camp. In August of the following year I was invited to return to Ontario Pioneer as the speaker at a week-long Family Camp, and I decided to expand the same material into five addresses, each an hour in length. Notwithstanding considerable delay and considerable expansion, these five addresses provided the initial basis for the chapters that follow. These chapters in turn furnished material for graduate-level courses outlining a biblical theology of God that I have taught at McMaster Divinity College since 2005; my deliberations have been further enriched by discussions arising within that context.

I am indebted to McMaster Divinity College for having provided thoughtful and thorough student research assistants in Michael Ford (who compiled masses of background material), Luz Iglesias (who read the entire text and offered many probing comments), and Matt Lowe (who helped prepare an initial draft of the indexes). Their contributions have proven invaluable. While the customary authorial assumption of responsibility for errors applies in this case also, I wish to thank John Bowen and Kurt Richardson for providing helpful comments and corrections to early versions of particular sections or chapters. My colleague Mark Boda read a much earlier draft of the study, and on that basis he commended me to IVP Academic. Eleanor Filyer (now Emmott) was kind enough to read the entire typescript, providing valuable suggestions for improvement, while Ronit Kaufman found a number of errors that had evaded many previous readings. Suk Mun Lum (who also worked her way through a complete first draft) asked difficult questions and challenged me to consider a wider range of audiences. Father David Burrell offered encouragement and helpful advice regarding my use of Islamic materials, as did Daniel Brown of Walden, Massachusetts. I am also deeply grateful for the prayers and encouragement offered at various times and in various ways by Janet Clark, Robin Ellis, Craig Evans, Sylvia Keesmaat, Ken Morgan, Christine Shalaby and Kent Sparks. A number of colleagues and students brought particular texts to my attention, and I have endeavored to acknowledge their contributions wherever possible. The resulting text provides wonderful proof that the best learning takes place in community.

Even after all the colleagues and friends mentioned above had contributed to the shaping of this study, it would never have seen the light of day had it not been for IVP Academic senior editor Dan Reid and his staff, whose assistance and encouragement I am grateful to acknowledge.

A study guide for this book may be found at the IVP Academic website page for *The Unfolding Mystery of the Divine Name* (www.ivpress.com). It includes suggestions for individual or corporate prayer, questions for group discussion, guidelines for meditation, thought-provoking quotations from saints and mystics of generations past, and practical proposals for imitating the ways of God.

# Introduction

## How Many Names Does God Have?

### Exodus 34:5-9

*5 The Lord descended in the cloud and stood with him there, and proclaimed the name, "The Lord."*

| | |
|---|---|
| *6 And the Lord passed before him and proclaimed,* | וַיַּעֲבֹר יְהוָה עַל־פָּנָיו וַיִּקְרָא |
| *"The Lord, the Lord, a God compassionate and gracious,* | יְהוָה יְהוָה אֵל רַחוּם וְחַנּוּן |
| *slow to anger, and abounding in steadfast love and faithfulness,* | אֶרֶךְ אַפַּיִם וְרַב־חֶסֶד וֶאֱמֶת |
| *7 keeping steadfast love for thousands,* | נֹצֵר חֶסֶד לָאֲלָפִים |
| *forgiving iniquity and transgression and sin,* | נֹשֵׂא עָוֺן וָפֶשַׁע וְחַטָּאָה |
| *but who will by no means clear the guilty,* | וְנַקֵּה לֹא יְנַקֶּה |
| *visiting the iniquity of the parents* | פֹּקֵד עֲוֺן אָבוֹת |
| *upon the children and the children's children,* | עַל־בָּנִים וְעַל־בְּנֵי בָנִים |
| *to the third and the fourth generation."* | עַל־שִׁלֵּשִׁים וְעַל־רִבֵּעִים |

*8 And Moses quickly bowed his head toward the earth, and worshiped.*

*9 He said, "If now I have found favor in your sight, O Lord, I pray, let the Lord go with us.*

*Although this is a stiff-necked people, pardon our iniquity and our sin, and take us for your inheritance."*

I remember reading, as a teenager, a short story by science fiction writer Arthur C. Clarke entitled "The Nine Billion Names of God."[1] In this story a group of Buddhist monks believes that history will come to an end when they have recited every divine name possible, some nine billion in total. They realize, of course, that such a project would require an inordinately long time to accomplish. So after arranging for such essential details as the provision of electricity at their remote monastery, they delegate this responsibility to a group of computer consultants who come up with the necessary software and hardware to carry out the task (a complex endeavor considering the state of computer technology in 1953, when the story was first published). The program is entered and executed. Then, as consultants and monks alike look up into the night sky, the stars begin blinking out one by one.

I even recall that the introduction to the particular edition in which I first read this story included a brief reflection on the plausibility of the task, presumably hinging on the question of whether human beings have it in their power to conclude history. Now, years later, the story raises for me a different question: that of the true name, or names, of God. For there to be nine billion in all would surely encompass every religious thought and tradition that human history has ever known. To make up such a total, our notion of God would need to include everything that we have ever imagined God to be, and then some. It is, indeed, the kind of radical inclusiveness that only Buddhism could accommodate. Viewed from a slightly different perspective, however, both the comprehensiveness and therefore the virtual incomprehensibility of God having nine billion names pose the question of how much we can actually know, or know about, God.

Islamic tradition, while acknowledging that the full range of divine attributes ultimately exceeds this number, identifies "Ninety-Nine Beautiful Names" or "Attributes of Perfection." This list, said to have been drawn up by Muhammad but conveyed by his companion Abu

[1]Arthur C. Clarke, "The Nine Billion Names of God," *Star Science Fiction Stories No. 1*, ed. Frederik Pohl (New York: Ballantine, 1953), 188-95; reprinted in Arthur C. Clarke, *The Nine Billion Names of God: The Best Short Stories of Arthur C. Clarke* (New York: Harcourt Brace Jovanovich, 1967), 3-11; also *The Collected Stories of Arthur C. Clarke* (New York: Tom Doherty Associates, 2000), 417-22.

Hurayrah (603-681 CE), provides a rich resource for prayer and meditation among pious Muslims. In particular, Muslims meditate on the divine attributes using the string of ninety-nine beads known as the *subha* or *tasbih*, thus recalling that God is, for example, "All-Merciful" and "All-Compassionate"; the "All-Holy" and "Source of Peace"; "Ever-Providing," "All-Hearing," and "All-Seeing"; "Just" and "Forgiving."[2] Devotional recitation of the divine names is particularly significant within Sufism, the Islamic mystical tradition.[3] Indeed, an influential treatise by the medieval Sufi theologian Abu Ḥamid al-Ghazālī (1058-1111 CE) not only expounds the significance of each attribute, but also adds instructions that will enable the devout to conduct themselves in a like manner.[4] For whoever faithfully enumerates these names, it is said, will enter paradise.[5] In fact, there is little in this list that could not be affirmed by adherents of all three monotheistic faiths: Judaism, Christianity, and Islam.[6]

Although metaphors and images for God abound in Scripture, there is no similarly definitive list of names or attributes to command universal assent within either Judaism or Christianity. Exodus 34:6-7, however, describes a series of names, or characteristics, of God; these are known in Jewish tradition as the "thirteen attributes [*middot*; lit., 'measures'] of love."[7] Indeed, so foundational has this passage proven for Judaism's understanding of God that it is widely echoed throughout the remainder of the Hebrew Scriptures and has been profoundly influential in shaping Jewish devotional tradition. The same characteristics

---

[2]For a brief introduction (by a Christian author) to the ninety-nine names, see Kenneth Cragg, *The Call of the Minaret* (New York: Oxford University Press, 1956), 40-44; a broader explanation of the Islamic concept of God is offered by S. H. Nasr, "God," in *Islamic Spirituality: Foundations*, ed. S. H. Nasr (WS 19; New York: Crossroad, 1997), 311-23.

[3]"Sufis incorporated the litany of divine names into their regular *dhikrs*, or group 'séances,' and mystics eagerly sought out the unique 'true' name of God, assumed to be one among the canonical ninety-nine, that would reveal his inner being" (F. E. Peters, *Islam: A Guide for Jews and Christians* [Princeton, NJ: Princeton University Press, 2003], 3).

[4]See David B. Burrell and Nazih Daher, trans., *The Ninety-Nine Beautiful Names of God: al-Maqṣad al-asnā fi s_harh asmā' Allāh al-ḥusnā* (Cambridge: Islamic Texts Society, 1995).

[5]Ibid., 21-22, 49.

[6]See David B. Burrell, "Naming the Names of God: Muslims, Jews, Christians," *Theology Today* 47 (1990): 22-29.

[7]These are not to be confused with the thirteen exegetical middot, or rules for interpreting Scripture, attributed to Rabbi Ishmael b. Elisha (ca. 90-130 CE), on which, see *EncJud* 8:366-72.

are likewise reflected in the New Testament, due no doubt to the fact that the earliest followers of Jesus, who saw in him the fullest expression of God's character, had been deeply influenced and formed by the devotional traditions of Israel. Although it would be an exaggeration to claim that Exodus 34 alone had been foundational for either Jewish or Christian spirituality in general, I have found this passage to be deeply illuminating and determinative for my own, specifically Christian understanding of God.

## Knowing and Being Known

Only when we have an initial grasp of the nature and character of God can we begin to understand how and why prayer, mission, worship, social action, or any number of other pious actions are either appropriate or even possible. The process of discovering who God is, what kind of God this is, and how this God acts must surely inform any attempt to respond to or serve such a God. To put it differently, the faith that lies at the heart of the Judeo-Christian response to God depends, in the final analysis, on "knowledge" of a certain sort—on an awareness, understanding, and practical engagement with the character of God. Only to the extent that we have some clear sense of what God is like can we conceive either of what such a God might want from us or of how this God might respond to our own sense of want. Granted, discipleship does not depend on a complete understanding of God's ways; sometimes the very opposite is required. Yet the better we come to know God (which is not at all the same thing as thinking or knowing *about* God, or *hoping* to know God), the clearer and more certain our faith is likely to be.

Still, a crucial qualification is in order here. "Knowledge" of God is ultimately more practical than conceptual, and it is acquired more by the interplay of thinking and doing than by thinking alone. So when Scripture and theology present us with language about God, even those who have a high estimation of biblical truth must invariably "field test" such descriptions to determine their validity in practice. In fact, what Scripture presents is less a series of statements *about* God than a practical invitation to respond that reflects Israel's and the early church's experience *of* God. In short, it is not enough for us to discuss or speculate about God: we want to encounter and experience God for ourselves. What the following study proposes, therefore, is a description of the dynamics of the divine-human relationship, beginning with an encounter between God and Moses on Mount Sinai, then tracing the echoes and reverberations of that encounter throughout ensuing centuries as a guide to our own experience of God.

As one who is called to prepare students for ministries of leadership within the Christian church, I maintain (and my students doubtless are weary of hearing me say) that in the last analysis, congregations only want to know one thing about those who presume to lead them. They want to know whether this person, pastor, or leader actually knows God. They are not interested in merely factual knowledge, in the sense of the French verb *savoir*, to know a fact, to know about something with some degree of accuracy. Rather, this must be personal knowledge, *connaissance*, an experiential kind of knowing that entails a relationship, a certain mutuality, and an appropriate level of spiritual intimacy. I would contend, moreover, that congregations can be prevailed upon to excuse poor preaching, lack of interpersonal and administrative skills, and even the occasional lapse in pastoral judgment, as long as they are convinced that those whom they trust to lead them truly know, and can speak of, the God whom they gather to worship. Conversely, even the greatest of gifts and personal aptitudes are unlikely to compensate for lack of such knowledge or for an inability to address spiritual hunger with news of a God who can truly satisfy it.

Of course, our claims in this regard need to be suitably modest. Even the apostle Paul (of all people) insists, "Now I know only in part; then I will know fully, even as I have been fully known" (1 Cor 13:12). Perhaps, then, it would be fairer to say that this book is about the ways in which God knows and seeks to be known by us, indeed that we come to know God only because that is God's own insistent purpose, even when knowledge of God is the furthest thing from our minds. It is only as a result of such divine tenacity that the words of Zechariah ring true: "In those days ten men from the nations of every language shall take hold of a Jew, grasping his garment and saying, 'Let us go with you, for we have heard that God is with you'" (Zech 8:23).

There is currently abundant evidence within Western cultures both of spiritual yearning and of spiritual exhaustion (as much within the church as outside it). People long for spiritualities of authenticity and integrity that are able to provide what they promise. In short, we hunger for God. My hope is that in some way the chapters that follow can help point to Scripture, to the historical experience of God's people, and, ultimately, to the God who satisfies that hunger. This is the One who proclaims, "I am the LORD your God. . . . Open your mouth wide and I will fill it" (Ps 81:10); of whom Mary declares, "He has filled the hungry with good things" (Lk 1:53); and on whose behalf Jesus promises, "Blessed are those who hunger and thirst for righteousness, for they will be filled" (Mt 5:6).

## A Road Map to This Book

The following chapters seek primarily to describe the content and background of certain key passages from the Hebrew Bible. My proposal is to trace the same divine "attributes" through a variety of texts and biblical traditions that, whatever other dissimilarities they may demonstrate, consistently employ a very specific and narrow set of terms to describe the "ways" of God. From this it will be clear that I do not understand Scripture to contain symbolic expressions of universal human spirituality, to proclaim God's invitation to authentic human existence, to constitute a "language event" that makes things happen, or even to articulate a series of abstract propositions regarding divine truth—although these are among the many ways in which various theologians have appropriated the biblical text.[8] Rather, my approach has more in common with that of Karl Barth, for whom the primary purpose of Scripture is to delineate the *identity* of God. As I understand it, this regard for the divine character most fully explains the relational, covenantal emphasis of both Hebrew and Christian Scripture and most fully accounts for the wide range of genres, origins, and content represented by the various documents that make up the biblical canon.

[8]See David Kelsey, *The Uses of Scripture in Recent Theology* (Philadelphia: Fortress, 1975).

What follows is deeply rooted in Christian conviction and is addressed in the first instance to a Christian audience. This will explain why many of the illustrations derive from Christian tradition, and why much attention is given to tracing specific lines of thought from the Hebrew Bible to the New Testament, and to the person of Jesus in particular. Yet I hope that others who do not claim Christian allegiance will find the perspective offered here to be of benefit to their own journeys of spiritual discovery and learning.

Chapter 1 sets the stage by recounting the story of Moses and the people of Israel as they flee into the wilderness of Sinai to escape bondage in Egypt. It recalls how at Mount Sinai God reveals the divine name to Moses as a way of preparing the covenant people for the journey ahead. This chapter deals with the meaning and purpose of names within the biblical tradition, the question of how Moses comes to know God's name, and possible implications of this discovery for our own day. Chapters 2 through 6 deal with the "character" of God, examining in turn the characteristics and qualities said to have been revealed to Moses: compassion, mercy, forbearance, steadfast love, forgiveness, justice, and the like. Chapter 7 examines biblical and postbiblical appeals to the divine name and attributes in their entirety as a basis for prayer and religious or ethical conduct, and it attempts to draw some broader conclusions for the life of Christian faith.

It is not my purpose to offer a comprehensive account of the chronological or semantic development of these terms through various textual or confessional traditions; such complexity is well beyond the scope of the present study, and in a number of instances the task has already been undertaken elsewhere.[9] I am fully aware that the meaning of particular words depends in significant measure on the specific literary contexts in which they appear (as well as, in turn, the larger social, political, and historical settings of each). Yet the ultimate context for this language, I contend, is the God of whom it speaks. Although at some risk of historical inexactitude, I therefore endeavor

[9]One recent example is Karla R. Suomala, *Moses and God in Dialogue: Exodus 32-34 in Postbiblical Literature* (SBL 61; New York: Peter Lang, 2004).

to present a synthetic, thematic overview of each set of vocabulary as it appears first in Hebrew Scripture as a whole and thereafter in bodies of literature that echo such language. At various junctures I acknowledge areas of significant scholarly debate, but I do so without belaboring the point for readers whose primary interests lie elsewhere. This is not intended as a word study in the traditional sense, but rather as an inquiry into a theology of encounter. Without implying the same totality of meaning in every different literary and historical context, each set of vocabulary nonetheless offers a series of clues or markers indicating the scope, shape, and nature of God's engagement with the heirs of Abraham. Since each word group could merit an entire volume of its own (and several already have), there is space enough here to select only a few clarifying examples, although readers who wish to pursue a particular topic will be able to find many more illustrations with the assistance of a biblical concordance. This qualification applies all the more strongly in the case of citations from the long and rich history of Jewish biblical interpretation, a vast field of its own in which I claim no expertise. Yet merely to dip one's toes into the "sea of Talmud" (as it is known) is amply rewarded by the devotional insight that such a venture offers for Jews and Christians alike. No less varied and complex is the realm of Islamic tradition, but the few references to this abundant heritage that I have managed to include can do no more than affirm the significance of meditation on the divine character within certain streams of Islamic devotion.

While there will be little objection from Christians to the use of illustrative material from Jewish sources, I recognize that more than a few Christians will find any positive estimation of Islam to be offensive, all the more so in light of the radicalization of Islam currently ascendant in certain parts of the world and its geopolitical implications for Western nations. However, as will emerge more clearly in the concluding chapter, current conflicts (whether theological, political, or directly military) argue for rather than against including Islam (however briefly) in the present discussion. In the introductory chapter of *A Generous Orthodoxy*, Brian McLaren observes,

> Nearly all orthodoxies of Christian history have shown a pervasive disdain for other religions of the world. . . . A generous orthodoxy . . . while never pitching its tent in the valley of relativism, nonetheless seeks to see members of other religions and non-religions not as enemies but as beloved neighbors, and whenever possible, as dialogue partners and even collaborators. It seeks to remove splinters from the eyes of other religions only after removing its own planks.[10]

This study represents my own efforts in the direction of "a generous orthodoxy"; it is an attempt to remain faithful to my own religious tradition and faith convictions while at the same time learning from the convictions and traditions of others. While significant, and in some cases vast, differences in theological outlook among the three Abrahamic faiths cannot be ignored, the purpose of this work is to focus instead on certain points of overlap and commonality in their respective views of God.

What we will see played out in Hebrew Scripture, through various texts from the intertestamental period, then on into the pages of the New Testament, the Talmud, and well beyond, is something like a series of musical "variations on a theme." Specific vocabulary from Exodus 34:6-7 will recur time and time again, occasionally repeating the original language exactly, or with only minor changes, but much more frequently transposing, overlaying, and juxtaposing its motifs in different settings so as to highlight every possible nuance of meaning in each new context. What emerges is an extended series of meditations on the divine character, each recognizably different, yet each reflecting the constant features of God's manner of keeping covenant with his people and creation as a whole. Of course, there are far more of these than can be fully explored in a single volume, but I trust that what follows will provide a representative sample of the many ways in which the writers of canonical and extracanonical texts in the Abrahamic tradition continually return to the same essential divine qualities in which they find hope, meaning, and a foundation for their lives.

---

[10]Brian McLaren, *A Generous Orthodoxy* (Grand Rapids: Zondervan, 2004), 35.

*Do not approach the words of the mysteries contained in the Scriptures without prayer and without asking for God's help. Say, "Lord, grant that I may receive an awareness of the power that is within them." Consider prayer to be the key to the understanding of truth in Scripture.*

St. Isaac of Syria (d. ca. 700 CE)[11]

[11]A. M. Allchin, ed., *The Heart of Compassion: Daily Readings with St. Isaac of Syria*, trans. Sebastian Brock (London: Darton, Longman & Todd, 1989), 47.

# 1

# Names and the Naming of God

*"Pray then in this way: . . . hallowed be your name."*

Matthew 6:9

## What's in a Name?

In the world of the Hebrew Scriptures a personal name was often thought to indicate something essential about the bearer's identity, origin, birth circumstances, or the divine purpose that the bearer was intended to fulfill. Thus "Abraham" was taken to mean "father of many" or "father of a multitude" (Gen 17:4-5), for that is what he was destined to become. "Isaac" means "laughter," the name having been given because his mother laughed at the thought that she might conceive in her old age (Gen 17:19; 18:12-15). "Moses," according to the explanation given in Exodus 2:10, recalls a word meaning "to draw out," as the Egyptian princess had drawn him out of the water in which he would otherwise have perished. But not all personal names have such specific or complex origins: the name of Jacob's first wife, Leah, probably comes from a verb meaning "to be weary"; "David" means "beloved one"; the name "Hannah" derives from a word translated elsewhere as "grace"; and the last prophet of Hebrew tradition is designated as "Malachi," meaning "my messenger." Often Hebrew names declare an important theological truth: "Joshua" (*yĕhôšûaʿ* or *yōšûaʿ* [from which the name "Jesus" is derived]) means "Yah[weh] is salvation." In much the same way, "Isaiah" can be translated "Yahu is salvation," and "Hosea" means "salvation." My own name, "Michael," is at once a question and a declaration of worship: "Who is like God?" As a variation on the same theme, the name of the prophet Micah is a shortened form of "Micaiah," meaning "who is like Yah[weh]?" the God of Israel (see Mic 7:18). Hundreds of such biblical names reflect a rich and lengthy tradition of devout, and very practical, theological reflection. These names record the deep faith of ordinary people over many centuries, as mothers and fathers named their children according to the character and ways of Israel's God—according to their experience of God—thus declaring the same convictions to be true for the next generation.[1] A similar practice persists in the modern Muslim tradition of naming children after the "names" or attributes of Allah.

In the earliest period of biblical history most people believed there to be many gods, with many different names. To some extent, the descendants of Abraham and Sarah first adopt, then adapt the names of God that come from the culture in which they find themselves. Thus "El," the generic (and Canaanite) name for God, becomes El Roi (possibly "God who sees" [Gen 16:13]); El Shaddai ("God Almighty" [e.g., Gen 17:1, 35:11, 43:14, 49:25]), El Elyon ("God Most High" [Gen 14:18-19, 22]), and El Olam ("Everlasting God" [Gen 21:33]). It seems likely that many of these originally were names of Canaanite deities but subsequently came to be identified with Israel's God. More to the point, Israel's understanding of God was conditioned over time by particular encounters and experiences. This God is associated not only with specific locations (as in the name "El Bethel," meaning "God of Bethel" [Gen 31:13; 35:7]) but also with specific individuals. Thus the God of the patriarchs comes to be designated, for example, "the God of Abraham and the God of Nahor" (Gen 31:53) or, later, "El Elohe Israel" ("El the God of Israel" [Gen 33:19-20]) and "El Elohe Abika"

---

[1]"Since ... both Egyptian and Western-Asiatic sentence-names (i.e. names which form a sentence, as most unabbreviated Semitic names did in antiquity) represent utterances of a parent or person with authority at the birth of a child, it is easier to understand their connotation. Such names contain a vow or invocation to a god, or a statement of good omen connected in some way with a god" (W. F. Albright, *From the Stone Age to Christianity: Monotheism and the Historical Process* [2nd ed.; Garden City, NY: Doubleday, 1957], 245).

("El the God of your father" [Gen 46:3]). Yet further encounters yield the divine names "Kinsman [alternatively, 'Fear'] of Isaac" (Gen 31:42) and "Mighty One of Jacob" (Gen 49:24). Particularly because they arise out of a context of divine encounter, all of these names indicate something important not only about who God is but also about how God acts. Thus the name, or names, by which Israel calls on God are never arbitrary; they describe the nature or character of God and thereby suggest the kind of divine-human relationships that arise as a result. Likewise in Christian experience, to speak of God as "Lord," "Father," or "Savior" expresses the nature of a relationship with this God.

Likewise today, names often define relationships, and different names are deemed appropriate for different degrees of formality or familiarity. The family physician may be "Dr. MacPherson" to his patients, "Ian" to friends and colleagues, and "Dad" to his children, but likely answers to "Sweetheart" or "Beloved" when his wife calls. When I was a child, one summer vacation provided a rather painful lesson in the social significance of names. As we pulled into a campground in our family car, I recognized one of my father's workmates, already installed with his own family at a campsite. Without hesitation I leaned out of the car window and shouted, "Hey, Art!" It was the only name I had ever heard my father call him. How, then, was I supposed to know that the proper form of address for a seven-year-old to employ towards an elder was "Mister Johnson"? Suffice it to say that my ears rang for hours, I shed many tears, and I was exceedingly careful with names thereafter.

The names that we use for God are no less significant, whether in Scripture or in our own day. This study is about the "name," and names, of God. For Scripture has much to say about the names by which we address God, and about the names by which God addresses us. When God calls Abraham, God calls him by name. When God calls Samuel, God calls him by name. To Israel God says, "I have called you by name, you are mine" (Is 43:1 [cf. Is 45:4]). This implies that God knows them intimately and names those who serve him much as parents bestow a family name on their newborn in order to declare their relationship with and responsibility for that child. The prophets declare that God gives his own name to his people: "You are called by my name; I made you" (cf. Is 43:7; Jer 15:16). Just as God calls on the covenant people by name, so God in turn invites the people to call on his name. God says, in effect, "You can call on my name; you can call me by my name" (cf. Ps 80:18; 105:1, 3). And finally, to those who are faithful God promises to give a new name "that no one will know except the one who receives it" (Rev 2:17).

But what *is* God's name? Christians have always claimed that the one true God, the God of Abraham, Isaac, and Israel, is made known most fully in the person of Jesus, whose own name means "God saves" (Mt 1:21). At least to his followers this name sums up the very essence of who God is, what God is like, and what God does for us. For the Christian claim is that behind the name of Jesus lies a very specific person, with a very specific series of accomplishments, and that behind that person stands a God who has chosen to be revealed "in many and various ways" (Heb 1:1) but nowhere more fully than in Jesus himself. The task of the chapters that follow is to focus not only on the way in which Jesus exemplifies the name—and character—of God, but also to reflect at length on one particular episode of divine self-revelation within the history of Israel and on one set of themes (or divine characteristics) that derives from that episode. The setting for this revelation is God's call for Moses to lead his people out of slavery in Egypt, the national deliverance that ensues, and Israel's impatient relapse into idolatry at Mount Sinai. To these events, and to the leader who serves as the catalyst for God's purposes, we now turn.

## Moses and the Name of God

To set the stage for God's revelation of the divine name to Moses, it helps to begin with the story of Moses' own life, as recorded in the first chapters of the book of Exodus. Moses is born into slavery. An Israelite, he is born in the land of Egypt, possibly during the Nineteenth Dynasty (1350-1200 BCE), at a time when his entire nation has been forced into slave labor. Although the people of Israel originally had fled there to escape famine in their own land, the forces of political change have overtaken them, with the result that they become the victims of shrewd military strategizing on the part of their former benefactors. According to Exodus 1:8-10, the Egyptian leadership grows concerned that these resident refugees might form an alliance with a hostile power, thereby threatening to overthrow the new Pharaoh and his regime. An initial solution is to impose forced labor on the Israelites (apparently not uncommon in the ancient world). Suddenly they are no longer immigrants, but enemies; no longer guest workers, but slaves. When that cruel strategy fails to curb the birth rate, a new decree is issued: whenever these foreigners bear children, the boys are to be thrown into the river. Relying on the crocodiles of the Nile has long provided the solution to awkward social difficulties.

The story of how Moses himself is rescued from such a grim fate is one of the best-known episodes in Hebrew Scripture. In an attempt to save her son, Moses' mother first tries to keep the infant hidden, then, recognizing that such a strategy cannot succeed indefinitely, she floats her son in a basket past a member of the Egyptian royal family, a daughter of the Pharaoh. Moved to pity, the princess decides to take the "abandoned" boy for her own. Conveniently, the child's real mother is close at hand, offering to raise the boy until he is old enough to join his adopted family (Ex 2:1-10). So by a strange twist of fate, this slave-born child grows up as the adopted grandson of the very ruler who would have had him killed.

Perhaps it is princely curiosity that gets the better of Moses (for he can hardly have forgotten his true lineage), but one day years later he goes out to see how the "other half" lives and, with newly mature eyes, sees the extent to which his adopted nation oppresses the people of his birth. Such are the conditions under which they labor that harsh punishment is commonplace. When an overseer starts to beat a slave, no one else thinks to raise a hand in protest. But Moses, who has been raised to expect better treatment than this, rises up in defense of his own people, kills the Egyptian, and hides his body in the sand. The next day he goes out again, and this time he encounters two Israelites fighting with one another. Once again he tries to intervene. But his secret is out, and one of the combatants retorts, with unintended irony, "So who died and made *you* king? Are you going to kill me too?" (Ex 2:14). To the Egyptians, Moses has become an

Israelite. But to the Israelites, he is still an Egyptian. They are unimpressed by the noble prince come home to his people.

So Moses, the slave-born prince, must flee into exile. Having rejected a royal heritage for the cause of justice, he finds that his own people reject him in turn. Since everyone has turned against him (even Pharaoh, who now wants him dead), he must escape into the wilderness of Midian (immediately east of the Gulf of Aqaba, in what is now northwest Saudi Arabia). There he marries the daughter of a local (pagan) priest and manages to eke out a living by tending his father-in-law's sheep—this notwithstanding the fact that being someone else's servant is the very thing he has been trying to avoid all along.

It is at this point, when all seems lost, that Moses' life takes an unexpected turn. Again, the story of the burning bush in Exodus 3 is so well known as hardly to need retelling. What we cannot overlook, however, is that the God of Moses' ancestors appears to him and calls him to be an instrument of divine justice and deliverance at a point in his life when, for all intents and purposes, Moses has already failed utterly. He is no longer an Egyptian prince, no longer a defender of Israel, perhaps not even (if his marriage is any indication) overly scrupulous in his religious observances. The story provides some hint of this when God declares from the burning bush, "'I am the God *of your father*, the God of Abraham, the God of Isaac, and the God of Jacob.' And Moses hid his face, for he was afraid to look at God" (Ex 3:6). According to tradition (Ex 7:7; Acts 7:23, 30), Moses is already eighty years old when God calls him to lead his people out of bondage into freedom in their own land.

Moses' response to this unexpected call might seem curious. He asks, "If I come to the Israelites and say to them, 'The God of our ancestors has sent me to you,' and they ask me, 'What is his name?' what shall I say to them?" (Ex 3:13). It is not just that prevarication seems ill-advised in the presence of the divine. For us to understand this reply, it helps to reflect once again on how names—divine names in particular—apparently functioned for peoples of the ancient Near East. Notwithstanding his explanation, Moses' desire to know the name of God amounts to a bid for control, an attempt to gain some degree of power over this terrifyingly intrusive deity. In the world of Moses' day, to know someone's name is to know what is most true about that person; to know the name of your god grants access to the hidden identity, nature, and power of that god. If you know and can call on the name of a god, you have that god in your power. Conscious of his failures, and doubtless overwhelmed by the magnitude of what the God of his ancestors has called him to do, Moses attempts to regain some degree of control.

But the name with which this God replies amounts to a resolute evasion of the questioner's intent. God pronounces the divine identity in three stages: as "I am who I am" or "I will be who I will be" (Ex 3:14a); more simply as "I am" (Ex 3:14b); and, finally, in what is known as the Tetragrammaton (i.e., "four-lettered word"), the Hebrew יהוה (Ex 3:15). These four Hebrew consonants sometimes are transliterated as "YHWH," conjecturally reconstructed as "Yahweh," or are rendered (following ancient tradition) as "the Lord" (and distinguished from the more general term by the use of small capitals). The Hebrew language originally was written using consonants only, on the assumption that people knew how to pronounce the various words. But when, by reason of time and circumstance, the use of Hebrew diminished and the language became less familiar, vowels were added in the form of tiny dots and lines, most written beneath each consonant. But there was one significant exception: the name of God was (and to this day still is) deemed to be so unutterably holy that pious scribes omitted the necessary vowel markings. Or, to be more precise, they substituted the vowel pointing for another, less dangerous divine name ("Adonai" or sometimes "Elohim") as a reminder not to pronounce the word as it was written (see *b. Qidd.* 71a). So we are forced to conjecture, with the result that the scholarly literature on this question alone is voluminous. As Frank Moore Cross once commented, "The discussion of the meaning and origin of the name Yahweh constitutes a monumental witness to the industry and ingenuity of biblical scholars. Fortunately there is no space to review it here."[2] Although the question is still subject to debate, it is a

---

[2]Frank Moore Cross, "Yahweh and the God of the Patriarchs," *Harvard Theological Review* 55 (1962): 250-51. One influential proposal is that the name in Exodus 3:15 represents a causative form of the verb "to be" and means, in concert with the interpretation provided at Exodus 3:14, "I cause to be" or "I create, bring into being" (see David Noel Freedman, "The Name of the God of Moses," *Journal of Biblical Literature* 79 [1960]: 151-56).

reasonable assumption that the ancient writer understood the four consonants of God's name to mean, as suggested by the previous verse, "I am who I am" or "I will be who I will be."[3] In other words, the name that God pronounces gives nothing away until God chooses to define it further. It is its own guarantee: "I am." Each of God's answers to Moses makes clear that the nature, the identity, and the "name" of God are self-authenticating, not subject to limitation or control by those who call upon it, despite Moses' fervent wish to do just that.

Whereas some of the names that Hebrew Scripture uses for God are also common in Canaanite religion (e.g., "El" means "God," "Baal" is "Lord"), YHWH is the one name that Scripture uses for the God of Israel and for no other. It is the one name by which God's essential identity and way of acting with the people of Israel will be known for all time: "This is my name forever, and this is my title for all generations" (Ex 3:15).[4] According to Genesis 4:26, the name YHWH was known and honored almost from the beginning of human existence (cf. Gen 21:33; 28:16). Nonetheless, Exodus 6:2-3 asserts that this particular name represents something theologically distinctive, even unique, as God says to Moses, "I am YHWH. I revealed myself to Abraham, to Isaac, and to Jacob as El Shaddai, but was not known to them by my name YHWH" (Ex 6:2-3). Whatever its historical origins, central to the meaning of this name is the assertion that God is beyond human manipulation or control. For Moses, knowing, following, and serving the God of his ancestors assumes new theological dimensions at the point where he realizes that he cannot control God, that he hardly knows God, and that far from being in command of the situation, he must allow this uncontrollable God to direct him. More to the point, he must learn to obey, so that this gracious and merciful God can use him for the benefit of a suffering people.

---

[3]This reduplication is known technically as an *idem per idem* formula, the purpose of which is to emphasize the particular action to which the verb refers (Freedman, "The Name of the God of Moses," 153).

[4]In contrast to the names of fertility deities such as Baal ("husband, lord"), Dagon ("grain"), and Shamash ("sun"), this name is distinctive in that its meaning appears intentionally evasive, not associated with any element of the natural or social order (see Richard Elliott Friedman, *Commentary on the Torah: With a New English Translation and the Hebrew Text* [San Francisco: HarperSanFrancisco, 2001], 290).

## Israel and the Character of God

Moses' encounter at the burning bush is not meant to be an end in itself; rather, it serves as an introduction to an even more momentous series of events: the deliverance of Israel from bondage in Egypt (Ex 11–14). National liberation, in turn, provides the context for the establishment of the covenant and giving of the law. Yet it is important to recognize that, notwithstanding the centrality of Torah in Jewish thought and practice, the giving of the law does not by itself represent the essence of the covenant. Furthermore, to characterize the Mosaic covenant as merely "legal" or "legalistic" (as Christians often do) is at best reductionist and at worst an outright misrepresentation. Granted, the circumstances under which this covenant is established emphasize the unapproachable holiness of Israel's God (as Heb 12:18-21 also insists). The people, together with their priests and leaders, must carefully consecrate themselves lest God's holiness consume and destroy them (Ex 19:21-24). Yet the covenant obligations are promulgated only after the people have been "passed over" by the angel of death, rescued from oppression, guided by "a pillar of cloud by day and a pillar of fire by night" (Ex 13:22), led through the waters of the Sea of Reeds, fed with manna and quail, satisfied by water from the rock, delivered from Amalek, and brought at last to the mountain. As the Decalogue itself makes clear, the obligations that God requires of Israel do not themselves establish a relationship between them, but rather simply articulate the parameters of a relationship already established on other grounds. Thus the "ten words" (Decalogue) are intentionally prefaced by a declaration of God's foundational, saving work: "I am the Lord your God, who brought you out of Egypt, out of the land of slavery" (Ex 20:2); only then are the covenant obligations enumerated.

But what had looked like an excellent beginning now crumbles into failure. Rather than trust in the fact that the guardian of their ancestors has once more taken charge of them, the people apparently lose their nerve and return to the tried-and-true, practical theology that they had once held in common with the surrounding nations. In a manner reminiscent of Moses' own motives for wanting to know God's name, the people endeavor to reduce this deity to more conveniently visible, tangible proportions. Neither the momentous salvation that they have experienced, nor God's sustenance and provision, nor even terrifying holiness prevents the people from construing this deity as one whom they can (literally) manipulate—the intention of worship notwithstanding—by hand-fashioning a divine image out of precious metal. They mold the statue of a calf (presumably a young bull, in keeping with the fertility symbolism of Canaanite theology), declaring, "These are your gods, O Israel!" (Ex 32:4-6 [cf. 32:23; note the plural]). Ironically, all of this takes place while Moses is on the mountaintop in intimate communion with God. Clearly, the people neither know nor understand this God as God desires to be known, not even those (Aaron and the elders among them) who are said to have seen and dined in God's very presence (Ex 24:9-11).

The impatience and recalcitrance of the Israelites make God threaten to quit. "Go up to a land flowing with milk and honey," God tells them, "but I will not go up among you, or I would consume you on the way, for you are a stiff-necked people" (Ex 33:3). But with nowhere else to turn, Moses persists. "If I have found favor in your sight," he says, "show me your ways, that I might know you and find favor in your sight. Consider too that this nation is your people" (Ex 33:13). His request or petition is in four parts: first, "show me your ways" (how does God act?); second, "that I might know you" (who or what is God like?); third, "[that I might] find favor in your sight" (how can he maintain the right kind of relationship with God?). These questions are, surely, foundational for the life of faith. Fourth and finally, because he is not alone in this, Moses calls on God not to abandon responsibility for the people over whom God has already staked a claim of ownership.

### *Presence, Glory, Goodness*

In many respects, the situation in which Moses now finds himself is at least as difficult as when God first met him in the wilderness of Midian. His questions are not matters of abstract speculation or idle curiosity. He and the people of Israel have embarked on a theological escapade of unimaginable proportions; yet the entire venture is now at risk, together with the very lives of God's "chosen" people. Moses' concern, therefore, is entirely practical. By choosing to come before God, Moses acknowledges the One who has led them to this place; by asking the questions that he asks, Moses also acknowledges how little he knows this God. Indeed, by asking at this particular juncture to know God's "ways," Moses cannot be referring to God's holiness, "other-ness," wrath, or saving power. These are concepts that he and the people already know, in some measure at least. It appears that Moses needs to know something more basic than what he has already encountered.

So in response to Moses' pleading comes this reassurance: "My presence will go with you, and I will give you rest" (Ex 33:14). It is worth pointing out that the second half of this sentence is as important as the first: the message God intends to convey is "My presence will go with you *in order to* give you rest." This amounts to an assurance that God's presence is not merely passive or inert. It is an active and saving presence, a presence that makes following possible and leads to rest.

Moses knows that his own identity and future, and that of the entire nation, rest on what God has already begun to accomplish on their behalf. If Egypt has failed as a land of refuge, they need another place in which to "rest." So if God will not go with them, says Moses, they do not want to go either: "For how shall it be known that I have found favor in your sight, I and your people, unless you go with us?" (Ex 33:15-16). Again, his interest is entirely practical. If God will not accompany them after all, then neither they nor their neighbors will have any grounds for believing that this supposed God of Israel carries any cosmic—or theological—weight.

Curiously, Moses persists further, insisting, "Show me your glory," to which God replies, yet more curiously, "I will make all my goodness pass before you, and will proclaim my name, YHWH" (Ex 33:18-19). An answer like this, in reply to a question like this, suggests that God's "goodness" and God's "name" are in fact the essence of God's "glory." "And," continues God, "I will be gracious to whom I will be gracious, and I will show mercy on whom I will show mercy." If those scholars are correct who assert that the name of God, "Yahweh," means something like "I will be who I will be," then that insight helps clarify this otherwise puzzling statement. That is, the simple tautology "I will be who I will be" now becomes "I will be gracious to whom I will be gracious, and I will show mercy on whom I will show mercy" (Ex 33:19). Just as "I will be who I will be" asserts that God is beyond human manipulation or constraint, so God promises to be gracious and to show mercy not ultimately because of Moses, or Aaron, or the faithfulness or unfaithfulness of Israel. God is gracious and merciful simply because that is God's nature, God's "name," prior to and independent of whatever response Israel might choose to make. At least for Israel, the divine identity is not a matter of metaphysical abstracts; rather, it is expressed in terms that describe God's gracious manner of acting within the divine-human relationship. And that divine identity is expressed in concrete action.

Even the process of revelation expresses the same premise, for at this point God adds a strange condition: "You cannot see my face; for no one can see my face and live" (Ex 33:20). God proposes to hide Moses in a crevice on the mountainside, shielding Moses with his hand until his "glory" has passed by: "Then I will take away my hand, and you shall see my back," says God, "but my face shall not be seen" (Ex 33:21-23). It is impossible to say what mystical or visionary experience is being portrayed here, for the depiction of God with "face," "back," and "hand" resorts to anthropological imagery for concepts that cannot be expressed in any other way.[5] But, unmistakably, Moses is carefully shielded from encountering the full, unbearable reality of a glorious God. Even God's self-revelation as merciful and gracious is itself merciful and gracious to one who would be destroyed by any fuller exposure. In the words of the Puritan commentator John Trapp (1601-1669), "None can see more than these and live: and we need see no more than these that we may live."[6]

---

[5]Augustine of Hippo (354-430 CE) proposes an altogether imaginative solution: God's "posterior" is none other than the incarnate Christ, whom Moses must have seen (*Trin.* 2.17.32 [*NPNF*[1] 3:52-53]). The various Aramaic paraphrases of Exodus 34:6 indicate that it is the "Shekinah" (divine "Presence") that passes before Moses. See further Diana Lipton, "God's Back! What Did Moses See on Sinai?" in *The Significance of Sinai: Traditions About Divine Revelation in Judaism and Christianity*, ed. George J. Brooke, Hindy Najman, and Loren T. Stuckenbruck (TBN 12; Leiden: Brill, 2008), 287-311.

[6]John Trapp, *A Commentary on the Old and New Testaments*, ed. Hugh Martin (5 vols.; repr., London: Richard D. Dickinson, 1867-1868 [1662]), 1:225.

The logic of this passage is such that each exchange with Moses leads to a further unfolding of the meaning of the divine name. That God refuses to be externally constrained or controlled is not the same thing as saying that God is arbitrary, unpredictable, or unknowable. On the contrary, the implication is that God will be God in consistently demonstrating mercy and graciousness, as Israel has already discovered through their deliverance from captivity and oppression. God's "ways" (Ex 33:13), God's "goodness," God's graciousness and mercy (Ex 33:19), even God's "glory" (Ex 33:18)—all are expressions of the same divine character. As such, they are all summed up in the meaning of God's "name," soon to be articulated more fully in Exodus 34:6-7.

### *The Thirteen Attributes*

The symbol of Israel's newly established covenant is the "two tablets" with their "ten words," articulating the essence of Israel's covenant obligations. The original pair of tablets is said to have been inscribed directly by God, but Moses shatters them in anger upon learning of the Israelites' apostasy (Ex 24:12; 32:15-19). These are replaced by two more tablets, which Moses must supply (Ex 34:1, 4), on which the patriarch himself must once more record the commandments (Ex 34:27-28). But before he can do so, God intervenes with what amounts to the fullest explanation yet of the divine character (Ex 34:6-9):

> And the LORD passed before him and proclaimed,
> "The LORD, the LORD, a God compassionate and gracious,
> slow to anger, and abounding in steadfast love and faithfulness,
> keeping steadfast love for thousands, forgiving iniquity and transgression and sin,
> but who will by no means clear the guilty. . . ."
> Then Moses quickly bent his head to the earth, and worshiped, and said, "If I have found favor in your sight, do not abandon us the way we have abandoned you; forgive us and take us for your people."

These are the "ways" (or practical characteristics) of God that Moses has sought to know. According to the Babylonian Talmud (*b. Roš. Haš.* 17b), this text enumerates precisely thirteen divine attributes, although there is no agreement in Jewish tradition as to how that number is to be reckoned.[7] Later interpreters observe that the numerical value of the word *ʾeḥād* ("unity") and of the word *ʾahăbâ* ("love") is thirteen, and that the sum of the two represents the numerical value of "YHWH."[8]

All of this apparently suggested to pious interpreters the appropriateness of discerning exactly thirteen attributes within the text in question. According to one possible reading, the God of Israel is (1) YHWH (the One who simply is, unconstrainable and self-sufficient); (2) YHWH (repeated for emphasis); (3) God, who is (4) compassionate; (5) gracious; (6) slow to anger; (7) abundant in showing steadfast love and (8) truth (or faithfulness); indeed, (9) preserving steadfast love for thousands of generations; (10) forgiving with respect to iniquity, (11) to transgression, and (12) to sin; yet (13) by no means clearing the guilty.[9] Although in a simpler arrangement than is offered by this somewhat complex partitioning, the meaning of these attributes will provide the focus for the remainder of this study.

The device of framing this material between a first and a second provision of the ten core commandments implies that Israel's covenant obligations are best understood in light of a proper knowledge of the God who requires them. The same is true for all the essential details governing Israel's worship, which fill the chapters between God's initial promise of the Ten Commandments (Ex 24:12) and the end of the book. So striking is it in its present context that some have seen in Exodus 34:6-7 an Israelite "confession of faith," or a liturgical formula derived from ancient Israelite worship.[10] The narrative itself, however, suggests the opposite to be true: it is precisely God's revelation of his gracious character that gives rise to worship, much as obedience to God takes its cue from knowledge of God.[11] It need hardly be said that this

[7]Compare *Midrash Psalms* 93 §5 on Psalm 93:5 (William G. Braude, trans., *The Midrash on Psalms*, [2 vols.; YJS 13; New Haven: Yale University Press, 1959], 2:129), citing various opinions according to which there may be ten, eleven, or thirteen such qualities (Braude proposes an extensive period of development for this text, "from the 3rd century C.E. to the 13th century" [ibid., 1:xxxi]).

[8]André Chouraqui, *L'univers de la Bible*, vol. 1, *Genèse, Exode* (Paris: Éditions Lidis, 1982), 446.

[9]For an alternative division of the text, see A. Z. Idelsohn, *Jewish Liturgy and Its Development* (New York: Schocken, 1967 [1932]), 357n32.

[10]Robert C. Dentan, "The Literary Affinities of Exodus XXXIV 6f," *Vetus Testamentum* 13 (1963): 36-37.

[11]So R. W. L. Moberly, *At the Mountain of God: Story and Theology in Exodus 32-34* (JSOTSup 22; Sheffield: JSOT Press, 1983), 128-31; see further discussion in John I. Durham, *Exodus*

observation applies not only to those who keep the covenant of Moses, but also to all who call upon Israel's God, no matter what other religious convictions or conventions may otherwise divide them.

### *Speaking of God*

It might be good at this point to confess that traditional discussions of the nature of God leave me largely unmoved for the simple (if undoubtedly selfish) reason that they tend to leave humankind out of consideration altogether. Discussions of the classic sort typically focus on nonmoral qualities such as God's transcendence, eternity, aseity (nonderivative existence), unicity, and immutability (changelessness), or on the three great "omni's": omniscience, omnipotence, and omnipresence. The Westminster Shorter Catechism is typical: "God is a Spirit, infinite, eternal, and unchangeable in his being, wisdom, power, holiness, justice, goodness, and truth." Nor is a tendency to abstraction the unique domain of Protestant theology. At the end of his life the Flemish Jesuit Leonard Lessius (1554-1623), one of the most influential controversialists and teachers of his day, sums up his great erudition in a work that enumerates fifty divine perfections, from "divinity" itself to "God the Last End." Completed only a few days prior to his death, it was perhaps a fitting way of preparing to meet his Maker. Three years earlier, in 1620, Lessius had published another series of reflections on the nature of God, in which he felt compelled to explain the relevance of such study:

> Not a few theological students are under the impression that what is called Speculative Theology is of very little use. They pay no attention to it during their course, and when their studies are over drop it altogether. They say they want something practical; as if Speculative Theology were a barren field. . . . Although all Theology teaches what is conducive to a pious and holy life, nothing draws us so powerfully away from the love of perishable things and influences our heart with the desire of what is celestial and eternal as the meditation of the divine perfections.[12]

---

(WBC 3; Waco, TX: Word, 1987), 454.

[12]Leonardus Lessius, *The Names of God and Meditative Summaries of the Divine Perfections*, trans. T. J. Campbell (New York: America Press, 1912), 135-37.

Accordingly, fourteen extended meditations follow, each addressed directly to God and seeking to foster devotion on the basis of God's infinity, immensity, immutability, eternity, omnipotence, goodness, sanctity, dominion, providence, mercy, justice, and so forth.

Such abstract characteristics are intellectually profound, indeed essential; discussion of them constitutes an important feature of theological debate and, for scholars such as Lessius, offers an important devotional resource. Even so, most readers find it difficult to appreciate the significance of these qualities in personal or practical terms. Indeed, they are sufficiently abstract as to appear highly impersonal and therefore functionally irrelevant.[13] Dutch theologian Kornelis Miskotte goes even further in his own reflection on Exodus 34: "In these [philosophical aphorisms] lie the deepest cause of the ambivalence of religion and the rise of the atheistic reaction and the nihilistic rebellion of the human spirit."[14] Many centuries before our own the popular hymn writer and theologian Ephrem the Syrian (ca. 303-373 CE) warned against unfruitful speculations that probe beyond the explicitly revealed name, and names, of God:

> Father, Son, and Holy Spirit can be reached only by Their names;
> do not look further, to Their Persons,
> just meditate on their names.
> If you investigate the person of God, you will perish,
> but if you will believe in the name, you will live.
> Let the name of the Father be a boundary to you,
> do not cross it and investigate His nature;
> let the name of the Son be a wall to you,
> do not cross it and investigate His birth from the Father;
> let the name of the Spirit be a fence for you,
> do not enter inside for the purpose of prying into Him.[15]

[13]For similar sentiments from a contemporary theological perspective, highlighting in particular the historical engagement that underlies God's self-revelation to Israel, see Janet Martin Soskice, "The Gift of the Name: Moses and the Burning Bush," *Gregorianum* 79, no. 2 (1998): 231-46.

[14]Kornelis H. Miskotte, *When the Gods Are Silent*, trans. John W. Doberstein (London: Collins, 1967), 400.

[15]From Sebastian Brock, trans., *The Luminous Eye: The Spiritual World Vision of Saint Ephrem* (Kalamazoo, MI: Cistercian Publications, 1992), cited in Lorraine Kisly, ed., *Christian Teachings on the Practice of Prayer: From the Early Church to the Present* (Boston: New Seeds, 2002), 181.

To emphasize a pragmatic approach is not a concession to the narcissism of a consumer age, in which we measure the worth of all things solely in relation to ourselves. The God of Israel is certainly not a "personal God" in the sense that one might employ a "personal trainer" in order to meet some personal need. Yet Israel's God is indeed "personal" in the sense of being consistently interested in "persons"—not only individuals but also the nation of Israel as a collective whole. Israel's God is consistently revealed within the very concrete, practical, and specific context of human history and human relationships, as the exchange between God and Moses itself clearly demonstrates. This is hardly how we would imagine a conversation between a holy, almighty, utterly transcendent deity, on the one hand, and a mere mortal, on the other. Theirs is a conversation marked by give and take, as if God and Moses were near equals. As a practical demonstration of the gracious character that God desires to make known, their dialogue is marked by what one writer calls "an intimacy that is surprising, considering the interaction that takes place [is] between God and man. Moses wants to know more about who God really is, and God steps out on a limb to reveal more about himself."[16] Maintaining a predominantly abstract concept of God seems out of place in comparison to the biblical depiction of a deity who, despite great opposition, seems steadfastly fixated on maintaining a saving intimacy with one especially fractious set of ancient Near Eastern tribes and numerous individuals within it. Israel's God consistently proves to be a God of history, a God of covenant, and a God of relationships.

It is fashionable in some theological circles to complain that passages such as Exodus 34:6-7 are irredeemably anthropomorphic. Feminists in particular have raised the question of who has the right to "name" human experience, including the experience of God. They have rightly exposed the patriarchal bias of Hebrew and Christian Scriptures alike, both of which emerged out of cultural contexts beset by their own inevitable prejudices and limitations. Even so, the church's adoption of these writings into an authoritative canon of Scripture reflects the fact

[16]Karla R. Suomala, *Moses and God in Dialogue: Exodus 32-34 in Postbiblical Literature* (SBL 61; New York: Peter Lang, 2004), 36.

that God's people have consistently heard within them a word concerning God that ultimately transcends, indeed challenges, any number of merely cultural values. It soon becomes evident that neither Scripture nor the God of Scripture can be co-opted with nearly as much ease as is sometimes assumed. More than a few theologians assert that God is beyond gender, or even (in what is known as the apophatic tradition) beyond language itself.[17] But the divine "name" or "names" described in Hebrew Scripture articulate the nature of God in terms that go well beyond the limitations of gender roles and gender socialization, whether in the ancient Near East, in our own day, or at any time in between.

Moreover, this text in particular claims to represent an instance of revelation, of God's *self*-depiction in terms that mere humans can appreciate and appropriate. Karl Barth makes a similar point with regard to language about God as "Father." According to Barth, we do not name God as "Father" on the basis of our knowledge of human fathers or fatherhood. Rather, it is God, named by Scripture as "Father," who defines "fatherhood" for us.[18] By the same token, it would be a mistake to imagine that Israel's appeal to divine graciousness, mercy, compassion, and the like were no more than a projection of their own ideals onto a metaphysical canvas; the very fact that the characteristics named in Exodus 34 reflect ideals that neither Israel nor any other nation has been able to consistently exemplify suggests something other than a purely human origin for them. It is God, and not human beings alone, who most fully and definitively fills them with meaning.[19] Against the theological tradition that proclaims the inadequacy of all human language for God, even the agnostic postmodern philosopher Jacques Derrida insists that we may speak of God in particular human words only because those words are themselves the gift of God.[20]

---

[17]See, for example, Emmanuel Clapsis, "Naming God: An Orthodox View," *Ecumenical Review* 44 (1992): 100-112.

[18]See, for example, Karl Barth, *Prayer*, trans. Sara F. Terrien, ed. Don E. Saliers (2nd ed.; Philadelphia: Westminster, 1985), 45-46.

[19]On divine self-revelation and self-interpretation as the source of our theological description of God, see Karl Barth, *Church Dogmatics*, ed. G. W. Bromiley and T. F. Torrance, vol. 1.1, *The Doctrine of the Word of God*, trans. G. W. Bromiley (Edinburgh: T & T Clark, 1975), 304-33.

[20]See Soskice, "The Gift of the Name," 245-46.

To this may be compared, from Islamic tradition, the opening declaration of Abu Ḥamid al-Ghazālī's treatise on the names of God, which sets out the aim of the work as a whole:

> Praise be to God, alone in His majesty and His might, and unique in His sublimity and His everlastingness, who clips the wings of intellects well short of the glow of His glory, and who makes the way of knowing Him pass through the inability to know Him; who makes the tongues of the eloquent fall short of praising the beauty of His presence unless they use the means by which He praises Himself, and use His names and attributes which He has enumerated.[21]

This essential premise is, in fact, already implicit within the language of Exodus. As Walter Moberly observes, the language of Exodus 33:19 and Exodus 34:5-6 (in particular, the verb *qr*ʾ [קרא]) elsewhere typically describes worshipers who proclaim or "call on" the name of Yahweh (e.g., Gen 4:26). However, in a unique and striking reversal, these two passages make Yahweh the subject of the formula, thereby declaring that it is God who "proclaims" the divine name. By intentionally inverting the usual language of worship and supplication, the writer stresses that human beings can call upon the name and celebrate the attributes of God only because God has first chosen to declare them.[22] By virtue of such self-declaration, God is thus the author and instigator of the human worship that follows upon it.

### *Divine Discovery: Finding and Being Found*

The fact that the qualities listed in Exodus 34:5-7 are moral, relational, and, more precisely, covenantal characteristics leads to a number of observations. First, it appears from the context of this passage in the life of Moses and the history of Israel that discovering God's name and identity typically comes not at the pinnacle of one's spiritual experience, but rather in the depths, at points of failure. As Moses' own experience clearly demonstrates, it is only when we become aware of our failure, confusion, and

[21]David B. Burrell and Nazih Daher, trans., *The Ninety-Nine Beautiful Names of God: al-Maqṣad al-asnā fī s̱harḥ asmāʾ Allāh al-ḥusnā* (Cambridge: Islamic Texts Society, 1995), 1 (see also pp. 177-81).

[22]Moberly, *At the Mountain of God*, 77.

"need to know" that we begin to ask. Moreover, given that it is God's nature to be merciful and forgiving, and to demonstrate saving compassion to those who are oppressed and broken, human failure provides the necessary backdrop for such qualities to emerge. What Israel may have failed to recognize about the character of this God through being rescued out of slavery in Egypt, they are now given to understand by being delivered from the consequences of their own failure. The same divine character emerges in both instances; in both, the nature of the relationship that God desires to establish with these people remains the same.

Second, the example of Moses and Israel at Mount Sinai suggests that discovering the name and identity of God is not a matter of human beings turning God to their own purposes, but rather of God making people part of the divine purpose. When God reveals the divine character to Moses and the people of Israel, it is not simply in order to confirm their own hopes, aspirations, and intuitions. Nor has Israel has demonstrated that they are somehow especially worthy of knowing this God. In fact, just the opposite is true: divine revelation comes not because of their fidelity, but rather in light of its absence (cf. Deut 7:7-8). Thus when God declares, "I will be who I will be," and "I will be gracious to whom I will be gracious," it comes as a kind of shocking good news: unconstrainable divine mercy meets, but is not caused by, human need.

Third, this episode points to what is most essential in the life of faith. Actions are, to be sure, important (otherwise Israel's disobedience would itself be irrelevant). But in this instance Israel's actions in worshiping a false image of God are precipitated at least in part by a misunderstanding of God's true nature. Knowing God, and knowing God truly, lie at the heart of acting faithfully. And the qualities listed here imply, as we noted earlier, that such knowledge is not simply a matter of knowing facts about God, but rather involves actually knowing God, God's ways and glory, and of responding appropriately. In other words, the life of faith is all about knowing God's true nature and, on that basis, being drawn into God's ways and purposes, thereby beginning to live in a way that takes account of, and indeed comes to depend on, that reality.

Fourth, we have already observed that "YHWH" was considered the most sacred of all names. Imbued with holiness and power, it could be uttered only on the rarest of occasions (lest even inadvertent misuse blaspheme God and bring calamity upon the speaker [cf. *m. Sanh.* 7:5]). Only a priest in the Jerusalem temple could utter the "Ineffable Name," whether in pronouncing the Aaronic blessing (Num 6:24-26; *m. Soṭah* 7:6; *m. Tamid* 7:2) or (in the case of the high priest) on the Day of Atonement (*m. Yoma* 3:8; 6:2; *y. Yoma* 3:7; *b. Yoma* 39b).[23] New Testament authors sometimes exhibit a similar reluctance to name God directly (e.g., Mt 3:2; 4:17; Mk 14:61-62; Lk 1:32, 35; Heb 1:3; 8:1). Thus it is ironic that Moses' encounter with God, including the expansions of the divine name in Exodus 33:19 and 34:6-7, suggest that the "meaning" of God's name is, so to speak, ultimately no great mystery. It is revealed neither by grammatical nor by mystical speculation any more than it can ultimately be safeguarded by holy fear. Rather, it is both disclosed and guaranteed by the nature of God's relationship with Israel (and, indeed, with the whole of creation). God's "name" is expounded by God's acts, revealing this God to be, indeed, "compassionate and gracious, slow to anger, and abounding in steadfast love and faithfulness, keeping steadfast love for thousands, forgiving iniquity and transgression and sin, but by no means [clearing] the guilty." This is so not simply because God says so, but by virtue of the fact that God's response to national apostasy is to abstain from promised retribution, to renew the covenant (Ex 34:10), and to dictate a second copy of the commands that Moses, not God, had smashed in anger (Ex 34:27-28; cf. Ex 32:19).

## Walking with God

Within all three Abrahamic religions knowledge of God, which is the ultimate goal of the spiritual life, is to be expressed as much in practice as in belief. To borrow the words of Abu Ḥamid al-Ghazālī,

> It is inconceivable that a heart be filled with high regard for [a divine] attribute and be illuminated by it without a longing for this attribute following upon it, as well as a passionate love for that perfection and

[23]For a fascinating collection of references to the divine name and its treatment during the Second Temple period, see Ephraim E. Urbach, *The Sages: Their Concepts and Beliefs*, trans. Israel Abrahams (Jerusalem: Magnes, 1979), 125-34.

majesty, intent upon being adorned with that attribute in its totality—inasmuch as that is possible to one who so esteems it.[24]

Indeed, according to al-Ghazālī, it is in this manner, rather than by means of philosophical argument or speculation alone, that mere mortals may most truly "know" a transcendent God.[25] In similar fashion, the first-century Jewish apologist and historian Flavius Josephus considered imitation of divine virtue to represent the ultimate purpose of all that Moses had taught:

> [Moses] considered it the most necessary thing of all for the one who intends to regulate his life properly and to prescribe laws for others first to understand the nature of God and, after becoming an observer of His deeds . . . thus to imitate the best model of all and to try to follow it to the extent possible. (*Ant.* 1.19)[26]

As might be expected of a Christian text, 1 John focuses the matter more precisely on the person of Jesus: "By this we may be sure that we are in him: whoever says, 'I abide in him,' ought to walk just as he walked" (1 Jn 2:5-6). Jesus himself insists on as much:

> You have heard that it was said, "You shall love your neighbor and hate your enemy." But I say to you, Love your enemies and pray for those who persecute you, so that you may be children of your Father in heaven; for he makes his sun rise on the evil and on the good, and sends rain on the righteous and on the unrighteous. . . . Be perfect, therefore, as your heavenly Father is perfect. (Mt 5:43-45, 48)

In other words, Jesus is concerned to create a "family resemblance" between his Father, himself, and his followers. It is their gracious conduct that will reveal them to be "children of [their] Father in heaven."

With this in mind, we will proceed to a closer study of God's "name" as it is set out in Exodus 34:6-7. My basic thesis in doing so is at once conceptual, devotional, and practical. Not only do the characteristics

---

[24]Burrell and Daher, *Ninety-Nine Beautiful Names*, 31.

[25]So David B. Burrell, "Maimonides, Aquinas, and Ghazali on Naming God," in *The Return to Scripture in Judaism and Christianity: Essays in Postcritical Scriptural Interpretation*, ed. Peter Ochs (New York: Paulist Press, 1993), 247-51.

[26]Translation from Louis H. Feldman, trans., *Judean Antiquities 1-4: Translation and Commentary* (Leiden: Brill Academic, 2000), 8.

enumerated in this passage describe the ways of Israel's God, and not only do they delineate the character and conduct of Israel's Messiah, but also, in turn, the character of divine Father and Son alike is of profound importance both for how we relate to God and for how we may conduct ourselves in light of that relationship. My hope is that by meditating, longing for, and acting on the basis of what we discover to be true about God, our own "ways" will come to reflect, in some small degree, the "ways" of God; indeed, that we will begin to learn, step by step, what it means to "walk in all his ways, to love him, to serve the LORD [our] God" (Deut 10:12). To the extent that we can begin to do this, we too will find ourselves walking "just as Jesus walked."

*Blessed are you, merciful God!*
*Blessed is your name forever;*
*let all your works praise you forever.*
*And now, Lord, I turn my face to you,*
*and raise my eyes toward you.*

TOBIT 3:11-12 (CA. 200 BCE)

# 2

# A God Compassionate and Gracious

*And the* Lord *passed before him and proclaimed,*
*"The* Lord*, the* Lord*, a God* compassionate *and* gracious,
*slow to anger, and abounding in steadfast love and faithfulness,*
*keeping steadfast love for thousands,*
*forgiving iniquity and transgression and sin,*
*but who will by no means clear the guilty. . . ."*

Exodus 34:6-7

## God Most Compassionate, Most Merciful

So far we have looked briefly at the significance of human and divine names in the ancient Near East, and we have explored in general terms the theological, historical, and narrative contexts of God's self-revelation to Moses as recorded in the book of Exodus. Now we will look more closely at the content of that revelation and begin to trace its widespread influence in different theological and devotional traditions among the heirs of Abraham. What we will discover is that for all their differences, Jews, Christians, and Muslims share some remarkably similar convictions about the character of God, convictions that find their origin in Exodus 34.

A frequent invocation among Muslims, one that identifies them as adherents of the Islamic faith, is "Bismillah al-Raḥmān al-Raḥīm." It can be rendered into English as "In the name of God the Most Gracious [or 'Most Compassionate'], the Most Merciful," and it appears at the head of all but one of the 114 chapters of the Qur'an. Among the devout, this prayer is uttered prior to commencing a particular action as a way of consecrating to God what one is about to do. For example, sermons often begin with this phrase; it can be said as a prayer for someone who is sick; and it is the petition that accompanies *wudu*, ritual cleansing before worship. To commence an action in this manner implies that one's conduct, attitude, and relationships with others are to be governed by the gracious character of God.

In Islamic thought the three names that make up this phrase are generally held to be the most important of the "Ninety-Nine Beautiful Names" or "Attributes of Perfection." That is to say, while "Allah" is in Arabic the proper name for God, "al-Raḥmān" means the "the All-Merciful" or "the All-Gracious," and "al-Raḥīm" is variously rendered as "the All-Compassionate," "the All-Merciful," or "the Bestower of Grace."[1] Abu Saʿid al-Khudri (d. 693 CE), a companion of Muhammad, reported that the prophet had himself learned the meaning of God's merciful names from Jesus:

> The Messenger [i.e., Muhammad] of God said, "Jesus, the son of Mary, said: '*Al-Raḥmān* is the [One who is] Merciful in the next world as well as this world; *al-Raḥim* is the [One who is] Merciful in the next world.'"[2]

Other Islamic interpretations, of similar antiquity, distinguish between mercy shown to the whole of creation and to believers in particular, or between the attribute as it belongs to God alone and as applied to human conduct.[3]

---

[1]See the range of interpretations offered by the authoritative ninth-century commentator Abū Jaʿfar Muḥammad ibn Jarīr al-Ṭabarī (839-923 CE), *The Commentary on the Qurʾān; Being an Abridged Translation of Jāmiʿ al-bayān ʿan taʾwīl āy al-Qurʾān*, vol. 1, trans. J. Cooper (Oxford: Oxford University Press, 1987), 53-59.

[2]Quoted from Jarīr al-Ṭabarī, *Commentary on the Qurʾān*, 56. A rich exploration of the figure of Jesus in Islamic tradition is provided by Tarif Khalidi, ed. and trans., *The Muslim Jesus: Sayings and Stories in Islamic Literature* (Convergences; Cambridge, MA: Harvard University Press, 2001).

[3]Grammatically, the difference between the two is that the first "conveys the idea of fullness and extensiveness," whereas the second "denotes the idea of repetition . . . mercy limited in its scope but repeatedly shown" (Malik Ghulām Farīd, ed., *The Holy Qur'an: Arabic Text and English*

The appeal to a merciful God is also central to Jewish devotion. One of the most significant prayers in the Jewish household, the Birkat ha-Mazon ("Grace after Meals"), includes a series of petitions (from nine to fifteen, according to the traditions of different communities) addressed to "ha-Raḥaman"—"the Compassionate One" or "the All-Merciful One."[4] These petitions figure no less prominently in the liturgy for the Passover meal. While God's "mercy" or "compassion" is a recurrent theme throughout much of the Birkat ha-Mazon, its fourth section in particular declares,

> The Compassionate One—may he reign over us for ever and ever.
> The Compassionate One—may he be blessed in the heavens and on the earth.
> The Compassionate One—may he be lauded throughout all the generations.

Subsequent and more specific biddings call upon this same characteristic: "The Compassionate One—may he send much blessing to us in this house and to this table from which we have eaten"; "The Compassionate One—may he make us worthy of the days of the Messiah and of the life of the world to come."[5]

In similar fashion, Jewish penitential prayer includes an ancient Aramaic litany traditionally recited in preparation for the New Year and the Day of Atonement:

> O Merciful One, who answerest the poor, answer us.
> O Merciful One, who answerest the lowly in spirit, answer us.
> O Merciful One, who answerest the brokenhearted, answer us.[6]

The Day of Atonement concludes with the service of Neilah, sym-

---

*Translation with Commentary* [London: The London Mosque, 1981], 3). See also Kenneth Cragg, trans., *Readings in the Qur'ān* (London: Collins, 1988; repr., Brighton: Sussex Academic Press, 2004), 34-35. Cragg's "Introductory Essay" (pp. 14-82) provides a helpful and sensitive introduction to the Qur'an for English-speaking readers.

[4]The Talmud also refers to God by this title (e.g., *b. Ber.* 60b-61a; *b. Ketub.* 45a-b; *b. Giṭ.* 17a).

[5]Quoted from Nahum N. Glatzer, ed., *The Passover Haggadah: With English Translation, Introduction, and Commentary Based on the Commentaries of E. D. Goldschmidt*, rev. ed. (New York: Schocken, 1969), 65.

[6]Quoted from Abraham E. Millgram, *Jewish Worship* (2nd ed.; Philadelphia: Jewish Publication Society of America, 1975), 227.

bolizing the closing of the gates of the temple, of heaven, and of prayer.[7] Ashkenazi (i.e., European) Jews traditionally sing the first verse of a meditation on the thirteen attributes as part of the Neilah service. This hymn, known as Yisrael Nosha, is by the tenth-century liturgical poet Amittai ben Shephatiah:

> Lord, Lord, merciful and gracious God!
> Thou God of grace, of truth and of great righteousness. . . .
> Cover us with thy wings, thou attribute of Mercy! . . .
> I put my hope in thy divine word, I trust that the gates of mercy will not be closed before the streams of our tears.[8]

Likewise the Tahanunim ("Supplications"), recited in the course of midweek synagogue prayers and modeled after Nehemiah 9, include the following petition:

> Merciful and gracious One, I have sinned before thee;
> O Lord, who art full of compassion, have mercy on me and accept my supplications.[9]

In all five instances the ultimate source of such language is Exodus 34:6: "The Lord, the Lord, a God *compassionate and merciful* [*raḥûm wĕḥannûn*]." The rabbis took particular interest in the fact that God's mercy or compassion was the first characteristic to be named in this extended list of divine attributes. Since the passage as a whole was an exposition of the name "YHWH," they reasoned, this surely indicated a special connection between God's name and the attribute at the head of the list:

> Whenever Scripture says *the Lord* (יהוה) [Yahweh], it refers to His quality of mercy, as in the verse, *The Lord, the Lord, God, merciful and gracious* (Ex. 34.6). Whenever it says *God* (אלהים) [Elohim], it refers to His quality of justice. (*Sipre* Deut. 3:23 [§26])[10]

[7]Ibid., 258-61.

[8]Quoted from Israel Zinberg, *A History of Jewish Literature*, vol. 2, *French and German Jewry in the Early Middle Ages; The Jewish Community of Medieval Italy*, trans. and ed. Bernard Martin (Cleveland: Case Western Reserve University Press, 1972), 153.

[9]Quoted from Judith H. Newman, *Praying by the Book: The Scripturalization of Prayer in Second Temple Judaism* (SBLEJL 14; Atlanta: Scholars Press, 1999), 211.

[10]Quoted from Reuven Hammer, trans., *Sifre: A Tannaitic Commentary on the Book of Deuteron-*

To understand the inner logic of this interpretation, we must recall the foundational Jewish conviction that whereas other nations had many names for God ("El" and "Elohim" among them), "YHWH" was a unique name revealed to Israel alone. Thus, whereas the name "God" (and with it God's justice) might be evident to any and all nations, only Israel had been given the privilege of knowing the true name—and the compassionate mercy—of YHWH, "the LORD."

## God's Fierce Love

The adjective in question, together with the corresponding noun (*raḥămîm*, "compassion") and verb (*raḥam*, "to show compassion") are etymologically related to another word that means "womb" (*reḥem*).[11] For this reason, such language typically is explained as referring either to the intense, visceral love that a mother feels for the children whom she has brought into the world from her own body, or to the innate bond experienced by siblings who have shared the same womb. Whether or not such explanations are strictly accurate (since the meaning of a word can, over time, evolve considerably apart from its linguistic roots), "etymological" explanations have long appealed to biblical authors and interpreters. This sense of fierce maternal compassion emerges clearly in, for example, the famous story of the two prostitutes who come before King Solomon for judgment. Both have recently given birth, but one of their infants has died; each woman argues vehemently that the remaining son belongs to her and not the other. When Solomon chooses to settle the dispute by dividing the child in two—with a sword!—the woman whose baby has in fact died offers no objection. Why should she care if another child perishes? "But the woman whose son

---

*omy* (New Haven: Yale University Press, 1986), 49 (for further references, see p. 400, n. 14). Although generally thought to include traditions from the Tannaitic era (i.e., prior to 200 CE), *Sipre* likely was compiled "in the late third century" (H. L. Strack and G. Stemberger, *Introduction to the Talmud and Midrash*, trans. Markus Bockmuehl [Edinburgh: T & T Clark, 1991], 297). Elsewhere in rabbinic tradition the "Attribute of Mercy" (*Middat Raḥamim*) and the "Attribute of Justice" (*Middat ha-Din*) often are personified (e.g., *b. Meg.* 15b; *b. Sanh.* 97b) and represent the two essential aspects of God's response to a sinful creation.

[11]Although Phyllis Trible proposes that the literal term came first, giving rise to the more figurative or abstract sense ("On the Nature of God in the OT," *IDBSup* 368-69), others suggest that this may not have been the case (see the critique by Paul Mankowski, "The Gender of Israel's God," in *This Is My Name Forever: The Trinity and Gender Language for God*, ed. Alvin F. Kimel [Downers Grove, IL: InterVarsity Press, 2001], 35-61, esp. 47-52).

was alive said to the king—because *compassion* [*raḥămîm*] for her son burned within her—'Please, my lord, give her the living boy; certainly do not kill him!'" (1 Kings 3:26). The visceral love that "burns" within her for the child she has borne clearly demonstrates who the real mother is.

No less boldly, Isaiah 49:15 makes a similar claim regarding God: "Can a woman forget her nursing child, or show no *compassion* for the child of her womb? Even these may forget, yet I will not forget you [says the Lord]."[12] However fierce a mother's love may be, declares the prophet, God's love is even more powerful! Nor, according to Scripture, is such compassion limited to mothers alone, as Psalm 103:13 insists: "As a father has *compassion* on his children, so the Lord has *compassion* for those who fear him." This psalm is one of many scriptural passages that echo the language of Exodus 34 and expand devotionally on its meaning:

> *The Lord is merciful and gracious, slow to anger and abounding in steadfast love.*
> He will not always accuse, nor will he keep his *anger* forever.
> He does not deal with us according to our *sins*, nor repay us according to our *iniquities*.
> For as the heavens are high above the earth, so great is his *steadfast love* toward those who fear him;
> as far as the east is from the west, so far he removes our *transgressions* from us.
> As a father has *compassion* for his children, so the Lord has *compassion* for those who fear him.
> For he knows how we were made; he remembers that we are dust.
> As for mortals, their days are like grass; they flourish like a flower of the field;
> for the wind passes over it, and it is gone, and its place knows it no more.
> But the *steadfast love* of the Lord is from everlasting to everlasting on those who fear him,
> and his righteousness to *children's children*, to those who keep his covenant and remember to do his commandments. (Ps 103:8-18)[13]

[12]See also (albeit in a more negative context) Isaiah 13:18.

[13]On which, see Michael A. Fishbane, *Biblical Interpretation in Ancient Israel* (Oxford: Clarendon Press, 1985), 348-49.

In an extended meditation on the character of God the psalm makes it abundantly clear that God's fierce love for Israel, in all its manifold dimensions, is like that of a parent for a child, whose continued existence and well-being are utterly dependent on the one who first brought it into the world.

While neither Jewish nor Christian orthodoxy allows the idea of our being physically descended from God, the Scriptures of both consistently affirm that we are indeed the work of God's hands. Isaiah announces salvation to the exiled people of God: "Thus says the LORD, he who created you, O Jacob, he who formed you, O Israel: Do not fear, for I have redeemed you; I have called you by name, you are mine" (Is 43:1). In much the same way, although in a very different setting, the apostle Paul declares to the church in ancient Ephesus, "We are [God's] handiwork, created in Christ Jesus for good works" (Eph 2:10 [cf. 2 Cor 5:17]). The tender, intense, protective compassion of mothers and fathers at their best seems a fitting description for such a creative and creating, parenting God.

Nor is divine compassion limited to those who explicitly call on God's name. Not just Israel, but all nations; not human beings alone, but creation as a whole—all are embraced by God's loving concern, simply on the grounds that God alone has brought all of them into being. In Psalm 145:8-10 the psalmist begins by recounting the divine character revealed to Moses. But instead of citing an illustration from the life of Israel, the psalmist next declares that what God's people in particular have experienced in fact applies universally. Finally, the psalmist juxtaposes the universal and the particular: all God's "works" (i.e., creation as a whole) and all God's "faithful" (i.e., those who worship this God) together praise and thank the one God, on whom all of them depend:

> The LORD is *gracious and merciful*, slow to anger and abounding in *steadfast love*. The LORD is good to all, and his *compassion* is over all that he has made. All your works shall give thanks to you, O LORD, and all your faithful shall bless you. (Ps 145:8-10)

This, then, represents the ultimate scope of God's *raḥămîm*: even as the visceral "compassion" of human parents embraces their own children, so divine "compassion" extends not only to Israel, whom God has chosen and called, but also to the whole of God's creation without exception.

In three of these passages (Ex 34:6; Ps 103:8; 145:8) the terms describing divine compassion (the various forms and cognates of *rḥm*) appear in tandem with a second group of words that usually are translated in terms of "grace," "graciousness," "favor," or "mercy." For English speakers, this second set of terms (variously representing the Hebrew noun *ḥēn*, the adjective *ḥannûn*, or the verb *ḥānan*) will be familiar from the name "Hannah," which, as we observed in the preceding chapter, refers to "grace" or "favor." As will become obvious in the course of this discussion, descriptions of God in Hebrew Scripture frequently link "compassion" with the language of "grace" and "graciousness." While *raḥămîm* ("compassion") represents the commitment of those bound by prior ties of kinship and creation, this second set of terms expresses a sense of generous benevolence that, even among family members, is by nature freely given, unmerited, and unconstrained.[14] Thus the combination of "compassion" and "grace" or "favor" conveys a sense of God's commitment and generosity, fierce love and magnanimity, divine ownership and gratuitous kindness that are essential features of the covenant relationship.

## Compassion and Covenant

Despite the universal scope of Psalm 145:8-10, discussion of God's compassion and mercy more frequently focuses on their specific implications for the people of Israel and their covenant relationship with Yahweh. So, for example, in Deuteronomy 4:31 Moses declares to the people, even while he warns them of the dire consequences of apostasy, "Because the Lord your God is a *compassionate* God, he will neither abandon you nor destroy you; he will not forget the covenant with your

[14]With regard to human relations, "These words are descriptive of beneficent actions that are freely offered or received and contribute to the well-being of another or to the health of an ongoing relationship. [They represent] active kindness or generosity exhibited particularly toward those in need. . . . While such actions may be expected, usually (as with mercy or liberality) they go beyond what is just or customary and may be said to be a gift from one person to another. . . . Language for grace/favor among human beings is drawn on to speak of divine dispositions and actions" (Terence E. Fretheim, "חנן," *NIDOTTE* 2:204-5).

ancestors that he swore to them."[15] The book of Deuteronomy is widely thought to originate from the period of Israel's return from exile in Babylon and to reflect the nation's renewed appropriation of their ancient traditions. So it is fitting that we find Ezra recounting Israel's history in similar terms, as he prays to God in the presence and on behalf of the repentant exiles:

> Our ancestors acted presumptuously and stiffened their necks and did not obey your commandments; they refused to obey, and were not mindful of the wonders that you performed among them; but they stiffened their necks and determined to return to their slavery in Egypt. But you are a God ready to forgive, *gracious and merciful, slow to anger and abounding in steadfast love*, and you did not forsake them. . . . Many years you were patient with them, and warned them by your spirit through your prophets; yet they would not listen. Therefore you handed them over to the peoples of the lands. Nevertheless, in your *great mercies* you did not make an end of them or forsake them, *for you are a gracious and merciful God*. (Neh 9:16-17, 30-31 [see also Neh 9:27-28; Ps 78:38])[16]

In similar circumstances, Daniel openly acknowledges that the desolation that has come upon the people of Judah and Israel is their own fault, the result of disobedience and stubborn rebellion:

> Open shame, O Lord, falls on us, our kings, our officials, and our ancestors, because we have sinned against you. To the Lord our God belong *compassion* [*raḥămîm*] and forgiveness, for we have rebelled against him. . . . We do not present our supplication before you on the ground of our righteousness, but on the ground of your great mercies. (Dan 9:8-9, 18)

The prayers of Moses, Ezra, and Daniel appeal to God's covenant as an expression of God's character. Their prayers are based not simply on the conviction that God will adhere to the covenant even when the

---

[15]As indicated by the use of italics, the translations provided here and throughout the chapter make use of a single English equivalent in order to demonstrate to readers not fluent in ancient Hebrew or Greek that the same group of words is in view.

[16]As Judith Newman (*Praying by the Book*, 88-91) observes, selective recitation of the divine attributes serves as a unifying refrain throughout this prayer, emphasizing the graciousness of God and avoiding any mention of divine judgment or retribution.

people prove unfaithful; they pray knowing that such fidelity can be explained only in terms of the divine characteristics that gave rise to the covenant in the first place. The psalmist neatly captures this juxtaposition: "He has gained renown by his wonderful deeds; the LORD is *gracious and merciful.* He provides food for those who fear him; he is ever mindful of his *covenant*" (Ps 111:4-5). Thus divine covenant and divine character are mutually illuminating: each makes sense of the other, and together they explain God's insistence on drawing his people back to himself no matter how frequently they turn away.

This insight is particularly important in times of national crisis, whether occasioned by famine, plague, military defeat, or simple failure to obey God's will. On the assumption that the divine-human relationship is guided and undergirded by the character of God, the prophets explain that God responds to disobedience and rebellion with a temporary withdrawal of compassion and mercy. The most famous (or notorious) example is that of the name given by the prophet Hosea to his second child, a daughter. Hosea prophesies in the second half of the eighth century BCE concerning the infidelity of the northern kingdom of Israel, then at war with the regional powerbroker, Assyria. In order to symbolize in vivid terms the significance of Israel's turning away from the God of Abraham, Isaac, and Jacob to worship fertility gods as other nations do (see, e.g., Hos 2:13; 3:1; 4:12-19), Yahweh commands Hosea to marry Gomer, a prostitute. Gomer bears three children, two boys and a girl, each of whom Hosea furnishes with names that represent the plight of the nation as a whole. Thus when the daughter is born, Yahweh tells Hosea, "Name her Lo-ruhamah [*lōʾ ruḥāmâ*], for I will no longer have compassion [*lōʾ . . . ʾăraḥēm*] on the house of Israel or forgive them" (Hos 1:6 [cf. Hos 2:4]). The irony of the name comes from the fact that God considers the nation itself to be like his own child (Hos 11:1, 3-4), yet by virtue of their apostasy their spiritual paternity (like the paternity of Gomer's children) is rendered uncertain, calling into question the divine parental compassion so essential to Israel's covenant.

Roughly contemporaneous with Hosea is the prophet Isaiah, who speaks in similar terms of God's judgment: "This is a people without understanding; therefore he that made them will not have *compassion* on them, he that formed them will show them no favor" (Is 27:11 [similarly Is 9:17]). Jeremiah, on the other hand, prophesies at least a century later, at the time of the fall of the southern kingdom, Judah. Yet he too describes the consequences of national apostasy not as God's abrogation of the covenant itself, but rather as God's refusal to exercise the graciousness that gave rise to the covenant in the first place: "I have taken away my peace from this people, says the LORD, my steadfast love and *compassion* [*raḥămîm*]" (Jer 16:5 [cf. Jer 13:14]).

As is often the case, the book of Psalms reflects the same outlook in more personal terms. In Psalm 77 a troubled sufferer cries out in fear that God has betrayed his own nature: "Has his *steadfast love* ceased forever? Are his promises at an end for all time? Has God forgotten to be *gracious*? Has he in anger shut up his *compassion*?" (Ps 77:8-9). Likewise, in Psalm 40 the poet (said to be King David) pleads with God not to treat him as his sins deserve, but rather in the way God usually deals with the nation as a whole: "Do not, O LORD, withhold your *compassion* from me; let your *steadfast love* and your faithfulness keep me safe forever" (Ps 40:11).

Even when God does withhold mercy and compassion, however, it is not a stance that Israel's Savior maintains for long. Hosea looks forward to the day when God will again be bound to his people as a husband to his wife, "in righteousness and in justice, in *steadfast love* and in *compassion*" (Hos 2:19). Indeed, says God through the prophet, in that day, "I will have *compassion* on Lo-ruhamah," again punning on the same word (Hos 2:23). Much later, rabbinic commentators offer a more detailed explanation: God says to Hosea, in effect, "If you cannot abandon your own promiscuous wife and possibly bastard children, how can I abandon my people, the chosen offspring of Abraham, Isaac, and Jacob who have already proven their worth?" (*b. Pesaḥ.* 87ab). Much like Hosea, Isaiah also declares that Yahweh will soon reaffirm his love and renew his covenant with his chosen people: "For a brief moment I abandoned you, but with great *compassion* I will gather you. In overflowing wrath for a moment I hid my face from you, but with everlasting love I will have *compassion* on you, says the LORD, your Redeemer. . . . My covenant of peace shall not be removed, says the LORD, who has *compassion* on you" (Is 54:7-8, 10 [see also Ps 102:13-14; Zech 1:12, 16]).

Indeed, the people of Israel know that they can rely on God's mercy even in the midst of judgment, and it is the assurance of this gracious compassion that frequently motivates their repentance and return. Late in life, King David decides to conduct a census of the united kingdoms of Israel and Judah. To modern sensibilities, this seems innocent enough: surveys by research institutes, marketing groups, and even religious organizations are constantly taking the national pulse. Yet David's advisors are appalled at the idea, and they try to dissuade him from such foolishness. Why do they object? Perhaps because enumerating the people reflects both self-satisfaction on the part of the king at the extent of his empire and a desire to demonstrate how powerful he has become. Gad, a prophet, offers David (and the nation) one of three punishments for his presumption: three years of famine, three months of affliction at the hand of their enemies, or three days of plague. In choosing the last of these, David's observation is instructive: "Let us fall into the hand of the Lord, for his *compassion* is great; but do not let me fall into the hands of men" (2 Sam 24:14; 1 Chron 21:13). David knows God's character: whereas human enemies are liable to exact untold vengeance, divine mercy and compassion are such that God's punishment, however painful, will not prove overwhelming.

Even amidst judgment, God's compassion, and therefore God's covenant, prevail. This is so even when judgment comes in response to apostasy and outright rebellion, as is said to have happened in the days of King Jehoahaz of Israel. Although God delivers the nation into the hands of their enemies, such is God's mercy and compassion that the people need not remain there for long:

> Now King Hazael of Aram oppressed Israel all the days of Jehoahaz. But the Lord was *gracious* to them and had *compassion* on them; he turned toward them, because of his covenant with Abraham, Isaac, and Jacob, and would not destroy them; nor has he banished them from his presence until now. (2 Kings 13:22-23)[17]

So it is hardly surprising that in one of the prophet Isaiah's most eloquent and compelling passages, God's fierce love for his wayward

[17]See also Isaiah 14:1; 60:10; Jeremiah 12:15; 30:18; 33:26; Ezekiel 39:25; Zechariah 10:6.

people is what provides the motivation for their return:

> Seek the LORD while he may be found, call upon him while he is near;
> let the wicked forsake their way, and the unrighteous their thoughts;
> let them return to the LORD, and he will have *compassion* on them,
> and to our God, for he will abundantly pardon. (Is 55:6-7)

Still, the prophet makes it clear that divine mercy is the cause, not the consequence, of human penitence. If the people have waited for God to be merciful, God was already waiting long before them:

> Therefore the LORD waits to be *gracious* to you;
> therefore he will rise up to show *compassion* [*rāḥam*] to you.
> For the LORD is a God of justice; blessed are all those who wait for him. (Is 30:18)

No less famous is the prayer of Habakkuk (likely a contemporary of Jeremiah), who pleads with God at a time of national distress, "In wrath, remember mercy" (lit., "remember to be compassionate" [Hab 3:2]). Here, the language of God's fierce and faithful covenant love again provides the "turning point" for the religious allegiance of the nation as a whole. Joel too invokes the covenant character of God when, faced with the double catastrophe of drought and locusts (e.g., Joel 1:4-7, 17-18), he calls for the people to repent and call anew upon their God:

> Rend your hearts and not your clothing.
> Return to the LORD, your God, for he is *gracious and merciful*,
> slow to anger, and abounding in steadfast love, and relents from punishing. (Joel 2:13)

In each of these examples compassion and mercy are central to the divine-human relationship. Whether motivated by national or individual needs, calling upon the character of God ultimately represents the very essence of prayer.

## Prayer and the Character of God

Why, we might ask, should God answer prayer? Should God be faithful to us because we have been faithful to God? On the contrary, human history (and the history of God's people in particular) provides ample grounds for God not to answer prayer. Should we base our appeal instead on the urgency of a particular need, because the petition (rather than the petitioner) deserves a positive response? Is our cause worthy simply because we ourselves judge it to be so? This too seems presumptuous. Christians might respond that God answers prayers by virtue of Jesus' merit: God views favorably prayers offered "in the name of Jesus," in light of Jesus' accomplishment and the favor in which the Father holds the Son. But does God answer only the prayers of Jesus' followers? Although some would insist that this is indeed the case, broader human experience firmly indicates otherwise. On what basis, then, does God answer prayers generally, whether those of Jews, Christians, Muslims, or others, religious and nonreligious alike?

The simplest answer is that God answers prayer on the basis neither of who we are nor of the situations in which we find ourselves, but rather on the basis of who God is. This premise forms the core of the biblical—and Jewish—concept of prayer. The oldest section of the compendium of rabbinic teaching known as the Mishnah is a chapter called "The Sayings of the Fathers" (*Pirqe Aboth*). Although the Mishnah as a whole is thought to have been compiled around 200 CE, this chapter in particular appears to include much earlier material. The following tradition is attributed to Rabbi Simeon ben Yoḥai, who flourished around 130-160 CE:

> R. Simeon said: Be careful . . . in prayer, and when you pray, do not regard your prayer as an appointed routine but as an appeal for mercy [*raḥămîm*] and favor [*taḥănûnîm*] before the Omnipresent, for it is said: "For he is gracious and full of mercy, slow to anger and abundant in loving-kindness, and relenting of the evil decree." (*m. ʾAbot* 2:13)[18]

The text that he cites is an adaptation of Exodus 34:6-7 found in Joel 2:13, but the logic of his argument focuses on God's gracious and merciful character. It is clear that Simeon considers prayer to hinge not on

[18]Quoted from Samson Raphael Hirsch, trans., *Chapters of the Fathers* (Jerusalem: Feldheim, 1972). Although Mishnaic Hebrew differs somewhat from that of the biblical text, the use of the same vocabulary is evident even in transliteration.

the petition itself (although he is concerned to avoid rote repetition), but rather on the divine characteristics and qualities by which God is disposed to hear such petitions in the first place.

While Simeon implies that prayer appeals to the whole of the divine character, the present discussion is limited to prayers that specifically call upon God's "compassion" and "graciousness." Returning once more to prayers offered for the life of the nation as a whole, we note that Psalm 79 begins by lamenting that Jerusalem lies in ruins, trampled underfoot by nations that do not even know the name of Israel's God. Yet that same name represents the psalmist's hope:

> Do not remember against us the iniquities of our ancestors;
> let your *compassion* come speedily to meet us, for we are brought very low.
> Help us, O God of our salvation, for the glory of your name;
> deliver us, and forgive our sins, for your name's sake. (Ps 79:8-9)

In praying this way, God's people assume, even presume, that God will be true to his own compassionate nature. Isaiah too demands of God, "Where are your zeal and your might? The yearning of your heart and your *compassion*?" (Is 63:15), even as Jeremiah seems to offer God's reply:

> Is not Ephraim my dear son, the child in whom I delight?
> Though I often speak against him, remembering I still remember him.
> Therefore my heart yearns for him;
> *In compassion I have compassion* on him, declares the LORD. (Jer 31:20)[19]

In both passages it is God's own passionate compassion for his people that moves him to act on their behalf. Or as Daniel declares, while contemplating the fate of Jerusalem and the disgrace of the exiles,

> Incline your ear, O my God, and hear. Open your eyes and look at our desolation and the city that bears your name. We do not present our supplication before you on the ground of our righteousness, but on the ground of your great *mercies* [*raḥămîm*]. (Dan 9:18)

It should not surprise us, then, that the most distinctive character-

[19]In Hebrew both verbs, "to remember" and "to have compassion," are reduplicated in order to underscore the action in question. Although based on the NIV, the translation here has been amended to reflect this emphasis.

istic of biblical prayer is that it intentionally recites and explicitly invokes the divine qualities that the petitioner deems most relevant to the situation. In the following examples the psalmist offers prayer not on behalf of the nation as a whole, but rather in response to individual and personal need. Thus in Psalm 86 David describes himself as "poor and needy," surrounded by an ungodly "band of ruffians" (so NRSV) who seek to take his life. In his distress he can do no better than to recall and call upon the character of God as first revealed to Moses:

> But you, O Lord, are a God *compassionate and gracious*, slow to anger
> and abounding in steadfast love and faithfulness.
> Turn to me and be *gracious* to me; give your strength to your servant;
> save the child of your serving girl. (Ps 86:15-16 [cf. Ps 86:3])

Some of David's prayers are remarkably similar to, and probably modeled on, Moses' own appeal to God in Exodus 33:13: "Show me your ways, that I might know you and find favor in your sight":

> Make me to know your ways, O LORD; teach me your paths. . . .
> Be mindful of your *compassion*, O LORD, and of your *steadfast love*, for
> they have been from of old.
> Do not remember the sins of my youth or my transgressions;
> according to your *steadfast love* remember me, for your goodness' sake,
> O LORD!
> All the paths of the LORD are *steadfast love* and *faithfulness*, for those who
> keep his covenant and his decrees. (Ps 25:4, 6-7, 10 [cf. Ps 40:11])

David's approach is no different when he himself is to blame for his predicament. Psalm 51 (described as the king's prayer of distress upon being rebuked for stealing another man's wife and having the husband conveniently put to death!) opens with another bold appeal to the character of God:

> Have *mercy* [*ḥānan*] on me, O God, according to your *steadfast love*
> [*ḥesed*];
> according to your abundant *mercy* [*raḥămîm*] blot out my transgressions
> [*pešaʿ*].
> Wash me thoroughly from my iniquity [*ʿāwōn*], and cleanse me from
> my sin [*ḥaṭṭāʾt*]. (Ps 51:1-2)

Lest we miss his point, the language with which the petitioner confesses his multiple offenses is, once more, from Exodus 34:7.[20] In his moment of greatest failure David thus clings to the very letter of the sacred text, calling on God as the One who is merciful and compassionate, forgiving "iniquity and transgression and sin."

Petitioning God to be "gracious" is typical of psalms attributed to David,[21] but it is by no means unique to Davidic material, or even to the psalms in general. Psalm 123, for instance, is one of a group of psalms known as the Songs of Ascent, traditionally recited by pilgrims on their way up to Jerusalem. This particular psalm (whose author is not identified) eloquently calls upon God to show mercy to the humble yet faithful servants whom everyone else despises:

> As the eyes of servants look to the hand of their master,
> as the eyes of a maid to the hand of her mistress,
> so our eyes look to the LORD our God, until he is *gracious* unto us.
> Be *gracious* unto us, O LORD, be *gracious* unto us,
> for we have had more than enough of contempt. (Ps 123:2-3 [cf. Ps 119:58, 76-77, 132])

Of course, the proud independence and love of personal freedom so characteristic of Western cultures make the position of a servant or slave seem acutely unappealing, even as a spiritual discipline. Yet as we recite this psalm in church and synagogue, it would be difficult to find a more fitting image to describe both the profound difference in power between ourselves and the One whom we call "Lord," and the rapt devotion of those who, in brokenness and humiliation, desperately wait to be set free.

## THE DIVINE FULCRUM

But how exactly does this work? In what way does God demonstrate mercy and compassion? Here Scripture describes the operations of grace in quite precise terms. First, with regard to national enemies, even as they have served as instruments of divine judgment, so when

[20]To be precise, the third of these terms is the more common form (*ḥaṭṭāʾt*) of a closely related but rare word (*ḥaṭṭāʾâ*) that occurs only in Exodus 34:7; Isaiah 5:18.

[21]See Psalm 4:1; 6:2; 9:13; 25:16; 26:11; 27:7; 30:10; 31:9; 41:4, 10; 56:1; 57:1.

their task is complete (as it were), God causes these same foreigners to change their perception of their victims in specific and highly significant ways. Not only does the Lord himself show compassion in due time, but at the right moment he causes others to show compassion as well. A classic instance is that of King Hezekiah of Judah, who instigates a religious reform around the year 700 BCE in the face of threatened invasion from Sennacherib, king of Assyria. It is a time of great political uncertainty, when citizens of the northern kingdom (Israel) have already been taken into exile, and the southern kingdom of Judah is forced to pay crippling tribute. Yet Hezekiah promises that the mercy of God is mightier even than the ferocity of a foreign invader, providing a compelling reason for religious trust: "For as you return to the LORD, your kindred and your children will find *compassion* with their captors, and return to this land. For the LORD your God is *gracious and merciful*, and will not turn away his face from you, if you return to him" (2 Chron 30:9). This is a powerfully counterintuitive message to a troubled nation whose only expectation of their conquerors would otherwise be desecration, pillage, slavery, and death.

Scholars suggest that Solomon's prayer for the dedication of the temple, originally set in perhaps the tenth century BCE, was revised and "updated" in light of Israel's experience some four centuries later. In its present form the prayer explicitly envisages a situation in which the people, having been captured and taken into exile, repent of the sins that have brought them under judgment and cry out for deliverance:

> If they repent with all their heart and soul in the land of their enemies, who took them captive, and pray to you toward their land, which you gave to their ancestors, the city that you have chosen, and the house that I have built for your name; then hear in heaven your dwelling place their prayer and their plea, maintain their cause and forgive your people who have sinned against you, and all their transgressions that they have committed against you; and grant them *compassion* in the sight of their captors, so that they may have *compassion* on them. (1 Kings 8:48-50)

Solomon (or his editor) views it as a general principle that at the appropriate moment God lends divine compassion to the normally uncompassionate in order to reverse the effects of judgment and set his people free. Why? Because God remains bound to this nation by both the covenant of Sinai and his own unchanging character.

This same conviction gives Jeremiah hope in the face of national disaster. King Nebuchadnezzar of Babylon besieges the city of Jerusalem in 587-586 BCE, breaches its walls, captures King Zedekiah, blinds him and leads him into captivity, slaughtering the rest of his family and all his courtiers (Jer 39:1-8). A guerilla movement continues to resist, assassinating the local governor whom Nebuchadnezzar has appointed; further turmoil ensues (Jer 41:1-18). Fearing Babylonian reprisals, a ragtag remnant asks Jeremiah to pray for God's direction and deliverance. But the prophet's answer is the very opposite of what they expect: "Do not be afraid of the king of Babylon, as you have been; do not be afraid of him, says the LORD, for I am with you, to save you and to rescue you from his hand. I will grant you mercy [*raḥămîm*], and he will have mercy [*raḥam*] on you and restore you to your native soil" (Jer 42:11-12). Just when they want help to escape from Babylonian domination, Jeremiah counsels them to accept it, for even Nebuchadnezzar, he insists, comes under God's command. According to the prophet, knowledge of God's character and the mysterious ways of God's providence wins out over political expediency; divine mercy, he insists, is mighty enough even to make Nebuchadnezzar merciful. Sadly, the remnant rejects the guidance of God's prophet (Jer 43:1-7). Yet according to the prayer that Nehemiah offers up some seventy years later, events transpire precisely as Jeremiah has predicted. As he looks back on the ruin of Jerusalem and the continuing exile of God's people, Nehemiah begins to fast and pray. Although his prayer is theologically rich in its entirety, its opening and closing words take particular care to mention God's name and covenant character, for these are the basis on which Nehemiah, like Jeremiah before him, makes his appeal:

> O LORD God of heaven, the great and awesome God who keeps covenant and steadfast love with those who love him and keep his commandments; let your ear be attentive and your eyes open to hear the prayer of your servant that I now pray before you day and night. . . . O

> Lord, let your ear be attentive to the prayer of your servant, and to the prayer of your servants who delight in revering your name. Give success to your servant today, and grant him mercy [compassion, *raḥămîm*] in the sight of this man! (Neh 1:5-6, 11)

His prayer is answered, for God grants not only Nehemiah but also the nation as a whole compassion in the eyes of the king.

Certainly this is the conclusion offered by Psalm 106, which appears to date from the same era of national exile and offers a theological interpretation of Israel's national history. Here a series of parallel statements reflect the close relationship between God's mercy, the captors' mercy, and Israel's covenant. The psalmist confesses that despite God's many acts of deliverance on their behalf, the people have fallen into the snare of idolatry, until at last God has allowed them to be defeated and exiled by their enemies. Yet that is not the end of the matter, for Israel's deliverer remains attentive to their prayers for salvation:

> Nevertheless he regarded their distress when he heard their cry.
> For their sake he remembered his covenant
> and showed compassion according to the abundance of his steadfast love.
> He caused them to be pitied [viewed with *compassion*, *raḥămîm*] by all
> who held them captive. (Ps 106:44-46)

Here, as in Solomon's dedicatory prayer, the psalmist affirms that divine compassion ultimately prevails over divine judgment. The nations are no more than instruments in God's hands; if sometimes they are agents of divine justice, they can just as easily become the means of God's mercy and restoration.

If God changes the hearts of tyrants, how much more so those of his own people. Deuteronomy 30 describes, in now familiar terms, the compassion that characterizes God's restoration of the covenant people from exile. Although it is already clear that the motif of prayerful appeal to divine compassion extends across much of Hebrew Scripture, this passage develops the idea in a unique and compelling fashion. Notwithstanding the emphasis elsewhere on divine initiative, in this passage Moses is said to describe the conditions necessary for obtaining mercy following disobedience and punishment:

> When all these things have happened to you, the blessings and the curses that I have set before you, if you call them to mind among all the nations where the LORD your God has driven you, and return to the LORD your God, and you and your children obey him with all your heart and with all your soul, just as I am commanding you today, then the LORD your God will restore your fortunes and have *compassion* on you, gathering you again from all the peoples among whom the LORD your God has scattered you. (Deut 30:1-3)

Specifically, the people must be "wholehearted" in their intentions: they must return and obey "with all [their] heart and with all [their] soul." Although this latter phrase is typical of the book of Deuteronomy (e.g., Deut 6:5; 10:12), it is liable to be misunderstood by Western readers who (not unreasonably) assume the familiar equivalences of "heart = emotions" and "soul = inner life." However, the meaning of "heart and soul" in their ancient Hebraic context is more along the lines of what we would term "will and mind." This is important because of what follows in Deuteronomy 30:6, where Moses adds, "Moreover, the LORD your God will circumcise your heart and the heart of your descendants, so that you will love the LORD your God with all your heart and with all your soul, in order that you may live." Since the heart in particular is the seat of decision making and will power, the intent of this passage is a divine promise of God's intention to amend the will of his people, directly enabling them to obey and love in return. This theme, later developed by both Jeremiah and Ezekiel (e.g., Jer 31:33; Ezek 36:26), comes to fuller expression in the spirituality of the New Testament (e.g., Phil 2:13; Heb 8:8-13).[22] But the context implies that such change emerges only as a consequence of divine compassion: the people repent "wholeheartedly," acknowledging their sin; God responds with compassion, and this compassion causes the transformation both of the people's external circumstances and of their interior disposition. The ultimate expression of divine compassion is the mending of mind and will that led to disobedience in the first place. Whether, then, in the hearts of the people or in those of their foreign masters, compassion,

---

[22]See Peter C. Craigie, *The Book of Deuteronomy* (NICOT; Grand Rapids: Eerdmans, 1976), 364n2.

directly inspired by God, is the principle on which their destiny hinges, the point on which the nation's history turns.

### Love of God and Love of Neighbor

Israel's God therefore is not the only one bound by covenant to demonstrate graciousness and compassion. In the book of Exodus, amidst ordinances that deal with concerns ranging from slavery, accidental injuries and thievery to the treatment of foreigners, we find the following instruction:

> If you take your neighbor's cloak in pawn, you shall restore it before the sun goes down; for it may be your neighbor's only clothing to use as cover; in what else shall that person sleep? And if your neighbor cries out to me, I will listen, for I am *compassionate* [gracious, *ḥannûn*]. (Ex 22:26-27)

The implication seems to be that God declares, "I am compassionate, even if you are not so inclined." But precisely because this is the nature of the God with whom Israel must deal, they are obligated to follow suit.[23] Going well beyond the premise that divine graciousness is the basis on which God hears the cry of the needy and oppressed, here Torah boldly asserts that God's compassion demands social justice. There is no appeal here to the creditor's better nature; rather, fair treatment of the powerless is based on nothing more than fear of what a just and merciful God might do on behalf of those who have been denied justice or mercy.

Whereas Exodus sets forth the early foundations of Israel's religious and social identity, the first eight chapters of Zechariah represent an entirely distinct period of biblical history: the return from exile in Babylon.[24] Yet the same principle is evident, as the prophet instructs God's people regarding the essence of proper moral conduct:

> And the word of the Lord came again to Zechariah: "This is what the Lord Almighty says: 'Administer true justice; show *mercy* [steadfast love, *ḥesed*] and *compassion* [*raḥămîm*] to one another. Do not oppress the

---

[23]Compare the complaint of the prophet Malachi that the temple priests call upon God's graciousness while failing to honor or obey him (Mal 1:9).

[24]That is, around 520-518 BCE (see Ezra 5:1; 6:14). For discussion of the dating of Zechariah 1–8, see Carol L. Meyers and Eric M. Meyers, *Haggai, Zechariah 1-8: A New Translation with Introduction and Commentary* (AB 25B; Garden City, NY: Doubleday, 1987), xxix-xliv.

widow or the fatherless, the alien or the poor. In your hearts do not think evil of each other.'" (Zech 7:8-10)

Concern for widows, orphans, and the oppressed is typical of the prophets (e.g., Is 1:16-17; 10:2; 58:6-7, 10; Jer 7:5-6; 22:3; Ezek 22:7; Mal 3:5). But in this passage concern for the widow, the fatherless, the alien, and the poor appears to be specific application of a prior principle, prior both logically and in terms of its mention in the text. The double reference to God's ancient name ("YHWH," here rendered "the Lord") serves as an intentional reminder of the source of Zechariah's language: the people are commanded to imitate their God in demonstrating "steadfast love" and "compassion" toward one another. Even the reference to "*true* justice" echoes (as we will see in chapter 5) the word for God's "faithfulness" in Exodus 34:6.

Three brief examples further illustrate this point. The first is Psalm 112, which celebrates the virtues of the righteous, describing how those who fear Yahweh and obey his commandments will be blessed and remembered forever. All their dealings are characterized by justice and generosity, the psalmist declares: they are "*gracious*, *compassionate*, and righteous" (Ps 112:4). Leaving aside for the moment the more conventional term "righteous," we note that the adjective *ḥannûn* ("gracious") occurs thirteen times in the Hebrew Bible (including, of course, Ex 34:6). In every instance except for this one it describes the character of God. Likewise the term *raḥûm* ("compassionate") occurs just thirteen times (again including Ex 34:6); only here does it describe a human characteristic. It seems, then, that the highest possible praise that Scripture can offer the servants of the one true God is to describe them in terms normally reserved for the gracious and compassionate character of God. In case the reader might miss the point, the same description applies to God just a few psalms later on: "Gracious is the Lord, and righteous; our God is compassionate" (Ps 116:5).

No less striking is the language of Psalm 18. The Hebrew verb *raḥam* ("to have compassion") usually appears with God as its subject. Only rarely is it applied to human beings, and then in a negative sense, as Jeremiah, for instance, warns of kings and ravenous armies coming from the north who will show neither compassion nor mercy (Jer 6:23 [cf. 50:42]; 21:7). Only once (as we saw earlier) does Jeremiah allow that the king of Babylon will act with compassion in repatriating the exiled nation, and then only because God will be acting compassionately through him (Jer 42:12). Such comparisons render the opening words of Psalm 18 all the more arresting. In this psalm David is said to celebrate his deliverance "from the hand of all his enemies and from the hand of Saul." He does so by relating the many ways in which God has rescued and made him strong, painting God as the true warrior who brings victory from the heavens for his faithful servant and king. Accordingly, the psalm opens with an exultant shout, but the force of its language is entirely lost in the English translation:

> I *love* [*rāḥam*] you, O Lord, my strength.
> The Lord is my rock, my fortress, and my deliverer,
> my God, my rock in whom I take refuge,
> my shield, and the horn of my salvation, my stronghold. (Ps 18:1-2)

A more wooden (and theologically impossible) rendering of the opening phrase might be something like "I love you compassionately, O Lord."[25] Clearly this sense cannot apply, although it is difficult to find an alternative rendering that conveys the depth, intimacy, and vigor of the psalmist's fierce love for God. So great has been Yahweh's compassion and care for him that he evidently feels compelled to reciprocate in similar terms.

Finally, we may turn to the familiar wording of the Aaronic blessing in Numbers 6:24-26:

> The Lord bless you and keep you;
> The Lord make his face to shine upon you, and *be gracious* to you;
> the Lord lift up his countenance upon you, and give you peace.

This benediction has a central place in Jewish spirituality, having once formed part of the temple liturgy. How far back such popularity extends is apparent from the fact that Psalm 67:1 already incorporates

[25]This verb occurs forty-seven times in Hebrew Scripture, but only here in the form that is usual for verbs of action in Hebrew, making its exact meaning all the more difficult to determine.

the blessing into Israel's worship. It is rich in meaning, asking Yahweh for abundance, safety, and peace. But the original text is even more precise, for in Numbers 6:27 God stipulates that by pronouncing this blessing, the sons of Aaron "shall place *my name* on the sons of Israel." The one specific echo of the divine name is the petition for God to "be gracious" (*ḥānan*). From what we have already seen, this would be appropriate language for any prayer offered to Israel's God. But in this particular instance it is not exactly a prayer; rather, it is a blessing, whereby the sons of Aaron are granted authority to invoke and, at least indirectly, bestow divine favor upon the people. In other words, the Aaronic blessing is one way in which, with God's own help, the people of Israel enable one another to experience the graciousness of their God.

From the passages reviewed thus far, it is clear that "compassion" and "graciousness" are not only essential divine attributes, but also divine requirements. If these are the qualities by which God keeps covenant, so they must characterize the covenant faithfulness of God's people, as those who depend on divine compassion demonstrate the same compassion to others. Failure to do so invokes judgment, as those who have not shown mercy find mercy withdrawn from them also. But more typically, the children of Israel are moved to imitation and reflect in their own actions the gracious manner in which Yahweh has dealt with them.

## Grace, Favor, and the Mercies of God

In the Greek of the New Testament several different groups of words can be translated as "compassion" or "mercy." The first of these is *splanchnon*, a word that in our literature always occurs in the plural (the corresponding verb is *splanchnizomai*, "to show compassion," as in the case of the prodigal's father [Lk 15:20]). The plural form, *splanchna*, originally meant "guts" or "entrails" (as with the somewhat graphic description of Judas's innards falling out in Acts 1:18). This accounts for the otherwise incomprehensible language of the King James Version in texts such as Philippians 1:8, where Paul declares, "I long after you all in the *bowels* of Jesus Christ," or Philemon 20, where Paul tells the former slave owner, "Refresh my *bowels* in the Lord." Somewhat more self-explanatory is 1 John 3:17: "Whoso hath this world's good, and seeth his brother have need, and shutteth up his *bowels of compassion* from him, how dwelleth the love of God in him?" (similarly Col 3:12). Whichever translation we choose, the original Greek terms convey a sense of deep inner feeling; our contemporary idiom "gut-wrenching" has a similar flavor.

Thus it would be natural to assume that *splanchnon* and *splanchnizomai*, with their strongly visceral overtones, most closely represent the Hebrew *rḥm*, since the latter is also associated etymologically with "innards." But reality turns out to be rather more complex. In fact, the Greek version of the Hebrew Bible often translates *rḥm* and its cognates by means of *oiktirmos* ("mercy, compassion"), together with the verb *oiktirō* ("to show mercy, compassion") and the adjective *oiktirmōn* ("merciful"). The Hebrew verb *ḥānan* ("to be gracious") is rendered into Greek as *oiktirō* or *eleeō* (of which the latter also means "to show mercy"), or else by the corresponding adjectives, whether *oiktirmōn* or *eleēmōn*.[26] Although translation can never be exact, there is frequent overlap between these various terms in both languages, in addition to which later literature (i.e., after the completion of the Septuagint), indeed uses *splanchnizomai* and related vocabulary to translate Hebrew language of visceral compassion (*raḥam*, *raḥămîm*, etc.).[27] Even though tracing degrees of equivalence turns out to be both complex and confusing, the association of these Greek terms with the name and character of God suggests that we should pay closer attention to their appearance in the New Testament.

As might be expected given his religious heritage, Paul describes the One whom he worships as "the Father of *mercies* [pl. of *oiktirmos*] and

---

[26]By comparison, the nominal form, *ḥēn*, appears in the Septuagint as *charis* ("grace"). For a fuller treatment of these terms, see Rudolf Bultmann, "ἔλεος, κτλ.," *TDNT* 2:477-87; idem, "οἰκτίρω, κτλ.," *TDNT* 5:159-61; Hans Conzelmann and Walther Zimmerli, "χαίρω, κτλ.," *TDNT* 9:359-415, esp. 376-89. The Hebrew adjective that appears in Exodus 34:6, *ḥannûn*, is translated into Greek as *eleēmōn*, which consistently appears in ensuing echoes of this formula (2 Chron 30:9; 2 Esd 19:17, 31 // Neh 9:17, 31; Ps 86:15 [LXX 85:15]; 103:8 [LXX 102:8]; 111:4 [LXX 110:4]; 145:8 [LXX 144:8]; Joel 2:13; Jon 4:2), but also in nonformulaic contexts (Ex 22:27 [MT/LXX 22:26]; Ps 112:4 [LXX 111:4]; 116:5 [LXX 114:5]); it is characteristic of God even without a Hebrew equivalent (Tob 6:18; 7:12; 2 Macc 1:24; 8:29; 11:9; 13:12; 3 Macc 5:7; Sir 2:11; 48:20; 50:19; *Pss. Sol.* 5:2; 7:5; 10:7).

[27]Helmut Köster, "σπλάγχνον, κτλ.," *TDNT* 7:552.

the God of all consolation" (2 Cor 1:3)[28] (cf. Eph 2:4: "God, who is rich in mercy [*eleos*]"). These are sentiments that any pious Jew might echo. Nor should it come as a surprise that Paul uses similar language to express the essence of godliness: "As God's chosen ones, holy and beloved, clothe yourselves with compassion [*splanchna oiktirmou*], kindness, humility, meekness, and patience" (Col 3:12 [cf. Phil 2:1]). But what sets Paul apart is his identification, in Romans 12:1, of Jesus of Nazareth as the paradigmatic expression of divine mercy. Indeed, that he does so without drawing further attention to the move suggests that such an association is for him both automatic and self-explanatory. The particular location of this language is all-important. Almost without exception Paul's letters fall into two major parts. Once past the customary greetings and introductory formulas, Paul begins most letters with theological argument and exposition, invariably focusing on the person of Jesus. With these explanations complete, he moves on to exhortation (the technical term for which is "paranesis"), implying that theological conviction must issue in moral action. In this letter the first verse of Romans 12 represents the point of transition between theology and ethics, between Christian conviction and Christian conduct. Here, as elsewhere, Paul's appeal hinges on an essential "therefore":

> I appeal to you *therefore*, brothers and sisters, *by the mercies* [pl. of *oiktirmos*] *of God*, to present your bodies as a living sacrifice, holy and acceptable to God, which is your spiritual worship. (Rom 12:1)

His "therefore" recalls the previous eleven chapters of densely packed theological argument as the basis on which he offers the exhortation now to follow. But he also adds an essential qualification: "by the mercies of God." This simple phrase sums up the argument of the entire letter, serving as shorthand for the whole purpose and meaning of Christ and his ministry. Jesus of Nazareth, Paul declares, is not only the Messiah of Jewish expectation, not only the "Lord," before whom Greeks and Romans alike must bow; he is the very expression of divine mercy, divine compassion. This, he says, is the motivation for his

[28]On this verse and its resonances with Jewish liturgy, see C. K. Barrett, *The Second Epistle to the Corinthians* (BNTC; London: Adam & Charles Black, 1973), 59-60.

readers to offer themselves as living sacrifices unto God. Just as Jesus first offered himself as a living sacrifice on their behalf, thereby embodying God's mercy, so on account of Jesus, his followers offer their own lives in sacrifice and worship to God. Because God has shown them mercy, they become like the One through whom that mercy has been shown, rendering all the worship and adoration that God is due. This, Paul declares, is what God finds "acceptable."

Such convictions raise an important question. Why, if Jesus of Nazareth is indeed the long-awaited Messiah, have so many in Israel failed to recognize him as such? Does this perhaps reflect a lack of mercy on God's part, even a withdrawal of divine mercy toward the covenant people? In Romans 9–11 Paul insists that, contrary to appearances, divine mercy remains fully in force. He begins by asserting that there is more to being a recipient of God's promises than simply having been born into the right family—in this case, the family of Israel. Even if those promises were indeed made to the descendants of Abraham, the operative principle remains one of divine fidelity, not blood lineage or even faithful conduct. After all, he reasons, the validity of a promise depends not on the one who receives it, but rather on the one who makes the promise—in this case, God. Paul admits that this might sound unfair, as though an unjust God were depriving people (good and evil alike) of their just deserts:

> What then are we to say? Is there injustice on God's part? By no means! For he says to Moses, "I will have mercy [*eleeō*] on whom I have mercy, and I will have compassion [*oiktirō*] on whom I have compassion." So it depends not on human will or exertion, but on God who shows mercy. (Rom 9:14-16)

Had Paul ended there, with his quotation of God's words to Moses in Exodus 33:19, he might have prevented much subsequent controversy and confusion. But in order to further drive home his point, he goes on to cite the example of Pharaoh as one upon whom (with every appearance of arbitrariness) God chose not to have mercy. Paul concludes emphatically, "So then he has mercy on whomever he chooses, and he hardens the heart of whomever he chooses" (Rom 9:18). That, of course, sounds all the more unjust, as a result of which Paul must spend the next ten or so verses further justifying his explanation. By this point the reader may be forgiven for having lost sight of the original principle: salvation is based not on human qualifications or accomplishments of any sort, but solely on God's inherent willingness to demonstrate mercy and compassion.

Although ancient Egyptians might have thought otherwise, the apostle insists that God's ways with his people do not amount to injustice. With the exception of the ill-fated Pharaoh (who illustrates a subsidiary point), the only means by which one can disqualify oneself from divine mercy, says Paul, is by thinking and acting as though one were qualified to receive it. This, in fact, was precisely the original implication of Exodus 33:19. For there, as we saw in the preceding chapter, the repetition "I will be gracious to whom I will be gracious, and will show mercy on whom I will show mercy" (this is the NRSV translation from Exodus, versus Paul's reformulation of the phrase) expands on the divine name, "I will be who I will be," and explains God's self-sufficiency in terms of a divine insistence on mercy and compassion regardless of human will or worth. What Paul picks up on, then, is the very earliest, most basic exposition of the divine name and character contained in the Scriptures of Israel. In order to explain the inexplicable—the apparent hardening of Israel for the benefit of the Gentiles—Paul recalls a similar episode from the past: the hardening of a Gentile for the sake of Israel. Both, he insists, are ultimately rooted in divine compassion: God's ultimate independence from all human claims is at the same time God's unconstrainable freedom to be universally gracious and merciful.[29] This point cannot be passed over lightly, for it insists that what appears dangerously capricious is in fact the very opposite. We fear that God will mishandle divine power in such a way as to oppress defenseless creatures like ourselves. In fact, says the apostle, God's nature is such as to consistently err on the side of mag-

[29]Despite the ends to which it has been turned in the service of ultra-Calvinist views of general predestination, Paul's appeal to Pharaoh indicates only that in the course of demonstrating mercy for the sake of many (in this case, to Moses, Israel, and their spiritual inheritors), God may choose to withhold mercy to the few, even as in Paul's own day the otherwise inexplicable lack of receptivity on the part of a few in Israel has opened the way of mercy for many among the Gentiles. No more general principle than this is intended.

nanimity and forgiveness, a lesson that Jesus also taught in declaring that God "makes his sun rise on the evil and on the good, and sends rain on the righteous and on the unrighteous" (Mt 5:45).

Paul's argument is stunning in its simplicity. Going well beyond the ancient principle that God withdraws mercy from those who refuse to demonstrate it, Paul insists that neither obedience nor disobedience can curtail mercy, for if they could, God's mercy would be determined by human action. The only factor that can curtail divine mercy and compassion, says the apostle, is the belief that one deserves or has a right to it. That, he insists, is theological presumption, which denies the essential character of mercy *as mercy*, and of grace *as grace*. By reasoning in this manner, Paul is doing no more or less than what we have observed throughout the Scriptures of Israel. Every reversal that Israel suffers (as in the particular case that Paul is trying to explain) represents a potential challenge to the view that God is unfailingly merciful and compassionate. Paul is certain that God's mercy and compassion endure, even in the situation of his own people at the present time, for when they too recognize their need, mercy will once more be mercy—versus a right—and so God will bestow it as freely upon them as upon the Gentiles (Rom 11:31-32).

Nor, it must be said, is this a uniquely Christian conviction, as emerges with particular clarity from an illustration found in the early medieval commentary known as *Exodus Rabbah*.[30] According to the biblical account, when Moses asks to be shown God's ways, God's glory (Ex 33:13, 18), Yahweh responds, "I will make all my goodness pass before you, and will proclaim before you the name, 'The Lord'; and I will be gracious to whom I will be gracious, and will show mercy on whom I will show mercy" (Ex 33:19). To explain the scope and significance of divine goodness, *Exodus Rabbah* tells a story about how Yahweh answered Moses by taking him on a tour of the heavenly treasure house:

> Then it was that God showed him all the treasures in which the rewards of the righteous are stored away. Moses asked: "To whom does all this treasure belong?"

---

[30]On the dating of *Exodus Rabbah* (perhaps in the tenth century CE), see Strack and Stemberger, *Introduction to the Talmud and Midrash*, 336-37.

> And He replied, "To those who fulfill My commandments."
> "And to whom does this treasure belong?"
> "To those who bring up orphans." And so it was with every treasure.
> Later he saw a huge treasure and inquired: "Whose is this great treasure?"
> The Divine rejoinder was: "To him that has [such things to his credit] I give of his reward, but to him who has not, I have to supply freely and I help him from this great pile," as it says, 'And I will be gracious to whom I will be gracious,' namely, to him to whom I wish to be gracious. Similarly, 'And I will show mercy on whom I will show mercy.'" (*Exod. Rab.* 45:6)[31]

There are those, by this account, who earn their heavenly recompense by dint of obedience or acts of compassion. But outweighing all such rewards is the vast treasury of mercy that God reserves for those who can claim no merit, on whom God shows compassion simply because it is his nature to do so.

## Blessed Are the Merciful

The language of mercy and compassion appears frequently in the ministry and teaching of Jesus. Just so, Jesus has compassion on a leper (Mk 1:41), on a widow who has lost her only son and source of support (Lk 7:13), the sick (Mt 14:14), the blind (Mt 20:34), or those who have gone hungry in order to hear his teaching (Mt 15:32 // Mk 8:2) (all expressed with the verb *splanchnizomai*). In each case Jesus' heartfelt compassion is the prelude to healing and provision. The same language appears in Jesus' parables, describing the father of the prodigal son (Lk 15:20), the Samaritan who helps the victim of violent robbers (Lk 10:33), and the king who forgives his servant an impossible debt (Mt 18:27). Of particular relevance for Jesus' followers in later generations is the description of Jesus' response to the crowds as he travels from town to town: "When he saw the crowds, he had compassion [*splanchnizomai*] for them, because they were harassed and helpless, like sheep without a shepherd" (Mt 9:36 [// Mk 6:34]). Just as in earlier examples of God's

[31]Quoted from Karla R. Suomala, *Moses and God in Dialogue: Exodus 32-34 in Postbiblical Literature* (SBL 61; New York: Peter Lang, 2004), 141.

compassion inspiring compassion on the part of God's people, so here Jesus' compassion leads him to enlist others to share in his mission of proclaiming the gracious reign of God: "Then he said to his disciples, 'The harvest is plentiful, but the laborers are few; therefore pray the Lord of the harvest to send out laborers into his harvest'" (Mt 9:37-38). Both Jesus' own mission and his call for others to join him in it arise from his deep sense of compassion. Participating in Christ's mission is far more than accomplishing some particular task for the kingdom of God; it comes as a consequence of being swept up by the impetus of divine love.

Whereas much Christian piety focuses on the imitation of Jesus (e.g., 1 Cor 11:1; 1 Thess 1:6; 1 Pet 2:21), Jesus himself exhorted his followers to imitate the One whom he boldly called "Father":

> If you love those who love you, what credit is that to you? For even sinners love those who love them. If you do good to those who do good to you, what credit is that to you? For even sinners do the same. If you lend to those from whom you hope to receive, what credit is that to you? Even sinners lend to sinners, to receive as much again. But love your enemies, do good, and lend, expecting nothing in return. Your reward will be great, and you will be heirs [*huioi*, "sons"] of the Most High; for he is kind to the ungrateful and the wicked. Be merciful, just as your Father is merciful. (Lk 6:32-36 // Mt 5:44-48 [cf. Eph 5:1])

Although some modern translations, for the sake of gender inclusiveness, refer to "children of the Most High," the issue at stake here is not gender itself, but rather the right of inheritance. For this reason, even though the Greek text reads "sons," I prefer the word "heirs." In a patriarchal society it was the sons who retained the power, the authority, and the property (land and slaves alike) of their father. However we choose to translate it, Jesus' statement is powerfully antipatriarchal and radically inclusive, for it offers divine "sonship" to any and all who, with him, are generous, merciful, and forgiving after the manner of their heavenly Father. By graciously embracing rather than excluding the weak, the disprivileged, and the poor, this notion of fatherhood and sonship alike represents the very opposite of all that "patriarchy" has come to represent.

Jesus goes even further, declaring, "Blessed are the merciful [*eleēmōn*], for they will receive mercy" (Mt 5:7). The implication seems to be that only those who are merciful may obtain mercy. This should not surprise us, for Jesus will soon tell his followers, "If you do not forgive others, neither will your Father forgive your trespasses" (Mt 6:15 [cf. Jas 2:12-13]). The two verses testify that such conditions are characteristic of God's gracious reign: either one operates according to principles of mercy and forgiveness, both given and received, or one does not. There are no half measures, no possibility of invoking one set of terms for oneself while applying a different set to everyone else. As we will see in greater detail later on, the parable of the unforgiving debtor (Mt 18:23-35) makes the same point in even more arresting terms.

Whereas refusal to forgive can prompt God to do the same, our own exercise of mercy is not ultimately the cause of God's. If anything can be said to "cause" divine mercy, it is our need of it, as Cyprian, bishop of Carthage, points out in his own distinctive exposition of Matthew 5:4 ("Blessed are those who mourn, for they will be comforted"). In a letter written in 252 CE Cyprian compares the heavenly Father to human fathers:

> How much more does that one and true Father, good, merciful, and loving—yea, Himself Goodness and Mercy and Love—rejoice in the repentance of His own sons! Nor threatens punishment to those who are now repenting, or mourning and lamenting, but rather promises pardon and clemency. Whence the Lord in the Gospel calls those that mourn, blessed; because he who mourns calls forth mercy. (*Epist.* 51.23 [*ANF* 5:333])

Following Cyprian's view, then, the Beatitudes reflect both sides of this dynamic: mourning calls forth mercy, which the mourners then reciprocate in being merciful toward others. Once again, the mercy we offer mirrors the mercy we live by. According to Isaac of Syria, an ascetic of wide influence in the Eastern church and briefly bishop of Nineveh in the 660s CE, imitation of God's compassion is thus the truest mark of spiritual maturity:

> It is the same with all the saints: when they become perfected, they

> attain this accomplishment by imitating God in the outpouring of their love and compassion upon all humanity. . . . This shall be for you a luminous sign of the serenity of your soul: when, on examining yourself, you find yourself full of compassion for all humanity, and your heart is afflicted with pity for them, burning as though with fire.[32]

In this sense, the "sonship" of which Jesus speaks implies a measure of likeness or similarity in conduct and outlook. What, then, does it mean to be like God and unlike the sinful? Most answers to this question emphasize the obligations of moral purity and holiness. Just so, according to Matthew, Jesus tells his disciples, "You shall be perfect, as your heavenly Father is perfect" (Mt 5:48). But according to the parallel passage in Luke, Jesus tells them, rather, "Be merciful [*oiktirmōn*] as your Father is merciful [*oiktirmōn*]" (Lk 6:36). Scholars debate which of the two derives from Jesus, which of the evangelists may have been responsible for adapting the tradition, or whether the variants represent alternative renderings of a common original.[33] One possibility, proposed by W. D. Davies and Dale Allison, is that Jesus adapts Leviticus 19:2 ("You shall be holy, for I the LORD your God am holy") by substituting "mercy" for "holiness."[34] This would suggest that the holiness (or perfection) of God is none other than the mercy of God, and that those who wish to honor God by becoming holy and perfect can do no better than to imitate God in mercy and compassion toward others.

Jesus was not the first teacher to define true piety as the imitation of divine mercy. The *Letter of Aristeas*, likely dating from the second century BCE, tells the story of a banquet at which a king puts questions to his guests on the subject of godly kingship. Asked how a king might be a "friend" to his subjects, one guest responds that since human life

---

[32]Quoted from A. M. Allchin, ed., *The Heart of Compassion: Daily Readings with St. Isaac of Syria*, trans. Sebastian Brock (London: Darton, Longman & Todd, 1989), 14, 58.

[33]For discussion, see Matthew Black, *An Aramaic Approach to the Gospels and Acts* (3rd ed.; Oxford: Clarendon Press, 1967), 181; Robert H. Gundry, *The Use of the Old Testament in St. Matthew's Gospel, with Special Reference to the Messianic Hope* (NovTSup 18; Leiden: Brill, 1967), 74; idem, *Matthew: A Commentary on His Handbook for a Mixed Church under Persecution* (Grand Rapids: Eerdmans, 1994), 99-100; Martin McNamara, *The New Testament and the Palestinian Targum to the Pentateuch* (rev. ed.; AnBib 27A; Rome: Pontifical Biblical Institute, 1978), 133-38.

[34]W. D. Davies and Dale C. Allison Jr., *The Gospel According to Saint Matthew* (3 vols.; ICC; Edinburgh: T & T Clark, 1988-1997), 1:561 (although the injunction to imitate God's holiness is also found in Lev 11:44-45; 20:26).

"is constituted in pain and punishment," the king ought not to visit punishment on his subjects too quickly. By bearing this in mind, the guest tells him, "You will be inclined to mercy, even as God is merciful" (*Let. Aris.* 208). From the same era comes a series of documents known as the *Testaments of the Twelve Patriarchs*, in which the twelve sons of Jacob instruct their respective descendants on the virtues of a righteous life. The *Testament of Zebulon*, the sixth son of Jacob, counsels "compassion on all," man and beast alike; in particular by feeding the hungry, comforting the needy, and clothing the naked (*T. Zeb.* 5–7): "You also, my children, have compassion toward every person with mercy, in order that the Lord may be compassionate and merciful to you. In the last days God will send his compassion on the earth, and whenever he finds compassionate mercy, in that person he will dwell. To the extent that a man has compassion on his neighbor, to that extent the Lord has mercy on him" (*T. Zeb.* 8:1-3).[35]

Later tradition illustrates this principle with a dramatic tale told of Rabbi Judah ha-Nasi ("the Prince"), compiler of the Mishnah and foremost among the early generations of rabbinic scholars. Why, the sages wondered, did such a pious man suffer from intense physical pain for thirteen years of his life? For a man so close to God, they reasoned, such affliction could not have been accidental, so they recounted the following story:

> A calf which they were bringing to slaughter went [and] hung its head in the corner of Rabbi's garment and cried. He said to it: "Go. For this [i.e., to serve as food] you were created." [Thereupon] they said [in heaven], "Since he shows no compassion, let sufferings come upon him."

One day, long years of affliction later, the rabbi's maid comes upon some rats while sweeping the house, and she captures them:

> He said to her: "Let them go. It is written, 'And His mercies [*raḥămîm*] are over all His works'" [Ps 145:9]. They said [in heaven], "Since he shows compassion, we will have compassion on him." (*b. B. Meṣiʿa* 85a)[36]

[35]For further instances in Jewish literature, see the passages listed by Craig S. Keener, *A Commentary on the Gospel of Matthew* (Grand Rapids: Eerdmans, 1999), 166n17.

[36]Quoted from Adin Steinsaltz, *The Talmud: The Steinsaltz Edition*, vol. 5, *Tractate Bava Metzia Part V*, trans. Israel V. Berman (New York: Random House, 1999), 133-34. A different form of this story appears in *Genesis Rabbah* 33:3.

Thus his suffering ends. Appropriately, the words of heaven echo those of Rabbi Judah's own grandfather, Gamaliel of Yavneh (also known as Gamaliel II): "Whosoever has compassion on his fellow-creatures, upon him God will have compassion."[37]

Islamic tradition makes a similar point on the basis of Jesus' teaching in Matthew 5:7; 6:15:

> It is written in the Gospels, "Son of Adam, as you have mercy, so shall God have mercy upon you. How do you hope for God's mercy if you do not have mercy upon His servants?" (Abu al-Layth al-Samarqandi [d. 983 CE])
>
> Jesus said, "The [one who is] merciful in this world is the one who will be shown mercy in the next world." (Abu al-Hasan al-ʿAmiri [d. 992 CE])[38]

Even so, believers demonstrate mercy to others not so as to earn mercy, but rather because God has already shown mercy to them. The Qur'an insists, "But for Allah's grace and mercy, His compassion and forgiveness, you would have long since been punished" (Sura 24:20 [cf. 24:10, 14]). Thus it is God's generous and compassionate treatment of the faithful that inspires similar conduct on their part:

> Your Lord has neither left you nor despises you. . . .
> Did He not find you an orphan and take care of you?
> Did He not find you perplexed and show you the way?
> Did He not find you poor and enrich you?
> So do not oppress the orphan,
> And do not drive the beggar away,
> And keep recounting the favors of your Lord. (Sura 93:3, 5-11)[39]

Sura 28:77 puts the matter succinctly: "Do good to others as God has done good to you."

### *To Walk in His Ways*

The question of holiness and the imitation of God is later taken up by the great medieval Jewish philosopher Moses Maimonides (1135-1204 CE) in

---

[37]See Elijah Judah Schochet, *Animal Life in Jewish Traditions: Attitudes and Relationships* (New York: Ktav, 1984), 164n117, citing *t. B. Qam.* 9:30 and *Sipre* §96.

[38]Quoted from Khalidi, *The Muslim Jesus*, 134, 138.

[39]Quoted from Ahmed Ali, trans., *Al-Qur'ān: A Contemporary Translation* (Princeton, NJ: Princeton University Press, 1988), 540.

his own exposition of Leviticus 19:2, although tracing the details of his thought turns out to be a complex task. In about the year 1190 Maimonides completed the work known in English as *A Guide for the Perplexed*, which seeks to provide a systematic account of Jewish theology in terms of then-prevailing philosophical concepts and categories. Much of this work is devoted to explaining and systematizing various features of Jewish Scripture in light of rabbinic debate. According to one view, Maimonides finds the core of Mosaic theology in the thirteen divine attributes revealed on Sinai, which articulate the essence not only of God's character, but also of righteous human conduct.[40]

Maimonides discusses the imitation of God in a passage that has, appropriately, perplexed commentators:

> For the utmost virtue of man is to become like unto Him, may He be exalted, as far as [one] is able; which means that we should make our actions like unto His, as the Sages made clear when interpreting the verse, *Ye shall be holy* [Lev 19:2]. They said: *He is gracious, so be you also gracious; He is merciful, so be you also merciful.* (*Guide for the Perplexed* 1.54 [67a]; italics original)

The problem is that the interpretation that he quotes (itself an echo of Ex 34:6) is one that other ancient authorities apply not to Leviticus 19:2 ("You shall be holy, for I the LORD your God am holy"), but rather to Exodus 15:2 ("This is my God and I will glorify him" [*y. Peʾah* 1:1; *b. Šabb.* 133b; *Mek. Shirata* 3]), Leviticus 22:28 (the command not to slaughter a cow and its calf on the same day [*Tg. Ps.-J.* Lev. 22:28]), and especially the injunction that Israel "walk in the ways" of their God in Deuteronomy 11:22 (*Sipre* §49); 28:9 (*y. Ber.* 5:3; *y. Meg.* 4:9-10). To walk in the ways of Yahweh, say the rabbis, means "to walk after the attributes of the Holy One, blessed be He." Just as God is said to clothe the naked, visit the sick,

[40]Moses Maimonides, *The Guide of the Perplexed*, trans. Shlomo Pines (Chicago: University of Chicago Press, 1963), xxxiv. For Maimonides, these are attributes of action; they do not indicate actual divine emotions or affections, but merely describe the way God acts. Nearly a thousand years earlier the Christian apologist Origen of Alexandria (ca. 185-254 CE) had concluded (late in life and against the Hellenistic philosophical tradition within which he worked) that Exodus 34:6 indeed gave evidence of divine affections: "Does not the Father and God of the universe somehow experience emotion, since he is long-suffering and of great mercy?" (*Hom. Ezech.* 6.6) (quoted and discussed in Robert M. Grant, *The Early Christian Doctrine of God* [Charlottesville: University Press of Virginia, 1966], 30-31).

comfort mourners, and bury the dead, so the pious are to imitate God by doing likewise (*b. Soṭah* 14a, citing Deut 13:5). Along the same lines, an interpretation attributed to the second-century commentator Abba Saul takes Leviticus 19:2 to mean that it is the responsibility of the king's retainers to imitate their king (*Sipra* Kedoshim 1).[41]

Indeed, the interpretation of holiness as mercy and kindness toward others may already be implied by Leviticus 19. The commentary known as *Leviticus Rabbah* interprets Leviticus 19:2 in terms of divine justice, God's willingness to answer human need, and, with reference to human conduct, separation from unholy thoughts and deeds (*Lev. Rab.* 24).[42] It then goes on to explain how the injunctions contained in Leviticus 19:2-19 repeat every one of the Ten Commandments.[43] But in the course of doing so, these verses also discuss care for the poor and the stranger, for day laborers, the poor, and the blind; the passage begins, "You shall be holy, for I the LORD your God am holy" (Lev 19:2), and concludes, "You shall love your neighbor as yourself; I am the LORD" (Lev 19:18).[44] As the commentary implies, even if imitation of God's holiness begins with personal sanctity and religious observance, putting holiness into practice must include acts of mercy and justice as well, for love of neighbor is equally honoring to God.

Perhaps the fullest exposition of this view is to be found in the early medieval work of moral instruction and metaphysical speculation known as *Seder Eliyahu Rabbah*, a collection of traditions that appeals to the authority of the prophet Elijah. The passage in question expounds Deuteronomy 28:9 in light of Exodus 34:6-7, once more explaining what it means to "walk in the ways" of God:

> Finally, "If thou art to keep the commandments of the Lord thy God, and *walk in His ways*" (Deut. 28:9), in the ways of Heaven, so, as the

---

[41]See Jacob Neusner, trans., *Sifra: An Analytical Translation*, vol. 3, *Aharé Mot, Qedoshim, Emor, Behar, and Behuqotai* (BJS 140; Atlanta: Scholars Press, 1988), 87.

[42]For a full discussion of Leviticus 19:2 in rabbinic thought, see Solomon Schechter, *Some Aspects of Rabbinic Theology* (New York: Macmillan, 1909), 199-218. *Leviticus Rabbah* dates from about 400-500 CE (so Strack and Stemberger, *Introduction to the Talmud and Midrash*, 316).

[43]See the quotation and discussion of this passage in Jacob Neusner, *A Rabbi Talks with Jesus: An Intermillennial, Interfaith Exchange* (New York: Doubleday, 1993), 82-87.

[44]See ibid., 83.

> ways of Heaven are being *merciful and compassionate* toward the wicked and accepting them in repentance, you are to be compassionate toward one another.
>
> And, as the ways of Heaven are to be *gracious*, graciously bestowing gifts not only upon those who know Him but also upon those who do not know Him, so you are to bestow gifts upon one another.
>
> And, as the ways of Heaven are to be *long-suffering*, long-suffering with the wicked and then accepting them in repentance, so you are to be long-suffering [with the wicked] for their good and not impatient to impose punishment upon them.
>
> For, as the ways of Heaven are *abundant in loving-kindness*, ever leaning to loving-kindness, so are you ever to lean toward doing kindness to others rather than lean toward doing them harm. (*S. Eli. Rab.* 135)[45]

According to this tradition, to be a "holy people" is not a matter of simple adherence to the letter of the law; rather, it entails "walking in the ways" of God, which means patterning one's own conduct after the divine nature and treating others with all the compassion, forbearance, and magnanimity that govern God's dealings with us.

Perhaps it was this text from *Seder Eliyahu Rabbah* that inspired Maimonides' otherwise puzzling exposition of Leviticus 19, for in his commentary on the Talmud he also explains Deuteronomy 28:9 in light of Exodus 34:6-7, quoting Leviticus 19:2 in the process:

> Just as He is called "Gracious," you shall be gracious;
> Just as He is called "Merciful," you shall be merciful;
> Just as He is called "Holy," you shall be called holy.
>
> In a similar manner, the prophets called God by other titles: "Slow to anger," "Abundant in kindness," "Righteous," "Just," "Perfect," "Almighty," "Powerful," and the like . . . to inform us that these are good and just paths. A person is obligated to accustom himself to these paths and [to try to] resemble Him to the extent of his ability.[46]

---

[45]Quoted from William G. Braude and Israel J. Kapstein, trans., *Tanna Debe Eliyyahu: The Lore of the School of Elijah* (Philadelphia: Jewish Publication Society, 1981), 333 (italics and paragraph breaks added for clarity). Estimates of the date of this work vary widely (from the third to tenth centuries CE), on which, see ibid., 4-12; see also Strack and Stemberger, *Introduction to the Talmud and Midrash*, 369-70 ("a date of composition before the ninth century . . . is likely").

[46]Quoted from Eliyahu Touger, trans., *Mishneh Torah: A New Translation with Commentaries, Notes, Tables Charts and Index*, vol. 2, *Hilchot De'ot* (New York: Maznaim, 1989), 26-28.

In both passages, then, Maimonides' discussion of Leviticus 19:2, "You shall be holy," reflects a keen reading of the original text, one that (with or without the assistance of *Leviticus Rabbah* and *Seder Eliyahu Rabbah*) explains human imitation of divine holiness in terms of compassion for the weak, the poor, and the needy.

What, then, does it mean to be holy, the way Yahweh, the God of Israel, is holy, and on what basis do Jesus, the sages, and Maimonides link imitation of God's holiness with deeds of mercy and loving-kindness? If God's fundamental orientation toward his creation and his creatures is one of merciful engagement, then being faithful to the intrinsic nature (or "holiness") of God surely does not require separation or aloofness from the things that God has made. On the contrary, it requires an engagement with creation (with sinners, strangers, and the pious alike) exactly as God engages it: with graciousness and generosity. Of course, detachment is less complicated than involvement, but given the doctrine of the incarnation, according to which God embraces material creation in the person of Jesus of Nazareth, the latter is a definition of holiness that Christians should not find difficult to affirm.

### *The Prodigal Son*

The classic depiction of God's compassion in Christian literature occurs in what is arguably the most famous of Jesus' parables: the parable of the prodigal son (Lk 15:11-32). With some justification, this parable has also been called "the parable of the prodigal father," for the key to its meaning lies in the father's extravagant generosity toward his lost son. The story is, unfortunately, familiar: that of an individual who wants to become rich through little or no effort of his own, who believes the world owes him a living, and that the time has come for him to collect on the debt. So when eagerness to become master of his own destiny at last overcomes both patience and prudence, the son demands his share of the family estate. It was not unheard of that a father wishing to "retire" would entrust the management of his estate to the rightful heirs, on the understanding that he would be suitably cared for in his old age.[47] But the son does not wait for the father's offer; the impli-

[47]G. B. Caird, *Saint Luke* (PNTC; New York: Penguin, 1979), 182-83.

cation of his selfish demand is that he wants the old man to drop dead.[48] This amounts to a devastating revelation of the son's true character: in his greed and haste he demonstrates no concern for his father (whom he impoverishes and refuses to support), for his brother (who must now assume full responsibility for the family and remaining estate), or even for his own heritage and identity. Were this not enough, the unnamed son then proceeds to squander the whole of his birthright. He is as unsympathetic a character as can be imagined, the author of his own misfortune, and one who has systematically alienated the only people who might otherwise take pity on him. To any right-minded way of thinking, he is a dead loss, and he has no one but himself to blame.

Ironically, only when he has lost everything does he "come to himself" (Lk 15:17), so he heads back the way he first came, rehearsing his speech on the way. "But while he was still far off, his father saw him," says Jesus, "and was filled with compassion [*splanchnizomai*]" (Lk 15:20). In such a situation custom demanded that the one who had been wronged—in this case, the father—wait for the penitent to make the first approach, pleading for forgiveness. But the father makes precisely seven gestures that, singly and in concert, demonstrate the nature of his love. First, he runs to meet his wayward son. Second, the father embraces and, third, kisses him, public gestures not only of greeting but also (in this case) of forgiveness. Fourth, the father orders that his son be honored with the best garment in the house; fifth, he orders a ring for the son's finger, and, sixth, he provides sandals for his feet. Seventh and finally, the father orders a celebratory feast. A "fattened calf" cannot remain in that state for long; it quickly grows to maturity, all the more so for having been fed so well. It can only be that for as long as his younger son has been absent the father has fattened each calf to which his cows have given birth, each time hoping against hope to make a joyful banquet of it.

The extravagance of the father's gestures is as outrageous as the scandalous selfishness of the son's previous conduct. Much as the elder brother

[48]So Kenneth E. Bailey, *Poet and Peasant: A Literary-Cultural Approach to the Parables in Luke* (Grand Rapids: Eerdmans, 1976), 161-65. For a modern parallel, see Michael David Kwan, *Things That Must Not Be Forgotten: A Childhood in Wartime China* (Toronto: Macfarlane, Walter & Ross, 2000), 160.

seems peevish and unforgiving by comparison, his protests are certainly justified. The younger son has already received more than he deserves, and he has no further claim, either moral or material, upon his father. The father's generosity seems like throwing good money after bad, in which case the old man has no more common sense than his younger son! Yet there is no question that Jesus means this parable to represent the compassion of God, whom Scripture also depicts as a loving father (e.g., Ps 103:13; Is 63:15-16). Indeed, the description rings entirely true to all that we have seen, with Jesus describing his heavenly Father as one who watches, yearns, and carefully prepares for the return of his lost children. According to Jesus, God's compassion amounts to an offer more profligate than any wayward child, for it is the longing of a parent who cannot forget the children to whom he or she has given life. Although the younger son has done everything in his power to break his father's heart, in the end he fails to do so, for he discovers that his father is willing to bear more shame, sorrow, and loss than the son is able to inflict.

According to Luke, Jesus tells this and two other parables when certain religious authorities object to him welcoming and sharing table fellowship with "tax collectors and sinners" (Lk 15:1-2). The first is the somewhat improbable tale of a brainless shepherd who neglects the bulk of his flock in order to rescue the one sheep that has (no less foolishly) wandered away. Contrary to expectation, it asserts that God is less concerned with the righteous than with the wayward, however few the latter may be. Similarly, the second parable describes a woman searching for lost treasure, emphasizing her persistence in recovering the lost property. All three parables describe not only the character of God, but also, by implication, the kind of religious conduct that most honors God. All three parables represent Jesus' response to the concern expressed by his critics, addressing their fundamental sense of abhorrence at the disobedience and intransigence of the ungodly. The pious, Jesus implies, are more concerned with maintaining their own purity than with winning back those whom they consider lost. By contrast, the compassion of the prodigal's father is such that he yearns and longs for the return of his child; the fact that the father interrupts his son's well-rehearsed speech implies that reconciliation—with God—is effected not by repentance alone, but by the magnanimous generosity of the One who has been wronged. The implications would not have been lost on Jesus' hearers, righteous and unrighteous alike. The explanation for Jesus' own apparently scandalous conduct in associating with moral reprobates and religious outcasts is that in so doing Jesus seeks nothing other than to imitate the compassion of his heavenly Father, as should his hearers also. Here, in parabolic form, Jesus again offers a provocative definition of holiness and the imitation of God.

This is the remarkable conclusion to Henri Nouwen's book *The Return of the Prodigal Son*. After exploring the rich devotional implications of what it means to identify with both the younger son and the elder son, Nouwen contends that our ultimate responsibility is to become like the compassionate Father:

> Perhaps the most radical statement Jesus ever made is: "Be compassionate as your Father is compassionate" [Lk 6:36]. God's compassion is described by Jesus not simply to show me how willing God is to feel for me, or to forgive my sins and offer me new life and happiness, but to invite me to become like God and to show the same compassion to others as he is showing to me. If the only meaning of the story were that people sin but God forgives, I could easily begin to think of my sins as a fine occasion for God to show me his forgiveness. There would be no real challenge in such an interpretation. I would resign myself to my weaknesses and keep hoping that eventually God would close his eyes to them and let me come home, whatever I did. Such sentimental romanticism is not the message of the Gospels.
>
> What I am called to make true is that whether I am the younger or the elder son, I am the son of my compassionate Father. I am an heir. . . . Indeed, as son and heir I am to become successor. I am destined to step into my Father's place and offer to others the same compassion that he has offered me. . . . Being in the Father's house requires that I make the Father's life my own and become transformed into his image.[49]

Nouwen succinctly captures the heart, so to speak, of the message that Jesus intended to convey to his original hearers.

[49]Henri J. M. Nouwen, *The Return of the Prodigal Son: A Story of Homecoming* (New York: Doubleday, 1992), 123.

*Love divine, all loves excelling,*
*Joy of heaven, to earth come down,*
*Fix in us thy humble dwelling,*
*All thy faithful mercies crown!*
*Jesu, thou art all compassion,*
*Pure, unbounded love thou art;*
*Visit us with thy salvation!*
*Enter every trembling heart.*

CHARLES WESLEY (1707-1788)[50]

[50]Originally published in a collection titled *Hymns for the Use of Those That Seek, and Those That Have Redemption in the Blood of Christ* (London: Strahan, 1747).

3

# A God Slow to Anger

*And the* Lord *passed before him and proclaimed,*
*"The* Lord*, the* Lord*, a God compassionate and gracious,*
slow to anger, *and abounding in steadfast love and faithfulness,*
*keeping steadfast love for thousands,*
*forgiving iniquity and transgression and sin,*
*but who will by no means clear the guilty. . . ."*

Exodus 34:6-7

## God's Justice in an Unjust World

One of the great theological mysteries of all time is why, if God is both just and all-powerful, those who scorn God and/or oppress their fellow humans manage to get away with such conduct for so long. Or as Job succinctly puts the question, "Why do the wicked live on, reach old age, and grow mighty in power?" (Job 21:7). The framers of Scripture are in no doubt that God eventually will assert the cause of righteousness and punish the ungodly. What troubles them, however, is why God delays so long in doing so. This question emerges any time the innocent suffer, but especially so at times of widespread disaster, and never more acutely for the people of Israel than in response to assaults upon Jerusalem, its temple, and all that these represent. Each such incident gives rise to a "literature of crisis": the book of Lamentations agonizes over the fate of the city at the hands of Nebuchadnezzar in 587/586 BCE; 2 Maccabees offers a theological interpretation of the persecution and enforced Hellenization carried out under Antiochus Epiphanes IV (175-164 BCE); several of the pseudonymous *Psalms of Solomon* react to the defeat of Jerusalem by the Roman general Pompey in 63 BCE; and other extrabiblical works such as *4 Ezra* and *2 Baruch* (as well as, arguably, the Gospels of Mark and Matthew) try to make theological sense of Jerusalem's destruction by the Roman forces of Titus and Vespasian in the Jewish War of 68-70 CE.[1]

The book known as *4 Ezra* (included within the Roman Catholic canon in an expanded form as 2 Esdras) is both plaintive and theologically eloquent in this regard. Likely written around 100 CE, it depicts the biblical scribe bitterly lamenting the injustice of God's ways. God, says Ezra, has used the ungodly to chasten the chosen people, preserving evildoers and enemies of righteousness while destroying his own nation. Where is the justice, he repeatedly complains, not only in God judging those who have tried—and failed—to keep the commandments, not only in using the wicked to execute that judgment, but above all in God failing to enable a weak humanity to attain a righteousness of which they are otherwise incapable?

> How much better it would have been if the earth had never produced Adam at all, or, since it has done so, if he had been restrained from sinning! For what good does it do us all to live in misery now and have nothing but punishment to expect after death? O Adam, what have you done? Your sin was not your fall alone; it was ours also, the fall of all your descendants. (*4 Ezra* 7:116-119 NEB)

Ezra does not doubt that some, at least, are righteous and deserving of heavenly reward. Nor does he doubt that many more of God's people have earned the anger and righteous judgment that he sees exemplified in the destruction of the holy city. But how this serves the purposes of a just and holy God is by no means clear to him.

How, then, does *4 Ezra* explain God's justice and God's wrath? The evidence is complex, even contradictory in places, and continues to

---

[1]For an introduction to the theological issues raised in these works, see Michael E. Stone, "Reactions to Destructions of the Second Temple: Theology, Perception and Conversion," *Journal for the Study of Judaism* 12 (1981): 195-204.

evoke scholarly debate.[2] Even if he cannot account for the way in which God seems to judge some and leave others unpunished, the writer takes refuge in the character of God, offering an extended meditation on Exodus 34:6-7:

> I know that the Most High is called "compassionate," because he has compassion on those yet unborn; and called "merciful," because he shows mercy to those who repent and live by his law; and "patient," because he shows patience to those who have sinned . . . and "rich in forgiveness," because again and again he forgives sinners, past, present, and to come . . . and he is also called "judge," for unless he grants pardon to those who have been created by his word, and blots out their countless offences, I suppose that of the entire human race only very few would be spared. (*4 Ezra* 7:132-140 NEB)

Given that he perceives his own nation to be under judgment, these same considerations provide the basis on which Ezra appeals for mercy:

> What is man, that you are angry with him,
> or what is a mortal race, that you are so bitter against it?
> For in truth there is no one among those who have been born who has
> not acted wickedly, and among those who have existed there is
> no one who has not transgressed.
> For in this, O Lord, your *righteousness* and *goodness* will be declared,
> when you are *merciful* to those who have no store of good works.
> (*4 Ezra* 8:34-36 [cf. *4 Ezra* 8:45])[3]

Although *4 Ezra* has survived to the present day mostly in Latin translation, there is a general consensus that it was first written in either Hebrew or Aramaic, as a result of which we probably are justified in thinking that the actual vocabulary of Exodus 34 underlies these passages. Nor can it escape our notice that, once again, the writer under-

---

[2]See Michael P. Knowles, "Moses, the Law, and the Unity of 4 Ezra," *Novum Testamentum* 30 (1989): 257-74; and on the following passage, see Michael E. Stone, *Fourth Ezra: A Commentary on the Book of Fourth Ezra*, ed. Frank Moore Cross (Hermeneia; Minneapolis: Fortress, 1990), 256-58, 260-61.

[3]Translation (with italics added) from Bruce M. Metzger, "The Fourth Book of Ezra," *OTP* 1:543, with line divisions added for greater clarity. A still later work in the same tradition, known as the *Greek Apocalypse of Ezra*, also meditates on the name and character of God (see *Gk. Apoc. Ezra* 1:10-18; Michael E. Stone, "Greek Apocalypse of Ezra," *OTP* 1:569n36).

stands God's righteousness to be most fully expressed in God's mercy. Here, then, is yet another instance in which meditation upon the divine name provides a key ingredient not of theological debate at some abstract level, but rather of devotional reflection on the nature of God in light of the real suffering and sorrow that God's people experience.

Much clearer in its dependence on Exodus 34 is a passage from the early medieval work *Pirqe Rabbi Eliezer*, essentially a rewriting of the Pentateuchal narrative that includes the following imaginative reflection on the moral destiny of humankind:

> The Holy One, blessed be He, said to the Torah, "Let us create man." The Torah replied, "Master of the Universe, this man will be of few years and full of trouble [Job 14:1] and will sin, and if You are not patient with him, he will be as if he had not been born" [i.e., he would be condemned very early to death]. To which the Lord replied: "Is it, then, for naught that I am called 'slow to anger and rich in steadfast kindness'?" (*Pirqe R. El.* 11)[4]

Here too the writer takes refuge in the mercy and forbearance of a gracious God.

Biblical and postbiblical responses to the question of theodicy (the problem of suffering and evil in a moral universe) range from sorrow and repentance in the belief that historical reversals are God's just punishment for the sins of his people (as in *4 Ezra* and much of rabbinic literature), to an assertion that rather than being established here on earth, God's justice will emerge after death in the context of final judgment. As the two examples that we have seen suggest, the assertion in Exodus 34:6 that God is "slow to anger" provides a critical ingredient for this debate. The phrase in question, *ʾerek ʾappayim*, may be rendered (at least as to the sense of the individual words) as "long of nostrils," much like similar expressions that refer either to physical length (Ezek

[4]Cited in Simon Greenberg, "Some Reflections on God's Forbearance, Forgiveness, and Related Concepts," in *Perspectives on Jews and Judaism*, ed. Arthur A. Chiel (New York: The Rabbinical Assembly, 1978), 161. The text is found in G. Friedlander, trans., *Pirkê de Rabbi Eliezer (The Chapters of Rabbi Eliezer the Great): According to the Text of the Manuscript Belonging of Abraham Epstein of Vienna* (repr., New York: Hermon, 1970 [1916]), 76. I am grateful to Lois Dow for bringing this passage to my attention. *Pirqe Rabbi Eliezer* likely dates from the eighth to ninth centuries CE. See also *Genesis Rabbah* 12:15.

17:3) or to length of time (2 Sam 3:1; Jer 29:28). Even though the meaning of language cannot be reduced to its etymology, the intention of the metaphor is clear enough, both because it is used elsewhere of forbearance as a human character trait (Prov 14:29; 15:18; 16:32; 19:11) and by virtue of the parallel expression "long of spirit" (Eccles 7:8), which also refers to long-suffering patience.[5] George Knight suggests that its intended meaning may be that "it takes a long time for the snort of anger to come through God's nose."[6] Although this perhaps seems to us an odd sort of anthropomorphism, it apparently made sense to the ancient Israelites. One of the oldest poems in the Hebrew Bible, the so-called Song of the Sea, explains that the waters part to let the Israelites pass because of a blast from God's nostrils (Ex 15:8), while Psalm 18 describes God's anger as "the blast of the breath of his nostrils" (Ps 18:15 [cf. 2 Sam 22:16]). In any event, if the original metaphor furnishes God with a "long nose," we might have recourse to a more contemporary image, one drawn from military weaponry and also having to do with anger: our equivalent would be to say that God has a "long fuse."

## Fear and Anger

Although the phrase "slow to anger" is a dynamic equivalent rather than a word-for-word translation, it certainly is accurate in highlighting the assumption, implicit within the original, of divine wrath or anger. And much in Scripture confirms this emphasis, notwithstanding the modern preference for a more benign view of God. Examples abound: one of God's names in Genesis is "the Fear of Isaac" (Gen 31:42, 53), meaning, presumably, that Isaac's God inspires terror in all his enemies. People with a healthy sense of self-preservation do not cross Isaac or his

[5]Elsewhere the expression "long of nostrils" occurs (with reference to God) usually in recitations of the formula from Exodus 34:6 (Num 14:18; Neh 9:17; Ps 86:15; 103:8, 145:8; Joel 2:13; Jon 4:2), although Jeremiah 15:15 is an exception. For an exhaustive exploration of this and related metaphors, see Mayer I. Gruber, *Aspects of Nonverbal Communication in the Ancient Near East* (StP 12; Rome: Biblical Institute Press, 1980), 480-553, esp. 503-10.

[6]George A. F. Knight, *Theology as Narration: A Commentary on the Book of Exodus* (Grand Rapids: Eerdmans, 1977), 200. Gruber, on the other hand, argues that the primary reference is to frowning rather than "fuming": "it refers to the appearance of the face: tightening of facial muscles in anger and their relaxation in the person who is placated" (*Aspects of Nonverbal Communication*, 503).

descendants, since there is no telling what their God might do if they are wronged. This is precisely how Jacob uses the title in dealing with his uncle Laban: neither of them trusts the other, and Jacob is certain that God has taken his side in keeping Laban from cheating him of his due (Gen 31:36-42). "If the God of my father, the God of Abraham and the Fear of Isaac, had not been on my side," complains Jacob, "surely now you would have sent me away empty-handed. God saw my affliction and the labor of my hands, and rebuked you last night" (Gen 31:42). If respect for one's own blood relations is not enough to inspire honesty, divine wrath provides a highly effective alternative!

"Fear of God" is an integral aspect of biblical morality, as in the case of the poor person's cloak that has to be returned by nightfall because God hears the cry of the needy (Ex 22:26-27). What was implicit in that instance comes to fuller expression in moral injunctions that occur in both legal and nonlegal sections of the canon: "You shall not revile the deaf or put a stumbling block before the blind; you shall fear your God: I am the Lord"; "You shall rise before the aged, and defer to the old; and you shall fear your God: I am the Lord"; "You shall not cheat one another, but you shall fear your God; for I am the Lord your God" (Lev 19:14, 32; 25:17). The unspoken assumption is that God demands justice and punishes injustice. As with Isaac and Laban, should concern for one's neighbor prove insufficient to motivate fair dealing, fear of God will suffice. Such expressions are especially common in Deuteronomy:

> So now, O Israel, what does the Lord your God require of you? Only to fear the Lord your God, to walk in all his ways, to love him, to serve the Lord your God with all your heart and with all your soul, and to keep the commandments of the Lord your God and his decrees that I am commanding you today, for your own well-being. (Deut 10:12-13)

Of the five injunctions in this verse that spell out what God requires (to "fear," "walk," "love," "serve," and "keep the commandments"), godly fear comes first, and specific acts of legal obedience last. In a similar vein, according to the biblical wisdom tradition, "fear of the Lord" is the "beginning" both of wisdom (Prov 9:10) and of knowledge (Prov 1:7). On such a view, all human ingenuity, learning, and accomplishment amount to nothing unless set within the context of honoring and obeying the one true God. For by the fear of the Lord one may avoid evil (Prov 16:6), while the reward for humility and fear of the Lord is riches, honor, and life (so Prov 22:4; cf. Prov 10:27; 14:27). Thus the conclusion of Proverbs 23:17 (attributed to Solomon himself) is unequivocal: "Always continue in the fear of the LORD" (Prov 23:17).

As an aside, it is worth asking what provokes Israel's God to anger. Although the stereotype of an unremittingly angry and punishing God still prevails in some quarters, our study thus far reveals this to be a misrepresentation. But this is not to say that God is never angry with his people, for that is indeed frequently the case. Although further examples can be found that do not fit within the following categories, two basic causes of divine wrath appear in Hebrew Scripture: ingratitude and inconstancy. The first amounts to a failure to recognize the magnitude of all that God has done. For example, having been delivered out of slavery in Egypt, the people grumble at the difficulty of life in the wilderness: they are hungry and thirsty, and they have doubts about their leaders (Ex 16–17; Num 11–12). Besides, the land that God has chosen for them looks dangerous and inhospitable: it may be fruitful, but the present inhabitants are as terrifying as they are large (Num 13–14). God's response is to propose putting a complete end to the malcontents. Moses responds immediately by pleading with God on their behalf. Moses warns that if he destroys the people, Yahweh will suffer a loss of reputation in the eyes of Egypt and the surrounding nations. More to the point, says Moses, it will call God's own character into question,

> And now, therefore, let the power of the LORD be great in the way that you promised when you spoke, saying, "The LORD is slow to anger, and abounding in steadfast love, forgiving iniquity and transgression, but by no means clearing the guilty, visiting the iniquity of the parents upon the children to the third and the fourth generation." Forgive the iniquity of this people according to the greatness of your steadfast love, just as you have pardoned this people, from Egypt even until now. (Num 14:17-19)

In other words, not only is God's reputation at stake, but also God's word: Moses simply recites back the terms of God's self-revelation (and begins quoting in midsentence, at the most relevant point).[7] Nonetheless, the people are made to wander in the wilderness for another forty years (cf. Ps 78; 95; 106).

Ingratitude is followed, second, by infidelity. Once the chosen people have settled in the land of Canaan, they repeatedly anger God in precisely the same manner as at Sinai: apostasy. Deuteronomy in particular contains repeated warnings against provoking divine wrath through the worship of other gods; this is the essence of God's final words to Moses (Deut 31:16-17). Deuteronomy likely reflects this exact situation. Many scholars believe it to have been composed in connection with the religious reforms of King Josiah in the late seventh century BCE (2 Kings 22–23), a period that the biblical historians recall as one of constant vacillation between Yahweh and the gods of the surrounding nations. Josiah is one of only a few kings of either Judah or Israel to escape censure for leading the people astray. God's "anger" is a constant theme in the case of many others: Solomon (1 Kings 11:9), or Jeroboam, Baasha, Omri, Ahab, Ahaziah, and Jehoahaz in the northern kingdom of Israel (1 Kings 14:9, 15; 15:30; 16:2, 7, 13, 26, 30; 21:22; 22:53; 2 Kings 13:3); Amaziah, Ahaz, Manasseh, and Zedekiah in the case of Judah to the south (2 Kings 21:6, 15; 23:26; 24:20; 2 Chron 28:25; 33:6). The eventual defeat of both kingdoms, despite the penitence of a few faithful rulers, is consistently interpreted as God's wrathful response to their infidelity (e.g., 2 Kings 17:5-18; 22:17; 2 Chron 24:18-19).

Prophets such as Amos and Hosea in Israel, as well as Isaiah, Micah, Zephaniah, Jeremiah, Habakkuk, and later Ezekiel in Judah, insist that unfaithfulness to Yahweh typically is accompanied by social violence, injustice, and oppression among the people, particularly on the part of rulers and priests (e.g., Is 5:25; 9:12, 17, 21; 10:4; Jer 12:1-13; Ezek 22:20-31; Hos 12:1, 7; Amos 5:11-15; Mic 2:1-4; Hab 2:1-4; Zeph 3:1-8.). Such conduct is wrong in itself, but what rouses God to anger is the failure of those who are called by his name to be true to that name either in their religious allegiances or in their conduct and dealings with one another.

---

[7]So Judith H. Newman, *Praying by the Book: The Scripturalization of Prayer in Second Temple Judaism* (SBLEJL 14; Atlanta: Scholars Press, 1999), 35-37.

This is the logic that undergirds prophetic condemnation of both forms of infidelity: rejection of the God of Moses implies the rejection of God's covenantal character and the conduct that accompanies it. With perfect irony, therefore, refusal to embody mercy, kindness, or compassion brings to the fore the one divine characteristic that the wicked still seem to imitate: divine wrath. In response to such justice comes the passionate plea of Habakkuk, likely a contemporary of Jeremiah: "O Lord, I have heard of your renown, and I stand in awe, O Lord, of your work. In our own time revive it; in our own time make it known; in wrath may you remember [to show] mercy [*raḥēm*]" (Hab 3:2).[8]

As Johannes Fichtner aptly summarizes,

> The central motive for God's wrath against Israel . . . is found in all its breadth and depth in the prophets . . . [who] never weary of emphasizing what Yahweh has done for Israel with His election and guidance, and this is the background against which they bring their message of the wrath of Yahweh. At the back of every individual prophetic charge, whether it refers to the cultus, or to social injustice, to a policy which trusts in armaments and alliances, or even to the worship of other gods, there stands finally the one great complaint, namely, that the people has forgotten its God, turned from Him, and despised his love. This is the deepest root of the concept of wrath, and in this light one can understand the overwhelming force of the message. It is Yahweh's wounded love which awakens his wrath.[9]

## "In Wrath, Remember Mercy"

Though not difficult to imagine in principle, however, it seems at least unhealthy, if not also theologically unbalanced, to envisage a spirituality based on fear of divine wrath. Is this not precisely what gives certain kinds of religion such a bad name? Yet to imagine God as "loving and forgiving" without further qualification turns out to be a selective reading of the evidence. Jesus himself issues a categorical exhortation to

[8]The prophet is specifically appealing to the name "YHWH." Although following the NRSV rendering, I have added the material in brackets to indicate more clearly that the final word in the sentence is a verb rather than a noun.

[9]Johannes Fichtner, "ὀργή, κτλ.," *TDNT* 5:403.

holy dread, addressed in its original context to committed disciples and casual onlookers alike: "I tell you, my friends, do not fear those who kill the body, and after that can do nothing more. But I will warn you whom to fear: fear him who, after he has killed, has authority to cast into hell. Yes, I tell you, fear him!" (Lk 12:4-5 [// Mt 10:28]). No amount of qualification or pious reinterpretation can take the edge off these words.

The New Testament describes various kinds of fear, whether of rejection and condemnation (like the woman who touches Jesus' garment from behind [Mk 5:33]), of personal loss (as with Jairus's concern for his daughter [Mk 5:36]), or of suffering and death (something that the disciples share with Jesus [Mk 10:32; 14:33-34]), all of which seem reasonable. But in addition to these normal, human fears is the kind of fear that Zechariah and the shepherds experience (Lk 1:12; 2:9), as do the twelve disciples when they encounter the miraculous (Mt 14:26; Mk 9:6; Lk 5:8), or the women at the empty tomb (Mk 16:8; Lk 24:5). Their fear arises from a realization that God has broken into their world in a manner so holy and unexpected that all of their smallness, weakness, selfishness, and inadequacy are suddenly exposed. Unlike normal human fearfulness, this is "holy" fear, for when God shows up, it is right to tremble. And it is this latter sort of fear that Jesus unmistakably encourages in Luke 12 and Matthew 10. Even so, Jesus continues in that same passage, "Are not five sparrows sold for two pennies? Yet not one of them is forgotten in God's sight. But even the hairs of your head are all counted. Do not be afraid; you are of more value than many sparrows" (Lk 12:6-7 [// Mt 10:29-31]). Later in the same chapter Jesus reassures his that God will provide for all their needs, again concluding, "Do not be afraid, little flock, for it is your Father's good pleasure to give you the kingdom" (Lk 12:32).[10] Elsewhere in the Gospels the disciples (and others) are frequently admonished not to fear (e.g., Mt 17:7; 28:5, 10; Mk 5:36; 6:50; Lk 1:13, 30; 2:10; 5:10).

This leaves the reader in something of a quandary. Which set of injunctions ought to be obeyed, and what is the place of fear (holy or otherwise) within biblical religion generally and Christian discipleship

[10]The same Greek verb, *phobeō* ("to fear"), is used consistently throughout Luke 12.

in particular? The answer lies, surely, in the nature of God's character; in the fact that God is not only "compassionate" and "gracious" but also "slow to anger." This affirms, on the one hand, the reality of divine wrath, with its implication of divinely sanctioned religious or ethical norms and boundaries, together with the prospect of judgment and condemnation for those who transgress them. On the other hand, it suggests a temperate wrath and tempered judgment—precisely what Habakkuk's finely balanced prayer envisages: "In wrath, remember mercy" (Hab 3:2). Thus despite the persistence of negative stereotyping in some Christian circles, the "God of the Old Testament" can no more be characterized as exclusively angry and wrathful than the God of Jesus can be described as nothing but patient and forgiving. While divine anger and judgment are unavoidable realities in both Testaments, divine patience is also prominent in both.

What are God's people to make of this twofold emphasis? Already in the seventh century BCE, at least one biblical writer took pains to assert that delay of retribution implies neither denial of justice nor diminishment of God's power:

> A jealous and avenging God is the LORD, the LORD is avenging and
> wrathful;
> the LORD takes vengeance on his adversaries and rages against his
> enemies.
> The LORD is *slow to anger* but great in power,
> and the LORD will by no means clear the guilty. (Nah 1:2-3)

For Nahum, justice delayed is by no means justice denied. Later in the same century Jeremiah knows to call upon God's "long nostrils" (or, in this case, a singular "nostril" [Jer 15:15]). Yet the fact that he does so in the face of what he knows is divine judgment upon his nation acknowledges that God's patience is limited. In much the same vein, the book known as Sirach (or Ecclesiasticus, or the Wisdom of Ben Sirach), which dates from around 180 BCE,[11] offers careful advice regarding the apparently contradictory tendencies of

[11]Regarding the date of Sirach, see Patrick W. Skehan and Alexander A. Di Lella, *The Wisdom of Ben Sira: A New Translation with Introduction and Commentary* (AB 39; New York: Doubleday, 1987), 8-16.

the divine character, warning equally against forgetting God's justice and presuming upon God's mercy:

> Do not say, "I sinned, yet what has happened to me?" for the Lord is slow to anger.
> Do not be so confident of forgiveness that you add sin to sin.
> Do not say, "His mercy is great, he will forgive the multitude of my sins," for both mercy and wrath are with him, and his anger will rest on sinners. (Sir 5:4-6 [cf. Sir 16:11-12; 35:19; *4 Ezra* 7:33-34])

Here the writer envisages three possibilities: first, sinners might misinterpret the fact that God does not punish their errors immediately; second, they might take the promise of forgiveness as an excuse for sin; and third, they might mistake clemency for indulgence. The problem, it seems, boils down to focusing on one divine attribute at the expense of all the others, for knowing God's ways is a matter of appreciating the divine character as a whole rather than concentrating on particular characteristics in isolation.

Sirach has come down to us (with the exception of a few manuscript fragments in Hebrew) as part of the Septuagint, the Greek translation of the Hebrew Bible that dates (like Sirach itself) from the first or second centuries BCE.[12] In it we find further indications that at this period a lively debate is underway in Jewish circles about the relationship between divine justice and divine mercy. The Septuagint's rendering of the Hebrew phrase "slow to anger" in Exodus 34:6 avoids any awkward reference to God's "nostrils," preferring the simpler term "long-suffering" or "forbearant" (Gk. *makrothymos*) both here and in the many recitations of this formula within the corpus.[13] But there is at least one instance in which the translators have added a reference to divine forbearance where none is evident in the original. The Hebrew text of Psalm 7:11 reads, "God is a righteous judge, a God who displays his wrath every day" (NIV),

---

[12]On this question, see Melvin K. H. Peters, "Septuagint," *ABD* 5:1096-97.

[13]See, for example, LXX Numbers 14:18; 2 Esdras 19:17 (Nehemiah 9:17); Psalms 85:15; 102:8; 144:8; Joel 2:13; Jonah 4:2; and compare, in the postbiblical Prayer of Manasseh, "For you are the Lord Most High, of great compassion, long-suffering, and very merciful, and you relent at human suffering. O Lord, according to your great goodness you have promised repentance and forgiveness to those who have sinned against you, and in the multitude of your mercies you have appointed repentance for sinners, so that they may be saved" (Pr Man 7).

or "pronounces doom each day" (NJPS) or "has indignation every day" (NRSV). The Greek translation, by contrast, indicates just the opposite: "God is a judge righteous, mighty, and forbearing [*makrothymos*], not bringing down wrath every day." By any account, this is a bold theological move, one surely occasioned by a firm conviction that there is far more to God's ways than righteous anger alone. What else would have motivated the translators (or the tradition that they were following) to flatly contradict the plain sense of the original text before them?

The book of 2 Maccabees, on the other hand, balances divine forbearance and anger in a somewhat different manner. Having just recited a series of horrifying atrocities visited upon those Jews who resisted attempts to turn them from their ancestral faith, the author adds an editorial aside:

> Now I urge those who read this book not to be depressed by such calamities, but to recognize that these punishments were designed not to destroy but to discipline our people. In fact, it is a sign of great kindness not to let the impious alone for long, but to punish them immediately. For in the case of the other nations the Lord waits patiently to punish them until they have reached the full measure of their sins; but he does not deal in this way with us, in order that he may not take vengeance on us afterward when our sins have reached their height. Therefore he never withdraws his mercy from us. Although he disciplines us with calamities, he does not forsake his own people. (2 Macc 6:12-16)

In seeking to defend both divine justice and divine patience, the writer asserts that these principles are applied differently to Jew and Gentile. Members of both groups, he admits, are liable to sin. And the sins of both are justly punished by a just God. But whereas God allows immediate "calamities" upon the erring faithful in order to return them to obedience, God patiently delays in responding to Gentiles so that the sins of the latter may come to "full measure" and thus, at the last, receive full punishment. Gentile readers are unlikely to find much comfort in this assessment! But that should not prevent us from recognizing it as yet another attempt to understand the practical outworking of God's attributes of justice and mercy, with divine forbearance mediating between the two.

## God's Two Nostrils

In many ways, this argument anticipates the observations of rabbinic commentators who were intrigued that the word for "nostrils" (which can also mean "faces" or "aspects") in Exodus 34:6 occurs in the plural (or more precisely, the dual form, referring specifically to a "pair" of nostrils):

> R. Haggai (or as some say, R. Samuel b. Naḥmani) stated: What [was the purpose] when Scripture wrote, *Long-suffering* [in the dual form] where the singular might well have been used? . . . Long-suffering towards the righteous and long-suffering also towards the wicked. (*b. ʿErub.* 22a, italics original)[14]

The medieval Talmudist Solomon bar Isaac (1040-1105 CE), more commonly known as Rashi, interpreted this to mean that the biblical phrase refers to two divine dispositions, one for the righteous, for whom reward is postponed, and the other for the wicked, for whom punishment is postponed.[15] If nothing else, this amounts to an explicit admission that divine justice is not to be found in the present age—hardly a surprising conclusion for a man who lived in the era of the first Crusade.

Rashi's analysis likely depends on a long tradition of interpretation already represented by, for example, the Jewish apocalyptic work known as *2 Baruch*. This book dates from only a few decades later than *4 Ezra* and, like that account, wrestles with the painful injustice of the destruction of Jerusalem. In much the same way as Ezra argues with a heavenly messenger, Baruch (Jeremiah's scribe) complains about the wickedness and corruption of humankind and that God's long-suffering is widely perceived as weakness (*2 Bar* 21:19-21). A heavenly voice assures him that the deeds of the wicked have been duly recorded, even as are the deeds of the righteous, and that in due course all will be revealed:

> And it will happen at that time that you shall see, and many with you, the long-suffering of the Most High, which lasts from generation to

---

[14]Haggai belongs to the fourth generation of Palestinian Amoraim, from the fourth century CE; Samuel b. Naḥmani is of the third generation of Amoraim, from the third or early fourth century CE. In *b. B. Qam.* 50b this tradition is attributed to Rabbi Ḥama, and in *y. Taʿan.* 2:1 to Rabbi Jonathan, both of whom are plausibly dated to the third century CE.

[15]See Israel Drazin, trans., *Targum Onkelos to Exodus: An English Translation of the Text with Analysis and Commentary (Based on the A. Sperber and A. Berliner Editions)* (New York: Ktav, 1990), 313n5.

generation, who has been long-suffering toward all who are born, both those who sinned and those who proved themselves to be righteous. (*2 Bar.* 24:2 [cf. *2 Bar.* 59:6; 85:8])

As with the problem of *4 Ezra* being extant only in translation, so *2 Baruch,* although likely written in Hebrew or Aramaic, survives only in a Syriac translation of a Greek version. In other words, the original vocabulary has been well and truly obscured, and there is no possibility of establishing a direct link to Exodus 34. Nonetheless, the same set of ideas is unmistakably present, as the writer envisages two distinct aspects to God's forbearance in order to explain the apparent injustice of God's faithful having to suffer while the wicked prosper with impunity.

A different approach emerges from the various Aramaic renderings of Scripture known as the Targumim (or Targums), which typically offer multiple interpretations of a single phrase. Such is the case with the rendering of Exodus 34:6 in *Targum Neofiti I*: "O Lord, O Lord, gracious and merciful God, patient [lit., "long of spirit"], the One who makes anger distant and brings near compassion."[16] Here we find a triple reading: first, the Hebrew phrase "long of nostrils" becomes "long of spirit" (as we saw already in Eccles 7:8), then the idea of length is taken in a quasi-temporal or spatial sense to imply the distancing of anger, and finally, for good measure, the translator adds the implied opposite: God draws compassion near. Elsewhere in the Targumim repetitions of the formula from Exodus 34:6 receive similar treatment.[17] Estimations as to the date of particular Targumim vary between the first and eighth centuries CE, although specific readings may originate earlier.[18] This passage may provide a case in point, for already in a

[16]Cited in Martin McNamara, ed., *Targum Neofiti 1: Exodus*, translated with introduction and apparatus by Martin McNamara, notes by Robert Hayward; *Targum Pseudo-Jonathan: Exodus*, translated with notes by Michael Maher (ArBib 2; Collegeville, MN: Liturgical Press, 1994), 138n*n*.

[17]*Targum Neofiti I* Numbers 14:8 repeats the threefold exegesis (although one manuscript reads "long of mercies [*rḥmyn*]"); one or more of these features is found in *Targum Onqelos* and *Targum Pseudo-Jonathan* Exodus 34:6; *Targum Pseudo-Jonathan* Numbers 14:18; *Targum* Joel 2:13; Jonah 4:2; Nahum 1:3.

[18]According to Philip S. Alexander, "[*Targum Onqelos*] originated in Palestine in the 1st or early 2d centuries C.E."; "[*Targum Pseudo-Jonathan*] cannot have been redacted before the 7th/8th cent. C.E."; "There are no good grounds for dating anything in [*Targum Neofiti*] later than the 3d/4th cent. C.E." ("Targum, Targumim," *ABD* 6:320-31).

Jewish apocryphal work known as the Similitudes of Enoch, from the first century CE or earlier, the archangel Michael declares to a trembling Enoch that he should not fear to receive revelations of future judgment, for God has always "been merciful and long-suffering [lit., 'of distant wrath'] toward those that dwell upon the earth" (*1 En.* 60:5).[19] By emphasizing divine forbearance as a source of hope even in the face of terrifying judgment, this last reading of Exodus comes out at the opposite end of the spectrum from Nahum, with whose more threatening tones this discussion began.

Consideration of the length of God's nose concludes with a series of parables or stories that illustrate varying interpretative approaches to this issue, one from the Jerusalem (or Palestinian) Talmud, two more from the Talmud of Babylonia, and yet another from the later collection of exegetical traditions known as *Midrash Tanḥuma*. The first parable, which equates "length" with distance, is told in the name of a third-century rabbi from Palestine who was famous for his stories:

> Said R. Levi: "What is the meaning of 'slow to anger'? It means, 'Distant from wrath.' It may be compared to a king who had two tough legions. The king said, 'If they dwell here with me in the metropolis, if the city-folk anger me now, they will put them down [with force]. But lo, I shall send them a long way away, so that if the city-folk anger me, while I am yet summoning the legions, the people will appease me, and I shall accept their plea.' Likewise the Holy One, blessed be He, said, 'Anger and wrath are angels of destruction. Lo, I shall send them a long way away, so that if Israel angers me, while I am summoning and bringing them to me, Israel will repent, and I shall accept their repentance.'" (*y. Taʿan.* 2:1)

A second, anonymous Talmudic parable reflects on the report of the spies from Numbers 14 and considers, once again, the fine balance between God's justice and mercy. It addresses the question of whether God exercises patience only toward the godly or does so toward the ungodly as

[19]Although the date of *1 Enoch* 37–71 (the Similitudes) has itself been vigorously debated, the majority view is that this work dates from between the last half of the first century BCE and the third quarter of the first century CE. See E. Isaac, "1 (Ethiopic Apocalypse of) Enoch: A New Translation and Introduction," *OTP* 1:6-7.

well. The early Christian bishop and exegete Irenaeus of Lyons (ca. 130-200 CE) reflects on the same issue and concludes as follows:

> Moses declared that God was indeed a consuming fire [Deut 4:24] to the people that transgressed the law, and threatened that God would bring upon them a day of fire; but to those who had the fear of God, he said, "The Lord God is merciful and gracious, and long-suffering, and of great commiseration, and true, and keeps justice and mercy for thousands, forgiving unrighteousness, and transgressions, and sins." (*Haer.* 4.20.8 [*ANF* 1:490])

According to Irenaeus, human beings can be divided into two distinct groups: transgressors, on the one hand, and those who fear God, on the other. Whereas fire awaits the persistently disobedient, divine mercy and long-suffering are reserved for those whose godly fear makes them worthy of it. By contrast, the Talmudic story suggests that Moses himself, although initially sharing Irenaeus's opinion, ultimately experienced a change of heart:

> When Moses went up on high and ascended Mount Sinai, he saw the Holy One, blessed be He, sitting and writing the word "long-suffering" among His attributes, and he said to Him: "Master of the Universe, surely You mean that You are long-suffering only for the righteous." God said to him: "No, I am long-suffering even for the wicked." Moses said to God, "But surely the wicked should perish!" God said to him: "Now you will see what you will need." When Israel sinned with the spies who were sent out to scout the Land of Israel and Moses prayed to God on their behalf, God said to him: "Did you not once say to Me that I should be long-suffering only for the righteous? According to you, they do not deserve My pardon." Moses said to God: "Master of the Universe, did You not say to me that You are long-suffering even for the wicked?" And this is the meaning of the verse that states: "And now, I pray You, let the power of my Lord be great, as You have spoken, saying" [Num 14:17], which implies that Moses reminded God of his earlier promise. (*b. Sanh.* 111ab)[20]

[20]Quoted from the expanded version by Adin Steinsaltz, *The Talmud: The Steinsaltz Edition*, vol. 21, *Tractate Sanhedrin Part VII*, trans. Israel V. Berman (New York: Random House, 1999), 178-79. See also *Midrash Psalms* 93 §8.

There is nothing like a sense of one's own culpability—or the culpability of those whom we love—to inspire a change of heart on the matter of divine wrath.

The third story is a variation of the second and comes from a supplementary section of *Midrash Tanḥuma* to the book of Numbers.[21] When interceding on behalf of the people in the incident of the golden calf, Moses is careful to inquire as to the principles by which God rules the world (i.e., "Show me your ways" [Ex 33:13]). God answers that he governs creation by the principle of mercy, and he recites the thirteen attributes as proof. When Moses learns that God is "slow to anger," he makes no response until, much later, God threatens to destroy the nation for their grumbling and discontent:

> Moses said to the Holy One: Sovereign of the Universe, in the case of a servant, if his deeds are good so that his master looks at him with a friendly face, one does not give his master any credit. So when would they give him credit? When the servant's conduct is evil with his deeds being evil, and then his master looks at him with a friendly face. So also in your case, O Sovereign of the Universe, pay no attention to their stiff neck. . . . So the Holy One said to him: See, because of you I am forgiving them. It is so stated (in Numb. 14:20): *I have pardoned them as you asked*. (*Midr. Tanḥ*. Num. 14:26ff., Part VIII; Parashah 4a.14)[22]

---

[21]"This supplement comes from *Codex Vaticanus*, *Ebr.* 34. It is found neither in Buber's primary Oxford manuscript nor in the traditional version of the Tanhuma" (John T. Townsend, trans., *Midrash Tanhuma: Translated into English with Introduction, Indices, and Brief Notes [S. Buber Recension]*, vol. 3, *Numbers and Deuteronomy* [Jersey City, NJ: Ktav, 2003], 119n1). Accurate dating of *Midrash Tanhuma* is problematic. According to H. L. Strack and G. Stemberger, the work seems to have developed between the early fifth and ninth centuries CE (*Introduction to the Talmud and Midrash*, trans. Markus Bockmuehl [Edinburgh: T & T Clark, 1991], 332-33). See also John T. Townsend, trans., *Midrash Tanhuma: Translated into English with Introduction, Indices, and Brief Notes (S. Buber Recension)*, vol. 1, *Genesis* (Hoboken, NJ: Ktav, 1989), xii.

[22]Quoted from Townsend, *Numbers and Deuteronomy*, 127-28 (italics added); see also Parashah 4.24 (ibid., 112). A briefer version of the story appears in *Numbers Rabbah* 16:28. Although its wording is Mishnaic (so *m. ʾAbot* 1:15) rather than biblical, the key phrase "with a friendly face" nonetheless probably was suggested by Exodus 34:6, since *ʾerek ʾappayim* can be understood as referring to the face and its demeanor: "ארך אפים, lit. 'long of face' denotes happiness and friendliness" (Gruber, *Aspects of Nonverbal Communication*, 503, citing Prov 14:29; 15:18 [p. 485]). John Townsend comments, "The Hebrew reads *be-sebher panim yaphot*. A freer translation of these words would be 'cordially,' but in this translation I have leaned toward the literal" (personal communication to author, July 1, 2004).

According to this tradition, Moses succeeds by reminding God that true forbearance emerges most clearly in the face of contumacy and rebellion (not unlike Jesus telling his disciples in Lk 6:32, "If you love those who love you, what credit is that to you?"). The theological conviction underlying this story is that when God's servants fail in their appointed responsibilities, the only principle more powerful than divine wrath or mortal fear of it is God's adherence to his own gracious character and name. Just so, the appropriately named Rabbi Naḥman answers God's words in Ezekiel 20:33, "I will reign over you . . . with overflowing fury" (NJPS), with confidence in God's ultimate purpose: "Even with such fury let the Merciful [One] rage against us, but that He redeem us" (*b. Sanh.* 105a).

This indeed is the ultimate message of an episode from the Babylonian Talmud set at a time when the Jerusalem temple is still standing (i.e., prior to the first Jewish War in 68-70 CE). It concerns the most sacred duty of the high priest, when he enters alone into the holy of holies, into the very presence of God, to offer incense on the Day of Atonement. Even at this supremely holy and terrifying moment, mercy prevails:

> It was taught: R. Ishmael b. Elisha says: I once entered into the innermost part [of the Sanctuary] to offer incense and saw Akathriel Jah [the "crown of Yahweh"], the Lord of Hosts, seated upon a high and exalted throne. He said to me: Ishmael, My son, bless Me! I replied: May it be Thy will that Thy mercy may suppress Thy anger and Thy mercy may prevail over Thy other attributes, so that Thou mayest deal with Thy children according to the Attribute of Mercy and mayest, on their behalf, stop short of the limit of strict justice! And He nodded to me with His head. (*b. Ber.* 7a.)[23]

## Patience as Virtue

In summary, then, Jewish tradition provides evidence of many centuries of theological meditation upon the principles implicit within the

---

[23]The identity of this individual is controverted, whether Ishmael ben Elisha of rabbinic tradition or the high priest Ishmael who was in office for some ten years from 59 CE onward. See the discussion by B. M. Lerner in A. Zvi Ehrman, ed., *The Talmud with English Translation and Commentary: Berakhoth* (2 vols.; Jerusalem: El-ʿAm, 1965-1974), 1.i.110-11.

phrase "slow to anger" or, literally, "long of nostrils," ranging from affirmations of divine justice in the face of unjust suffering, to warnings against pride or presumption, and finally to an insistence that God's long-suffering and mercy are what keep judgment at bay. As was the case with divine compassion and favor, the ways of God serve in this respect also to inspire and guide human conduct. Once more the *Letter of Aristeas*, from the second century BCE, provides an important example of this principle, as the king asks his banquet guests what qualities will help him to retain his throne for as long as possible:

> When, after an interval, an opportunity offered, the king asked the man who occupied the first place at table . . . how he might preserve his kingdom unimpaired to the end. He paused for a moment and replied, "You would maintain it best by imitating the constant gentleness of God. For by exercising long-suffering patience [*makrothymia*] and dealing with those who merit punishment more gently than they deserve, you will turn them from wickedness and bring them to repentance." (*Let. Arist.* 187-189)[24]

In similar fashion, the Christian canon celebrates forbearance as a cardinal virtue, citing Abraham (Heb 6:12-15), the prophets (Jas 5:7-8, 10), and even Paul as examples (2 Cor 6:6; cf. 2 Tim 3:10).[25] James 1:19-20 counsels, "You must understand this, my beloved: let everyone be quick to listen, slow to speak, *slow to anger*; for your anger does not produce God's righteousness." Or as Paul himself famously declares, "Love is forbearing [*makrothymeō*] and kind" (1 Cor 13:4).

James encourages his readers to hold steady amidst the "various trials" that they encounter, appealing to the example of Job and the categories of God's character: "You have heard of the endurance of Job, and you have seen the purpose of the Lord, how the Lord is *compassionate* and *merciful*" (Jas 5:11). His logic is not easy to follow, however, and presents a number of exegetical knots to untangle. First, the Greek version of Exodus 34:6 describes God as both "compassionate"

---

[24]Translation from Moses Hadas, ed. and trans., *Aristeas to Philocrates (Letter of Aristeas)* (New York: Harper, 1951).

[25]However, in the New Testament the adjective *makrothymos* does not occur, but only the corresponding noun (*makrothymia*), verb (*makrothymeō*) and adverb (*makrothymōs*).

(*oiktirmōn*) and "very merciful" (*polyeleos*), whereas James combines *oiktirmōn* instead with *polysplanchnos*. Although *polysplanchnos* ("very compassionate") has essentially the same meaning as *polyeleos* ("very merciful"), it likely represents an independent translation of the Hebrew in keeping with the preferences of the New Testament era. The second difficulty is the confusing syntax of James 5:11, which reads, literally, "You have heard of Job's endurance, and you know the Lord's purpose [or, 'result'], for [or, 'that'] the Lord is compassionate and merciful." Yet the awkward syntax will likely resolve itself if we can tease out, third, the logical connection that James intends between Job, his "endurance," and God's compassionate mercy.

For a start, Job is one of four ancient "worthies" to whom James appeals: the others are Abraham (Jas 2:21), Rahab (Jas 2:25), and Elijah (Jas 5:17).[26] The mention of Job in the letter's concluding section illustrates a theme first introduced in the opening verses: "My brothers and sisters, whenever you face trials of any kind, consider it nothing but joy, because you know that the testing of your faith produces endurance; and let endurance have its full effect, so that you may be mature and complete, lacking in nothing" (Jas 1:2-4). Job, after all, is the biblical epitome of unmerited suffering and the endurance that it requires. His example is apt because endurance is likewise required of the letter's recipients in the face of their own tests and trials, whether these arise out of their own desires (Jas 4:1-6), at the hands of the wealthy in their midst (Jas 2:1-7; 5:1-6), or from the devil (Jas 4:7), who so afflicted Job. These reflections lead James to the following conclusion, which includes his next reference to Job:

> Be *patient*, therefore, beloved, until the coming of the Lord. The farmer waits for the precious crop from the earth, being *patient* with it until it receives the early and the late rains. You also must be *patient*. Strengthen your hearts, for the coming of the Lord is near. . . . As an example of suffering and *patience*, beloved, take the prophets who spoke in the name of the Lord. Indeed we call blessed those who showed endurance.

[26]This analysis follows Kurt A. Richardson, "Job as Exemplar in the Epistle of James," in *Hearing the Old Testament in the New Testament*, ed. Stanley E. Porter (Grand Rapids: Eerdmans, 2006), 213-29.

> You have heard of the endurance of Job, and you have seen the purpose of the Lord, how the Lord is *compassionate* and *merciful*. (Jas 5:7-11)

James's fourfold appeal for "patience" represents a verb (*makrothymeō* [Jas 5:7-8]) and a noun (*makrothymia* [Jas 5:10]) that recall the similar description of God as *makrothymos* ("long-suffering") in the Greek version of Exodus 34:6 and passages that follow its lead.[27] That James indeed has this passage in mind is obvious from the concluding phrase of the paragraph. We find his logic difficult to follow because he is referring to concepts that his Jewish Christian audience takes for granted and therefore (as he sees it) require no further explanation. His reasoning appears to be as follows. The essence of biblical piety is the imitation of God. Just as God is "compassionate," "merciful," and "long-suffering" or "patient," so should God's people be. The latter, of course, demonstrate such virtue not only when they are "slow to anger" (the sense of the Hebrew original articulated earlier in Jas 1:19), but also by remaining "patient" (Gk. *makrothymia*), and more especially, in keeping with the example of Job, by their "endurance" of unmerited suffering. Precisely by virtue of living out their relationship with God in this manner, the faithful will find themselves sustained in their trials. For they have the assurance that even in the midst of lengthy tribulation, God's character, and therefore also God's "purpose," endure. Even as God is long-suffering, and they remain patient, so by the same measure God continues to be "compassionate and merciful." In the end, therefore, Job is simply an example, an illustration, but not the source of the church's staying power. The true inspiration that James intends is the enduring character of the righteous, compassionate, and forbearing God.

Paul is equally confident regarding the purpose of divine forbearance. It would be a mistake, he argues, to imagine that the delay of God's judgment implies its irrelevance or absence: "Do you despise the riches of his kindness and patience [*anochē*] and forbearance [*makrothymia*]? Do you not realize that God's kindness is meant to lead you to repentance?" (Rom 2:4). This same premise is used in 2 Peter 3:9 to explain why Christ

---

[27]See Luke Timothy Johnson, *The Letter of James: A New Translation with Introduction and Commentary* (AB 37A; New York: Doubleday, 1995), 312-13.

has not yet returned to judge the earth: "The Lord is not slow about his promise, as some think of slowness, but is forbearing [*makrothymeō*] with you, not wanting any to perish, but all to come to repentance." The author acknowledges his dependence for such ideas upon Paul ("Regard the forbearance [*makrothymia*] of our Lord as salvation. So also our beloved brother Paul wrote to you" [2 Pet 3:15]), although here and elsewhere the letter for the most part simply repeats traditional Jewish doctrines.[28] But the ultimate focus of his argument is not on the delay of divine judgment or justice per se, or even on the opportunity for repentance that such delay affords, important as such principles may be in their own right. Rather, as Richard Bauckham contends, the use of vocabulary specifically echoing the Greek translation of Exodus 34:6 roots these doctrines in a proper apprehension of the character of God.[29]

In other words, a proper reading of salvation history and of the course of divine justice, as well as a proper sense of ethical motivation, depend ultimately on a proper "reading" of the divine nature. Above all in matters of wrath and justice, specifically theological ethics amount once more to the imitation of God. Thus in what Robert Wilken calls "the first treatise in the history of the church on a specific virtue," Tertullian of Carthage (ca. 160-225 CE) explains that Christian patience is ultimately modeled on the example of God.[30] For, says Tertullian, "It is God's nature to be patient. . . . When God's Spirit descends, patience is always at his side" (*Pat.* 3.11; 15.7).[31] Nowhere is this exemplified more fully than in God's own submission to human frailty at the incarnation, and to human evil, in Christ's crucifixion. Thus we too are to be patient, says Tertullian, both because of the example Christ has set us and because patience gives rise to other essential virtues: faith, hope, and love. "Patience," he says, is "the Mother of mercy" (*Pat.* 3.8 [*ANF* 3:708]). As Augustine will insist some two centuries later,

---

[28]So Jerome H. Neyrey, *2 Peter, Jude: A New Translation with Introduction and Commentary* (AB 37C; New York: Doubleday, 1993), 196-97.

[29]Richard J. Bauckham, *Jude, 2 Peter* (WBC 50; Waco, TX: Word, 1983), 312.

[30]Robert L. Wilken, *The Spirit of Early Christian Thought: Seeking the Face of God* (New Haven: Yale University Press, 2003), 283. See Tertullian, "Of Patience," *ANF* 3:707-17. Tertullian wrote this treatise around 200 CE.

[31]Cited in Wilken, *The Spirit of Early Christian Thought*, 284-85; see Tertullian, "Of Patience," *ANF* 3:708, 717.

> Christ exhorts us to imitate this long-suffering goodness of God, who makes the sun to rise upon the evil and the good, and sends rain on the just and on the unjust; that we may not be careful to revenge, but may do good to them that hate us, and so may be perfect, even as our Father in heaven is perfect. (*Faust.* 19.28 [*NPNF*[1] 4:251])

Likewise the Eastern Orthodox theologian John of Damascus (ca. 655-750 CE) explains how Christ epitomizes the long-suffering patience of God and thereby inspires his followers to imitate his virtue:

> He delivered all humanity from death's destruction and the tyrant that was sin. It was not by force that He led sinners to virtue, not by having them swallowed up by the earth, nor by having them burnt up by fire, nor by having them stoned to death; it was with gentleness and forbearance [*makrothymia*] that He persuaded men to choose virtue and for virtue's sake to undergo sufferings with rejoicing. (*An Exact Exposition of the Orthodox Faith* 4.4)[32]

The primacy of forbearance (both divine and human) may be illustrated, finally, by the appeal in Islamic devotion to God as Al-Tawwāb, "the Ever-Relenting." How, exactly, does God manifest this quality? Abu Ḥamid al-Ghazālī's explanation differs little from those of the Jewish and Christian writers whose voices we have already heard. God demonstrates forbearance, he says, "[by] facilitating the causes of repentance in His servants . . . conveying His counsel to them, and disclosing His deterrents and warnings to them—to the point where, once informed by His instruction of the dangers of their sins, they will begin to experience the fear occasioned by His deterrents and have recourse to repentance, so that the favour of God the most high will return to them." Indeed, similar conduct on the part of the pious will reflect their own experience of God: "Whoever accepts time and again the excuses of those who do wrong among those entrusted to his care, as well as those of his friends and acquaintances, is indeed characterized by this quality and has gained a share of it."[33]

---

[32]Quoted from Frederic H. Chase Jr., trans., *Saint John of Damascus: Writings* (FC 37; New York: Fathers of the Church, 1958), 339. I am grateful to Sandra Smith for having brought this quotation to my attention.

[33]David B. Burrell and Nazih Daher, trans., *The Ninety-Nine Beautiful Names of God: al-Maqṣad*

## Perfect Love Casts Out Fear

In practical terms, what difference does it make whether one acts out of fear of divine punishment or on the basis of gratitude for God's unfailing forbearance? Either approach may inspire repentance, but surely it is the latter that most closely corresponds to the character of God. In order to prepare readers for the day of judgment, 1 John 4:16-18 makes this point:

> God is love, and those who abide in love abide in God, and God abides in them. Love has been perfected among us in this: that we may have boldness on the day of judgment, because as he is, so are we in this world. There is no fear in love, but perfect love casts out fear; for fear has to do with punishment, and whoever fears has not reached perfection in love.

According to this passage, God is most aptly characterized by "love" (*agapē*); this is not the idealized, romantic love of popular culture, but rather a love specifically defined and illustrated by the fact that "the Father has sent his Son as the Savior of the world" (1 Jn 4:14). Since God's essential character is unchanging, God's love extends even to the day of judgment, thereby answering our fear of punishment. This does not imply that human beings (including followers of Jesus) do not deserve judgment. On the contrary, John freely confesses that his readers have "sinned"; that is, they have offended against God and incurred condemnation. He summarizes their condition as a general failure to "love God." This is the point at which the divine character becomes all-important, for, John declares, "In this is love, not that we loved God but that he loved us and sent his Son to be the atoning sacrifice for our sins" (1 Jn 4:10). Boldness on the day of judgment, then, has nothing to do with self-assurance, still less with moral rectitude; instead, it has to do with the assurance that the character of God graciously prevails over the manifold failings of human character. John's word of consolation for the present moment is that as we experience divine love—as we encounter a God who is gracious, compassionate, and slow to anger—our fears begin to diminish as the conviction of God's true nature begins to replace them: "perfect love casts out fear" (1 Jn 4:18).

The reconciliation of God's justice and mercy in the person of Jesus,

---

*al-asnā fī sharḥ asmāʾ Allāh al-ḥusnā* (Cambridge: Islamic Texts Society, 1995), 137-38.

as the ultimate expression of divine "patience" (*anochē*) and "forbearance" (*makrothymia*) (Rom 2:4), is likewise at the heart of Paul's vision of salvation. The first three chapters of his most famous letter, in which he summarizes the content of the gospel that he preaches, contend that "all have sinned and fall short of the glory of God" (Rom 3:23). Romans 3:21-26 represents the climax of this argument, for here Paul proposes that divine righteousness is now revealed, not in the just judgment of a sinful humanity, but rather in God's own justification of the unrighteous through the sacrifice of Christ:

> But now, apart from law, the righteousness of God stands revealed, attested by the law and the prophets, the righteousness of God through faith in Jesus Christ for all believers.
>
> For there is no distinction, since all have sinned and fall short of the glory of God; they are now justified by his grace as a gift, through the redemption that is in Christ Jesus, whom God put forward as a sacrifice of atonement, through faith in his blood.
>
> He did this to demonstrate his righteousness, because in his divine forbearance [*anochē*] he had passed over [*paresis*] the sins previously committed;
>
> it was to prove at the present time that he himself is just and that he justifies the one who has faith in Jesus.

God, concludes Paul triumphantly with a carefully crafted play on words, is thus both "just and justifying" (Rom 3:26). In so saying, he contends that the sacrifice of Christ finally solves the dilemma with which so many of his fellow Jews had wrestled for so long: how to reconcile the imperative of divine justice with the assertion of divine clemency and forbearance.

Admittedly, the grammar and logic of this passage are complex, and Paul's argument is subject to more than one interpretation. One possible sense of Romans 3:25-26 is that the sacrifice of Christ constitutes a demonstration of divine righteousness insofar as God's "forgiveness" (*paresis*) of sins furnishes a prime example of the divine "patience" (*anochē*) to which Paul had earlier referred in Romans 2. A slightly different reading emerges if we understand the key term *paresis* "to express the idea of passing over, leaving unpunished" sins committed in a former age.[34] This, for example, was the interpretation offered by Peter Abelard (1079-1142)—the brilliant medieval theologian better known today for his costly love affair with one of his pupils, Héloise—in his commentary on this passage:

> I maintain emphatically that remission is granted even for previous sins *in the forbearance of God*—because of the patience of God, who does not immediately punish the guilty and destroy the sinners, but waits for a long time so that they may return to him again through penitence, leave off sinning, and so obtain forgiveness.[35]

This is the sense that Joseph Fitzmyer's translation of the passage seeks to express: "This was to be a manifestation of God's uprightness for the pardon of past sins committed in the time of his forbearance, a manifestation of his uprightness also at the present time to show that he is upright and justifies the one who puts faith in Jesus."[36] Or, as C. E. B. Cranfield explains, "The idea of God's patiently holding back his wrath is familiar in Judaism. But for God simply to pass over sins would be altogether incompatible with His righteousness. . . . God has in fact been able to hold His hand and pass over sins, without compromising His goodness and mercy, because His intention has all along been to deal with them once and for all, decisively and finally, through the Cross."[37]

For Paul, the demands of both justice and mercy alike are fully served by the cross of Christ. Thus at the heart of Paul's complex theological exposition, providing the origin and motivation for the cross itself, stands the character of God, now revealed in both forbearance and justice for all to see. As was the case in 1 John, if the justice and righteousness of God at first inspire terror in light of coming judgment, here Paul insists that it is precisely these divine characteristics that God imparts to the ungodly. God, as the apostle puts it so succinctly, is both "just" and "justifying."

---

[34]C. E. B. Cranfield, *A Criticial and Exegetical Commentary on the Epistle to the Romans* (2 vols.; ICC; Edinburgh: T & T Clark, 1979), 1:211.

[35]Quoted from A. D. Galloway, ed., *Basic Readings in Theology* (Cleveland: World, 1968), 103.

[36]Joseph A. Fitzmyer, *Romans: A New Translation with Introduction and Commentary* (AB 33; New York: Doubleday, 1993), 341.

[37]Cranfield, *Romans*, 1:211-12; similarly, Fitzmyer, *Romans*, 351-52, citing a range of further opinion.

In some respects, then, the New Testament writers are content to repeat what they have already learned from Judaism: Israel's God is indeed "slow to anger," as divine mercy delays divine justice and affords ample opportunity for Jews and Gentiles alike to amend their ways. But as they reflect on the meaning of Jesus' death, the earliest Christians come to a bold conclusion: the cross represents a new resolution to this ancient dilemma, one that not only reconciles justice with mercy, but also results in the transformation of the faithful into the divine image: "And all of us, with unveiled faces, seeing the glory of the Lord as though reflected in a mirror, are being transformed into the same image from one degree of glory to another" (2 Cor 3:18).

*We beseech Thee, Almighty God, to receive with Fatherly tenderness*
*Thy people fleeing from Thine anger to Thyself; that they who dread*
*the scourge that comes from Thy Majesty may be enabled to rejoice*
*in Thy forgiveness; through Jesus Christ our Lord. Amen.*

GELASIAN SACRAMENTARY (EIGHTH CENTURY CE)[38]

[38]Quoted from J. Manning Potts, ed., *Prayers of the Early Church* (Nashville: Upper Room, 1953), 89.

# 4

# A God of Steadfast Love

*And the* Lord *passed before him and proclaimed,*
*"The* Lord, *the* Lord, *a God compassionate and gracious,*
*slow to anger, and* abounding in steadfast love *and faithfulness,*
keeping steadfast love for thousands,
*forgiving iniquity and transgression and sin,*
*but who will by no means clear the guilty. . . ."*

Exodus 34:6-7

## Deeds of Loving-kindness

In one of the earliest traditions recorded by the Mishnah a teacher named "Simeon the Just" declares, "The world rests on three things: *Torah*, *Avodah*, and deeds of *Ḥesed*" (*m. ʾAbot* 1:2). It is not clear whether the attribution refers to the high priest Simeon who lived around 300 BCE, or to another high priest by the same name who flourished a century later.[1] Whichever the case, there is no question either of the antiquity or of the importance of this tradition in Jewish thought: deeds of "loving-kindness" (or "steadfast love") are seen to be, in every sense, foundational. They are as essential to the righteous life, according to Simeon, as are Torah, which is God's revelation of the norms and boundaries of human conduct revealed to Moses, and Avodah, which is the service and worship of God exemplified by the liturgy of temple and synagogue. According to Asher

[1]So Philip Blackman, trans., *Mishnayoth: Pointed Hebrew Text, English Translation, Introductions, Notes, Supplement, Appendix, Indexes, Addenda, Corrigenda*, vol. 4, *Order Nezikin* (New York: Judaica, 1963), 490. See also *Pirqe Rabbi Eliezer* 11, 17.

Finkel, this threefold declaration sets out the essence of what it means to live under the direct rule and gracious sovereignty of God.[2] That is, creation as a whole and God's people in particular are called to worship and honor God, they are called to obey God's revealed will, and they are called to imitate God by reflecting in their treatment of one another God's characteristic way of dealing with them.

Since neither the Palestinian nor the Babylonian Talmud includes this particular tractate, the task of commenting on Simeon's maxim is taken up by a work known as *The Sayings of the Fathers According to Rabbi Nathan*, which proposes that it was originally God's "loving-kindness" (rather than human actions motivated by it) that provided the foundation of the world. In support of this view, "Rabbi Nathan" cites Psalm 89:2, translated rather creatively as "The world is built with mercy [*ḥesed*]; in the very heavens Thou dost establish Thy faithfulness" (*ʾAbot R. Nat.* §4).[3] The same commentary goes on to explain that deeds of loving-kindness performed by the people of God provide a substitute for the worship and sacrifice that can no longer be carried out following Rome's destruction of the Jerusalem temple. It illustrates this point with a story about a preeminent rabbi of the postwar period (the last quarter of the first century CE, around the same time the Synoptic Gospels were written) and one of his disciples:

> Once as Rabban Joḥanan ben Zakkai was coming forth from Jerusalem, Rabbi Joshua [ben Ḥananiah] followed after him and beheld the Temple in ruins. "Woe unto us," Rabbi Joshua cried, "that this, the place where the iniquities of Israel were atoned for, is laid waste!" "My son," Rabban Joḥanan said to him, "be not grieved; we have another atonement as effective as this. And what is it? It is acts of loving-kindness [*gĕmilût ḥăsādîm*], as it is said, 'For I desire mercy [*ḥesed*] and not sacrifice' [Hos 6:6]."[4]

[2]Asher Finkel, "Prayer in Jewish Life of the First Century as Background to Early Christianity," in *Into God's Presence: Prayer in the New Testament*, ed. Richard N. Longenecker (Grand Rapids: Eerdmans, 2001), 44-49.

[3]Judah Goldin, trans., *The Fathers According to Rabbi Nathan* (YJS 10; New Haven: Yale University Press, 1955), 34, quoted from W. D. Davies, *The Setting of the Sermon on the Mount* (Cambridge: Cambridge University Press, 1966), 306 (cf. Maimonides, *Guide for the Perplexed* 3.53). This work dates from the third to fourth centuries CE (see Goldin, *The Fathers According to Rabbi Nathan*, xxi).

[4]Davies, *Setting of the Sermon on the Mount*, 306. Compare the interpretations offered by Maimonides and by Isaac Abrabanel (1437-1506): see Moses Maimonides, *The Commentary to*

Here, deeds of loving-kindness include celebrating with a wedding party, mourning with a funeral procession, giving alms to the poor, and remaining faithful in prayer. That acts of charitable piety, or *ḥesed*, might atone for sin should not be too quickly dismissed as "salvation by works." Rather, a more profound logic undergirds this view. For atonement itself—the process whereby God is willing to welcome back offenders and renegades—depends entirely on divine kindness and generosity. Hence God "desires mercy" because that is God's very nature. As Hosea 6:6 clearly implies, it is this inner logic, and not the external gesture alone, that makes sense of human worship as a whole. What Joḥanan proposes, therefore, in keeping with the words of the prophet, is that in the absence of atoning sacrifice to cleanse them from their sins, God's people can hardly do better than to pattern their own lives after the divine loving-kindness that makes reconciliation possible in the first place. As God has been merciful to them, so they are to act mercifully toward others (a principle already explored in previous chapters). Because they reflect the very nature of God, deeds of loving-kindness take precedence over liturgy and sacrifice alike.

Allusions to Hosea 6:6 are rare in Jewish sources prior to the destruction of the temple.[5] In Matthew's Gospel, however, Jesus cites this verse twice: once when he is criticized for consorting with the ungodly (Mt 9:13), and a second time in defense of his failure to rebuke the disciples for laxity in matters of Torah (in this particular case, Sabbath observance) (Mt 12:7). "Go and learn what this means," Jesus responds, "'I desire mercy, not sacrifice.' For I have come to call not the righteous but sinners." The only difficulty with this line of reasoning is that neither failure to observe the Sabbath nor table fellowship with sinners has anything to do with "sacrifice"—that is, with temple liturgy, worship, or sacrificial offerings. What, then, is the logic of Jesus' reply? The saying attributed to Simeon provides the implied link: obedience, worship, and demonstrations of *ḥesed* belong together as the foundations of a righteous life. But even as, according to Hosea and Joḥanan,

*Mishnah Aboth*, trans. Arthur David (New York: Bloch, 1968), 2; Abraham Chill, trans., *Abrabanel on Pirke Avot: A Digest of Rabbi Isaac Abrabanel's "Nahalat Avot" with Selections from Other Classical Commentaries on Pirkei Avot* (New York: Sepher-Hermon, 1991), 27-28.

[5]See W. D. Davies and Dale C. Allison Jr., *The Gospel According to Saint Matthew* (3 vols.; ICC; Edinburgh: T & T Clark, 1988-1997), 1:135.

"loving-kindness" (*ḥesed*) takes precedence over Avodah (sacrifice and worship), so also, says Jesus, it takes precedence over Torah (strict obedience to the Mosaic commands). In practice, Jesus and Joḥanan concur that *ḥesed* is the preeminent characteristic of a pious life: "loving-kindness" is the first foundation on which the world is based.

According to the Babylonian Talmud, "Torah [i.e., the Pentateuch] begins with deeds of loving-kindness and ends with deeds of loving-kindness" (*b. Soṭah* 14a).[6] This saying arises much later than either Simeon or Jesus, as it is attributed to a Palestinian teacher of the third century CE, Rabbi Simlai. But it is nonetheless striking that according to Simlai, the "deeds of loving-kindness" that frame Torah (itself the central expression of Israel's covenant obligations) are performed not by Israelites, but by God. According to this interpretation, it is God who first made clothes for Adam and Eve (Gen 3:21), and God who eventually buried Moses in the land of Moab (Deut 34:6). The purpose of the Talmud, we recall, is to spell out in careful detail how the pious can observe all 613 injunctions contained in Torah. As we noted briefly in the discussion of Maimonides and the imitation of God in chapter 2, a close contemporary of Simlai, Rabbi Ḥama ben Ḥanina, spells out this principle in greater detail in relation to Deuteronomy 13:5:

> What means the text: Ye shall walk after the Lord your God? . . . [The meaning is] to walk after the attributes of the Holy One, blessed be He.
>
> As He clothes the naked, for it is written: And the Lord God made for Adam and for his wife coats of skin, and clothed them [Gen 3:21], so do thou also clothe the naked.
>
> The Holy One, blessed be He, visited the sick, for it is written: And the Lord appeared unto him by the oaks of Mamre [Gen 18:1], so do thou also visit the sick.
>
> The Holy One, blessed be He, comforted mourners, for it is written: And it came to pass after the death of Abraham, that God blessed Isaac his son [Gen 25:11], so do thou also comfort mourners.

[6]Employing the literal translation from the footnote to the Soncino edition, referring to *gĕmilût ḥăsādîm*, as in both *m. ʾAbot* 1:2 and Joḥanan ben Zakkai's interpretation of Hosea 6:6. Similarly *Midrash Psalms* 25 §11, on Psalm 25:10.

> The Holy one, blessed be He, buried the dead, for it is written: And He buried him in the valley [Deut 34:6], so do thou also bury the dead. (*b. Soṭah* 14a)

Thus as the rabbis continue to reflect on the meaning of *ḥesed*, the principle of imitating God's own "loving-kindness" provides the inner logic of Torah obedience and represents the essence of keeping covenant with God.

## The Sermon on the Mount

The Sermon on the Mount (Mt 5–7) follows a similar logic. These chapters have long presented difficulties for interpreters: are Jesus' commands to be taken literally; do they merely describe, in prophetic fashion, the future conditions of "the kingdom of heaven"; or do they (as Martin Luther partly held) set a standard for pious conduct so impossibly high as to demonstrate our need of grace?[7] We have already noted at several junctures that for Jesus, imitation of God constitutes the essence of true piety (Mt 5:43-48). Yet however we interpret particular aspects of the "higher righteousness" (Mt 5:20) that he expounds, it is clear that the center and focus of Jesus' moral vision are located in *God's* righteous acts, as the source from which righteous human action is derived. Jesus explains as much in one of the most famous and poetic passages of Matthew's Gospel:

> Therefore I tell you, do not worry about your life, what you will eat or what you will drink, or about your body, what you will wear. Is not life more than food, and the body more than clothing? Look at the birds of the air; they neither sow nor reap nor gather into barns, and yet your heavenly Father feeds them. Are you not of more value than they? And can any of you by worrying add a single hour to your span of life? And why do you worry about clothing? Consider the lilies of the field, how they grow; they neither toil nor spin, yet I tell you, even Solomon in all his glory was not clothed like one of these. But if God so clothes the grass of the field, which is alive today and tomorrow is thrown into the oven, will he not much more clothe you—you of little faith? Therefore do not worry, saying, "What will we eat?" or "What will we drink?" or

[7] For a brief summary of the history of interpretation of the Sermon on the Mount, see Graham N. Stanton, *A Gospel for a New People: Studies in Matthew* (Louisville: Westminster John Knox, 1993), 289-97.

"What will we wear?" For it is the Gentiles who strive for all these things; and indeed your heavenly Father knows that you need all these things. But strive first for the kingdom of God and his righteousness, and all these things will be given to you as well. (Mt 6:25-33)

Jesus' logic does not differ in principle from that of Simeon, Simlai, or Ḥama ben Ḥanina. But whereas the rabbis argue on the basis of God's acts of *ḥesed* toward the patriarchs, recorded in Scripture, Jesus pursues a more pragmatic line of reasoning, in keeping with the pastoral setting of his ministry. To begin with, he appeals directly to the needs and concerns of his hearers rather than to the more lofty and pious ideal of *imitatio Dei.* If, he says, his heavenly Father feeds the birds and clothes the grass and lilies with splendor, how much more will God perform *gĕmilût ḥăsādîm*, deeds of loving-kindness, for those who seek his reign?[8] "All these things," he assures them, "will be given to you as well." The focus of Jesus' ethical orientation is not a creation-based spirituality, nor does it stem from a love of nature for its own sake; rather, he insists, much like the familiar gifts of sunshine and rain, the birds of the air and the lilies of the field rely on and reveal the *ḥesed*, or loving-kindness, of an abundantly generous God.

In later centuries Christian exegetes likewise ponder the meaning of *ḥesed*, both human and divine. Among them is the fourth-century exegete, preacher, and eventual patriarch of Constantinople, John Chrysostom (ca. 347-407 CE). Although hundreds of his "homilies" on Genesis, the Gospels, and the letters of Paul are extant, only fragments survive from Chrysostom's study of the Letter of James. Included among these is a reflection on James 1:27: "Religion that is pure and undefiled before God, the Father, is this: to care for orphans and widows in their distress, and to keep oneself unstained by the world." James avers that "deeds of loving-kindness," not belief alone, are essential features of Christian obedience; that "faith" and "faithfulness" go hand in hand. Chrysostom comments,

> It is this by which we are able to be like God: in being merciful and compassionate. But should we not have this, we are lacking altogether. He did not say, "If you fast, you are like your Father"; for no such things

[8]Jesus' emphasis on *gĕmilût ḥăsādîm* is identified by Davies, *Setting of the Sermon on the Mount*, 307-8.

are of God, nor does God do anything like them. But what does it say? "Be merciful like your Father in heaven." *This* is the work of God. . . . "I desire mercy," he says, "and not sacrifice." (*Fr. Ep. Cath.* [my translation])[9]

Chrysostom too believes that piety consists essentially of imitating God, quoting first a combined paraphrase of Matthew 5:48 and Luke 6:36, then Hosea 6:6, to prove his point. In fact, the opening sentence of the quoted passage could almost be translated, "It is this by which we are able to *be equal* to God," although such a rendering might be too bold for Chrysostom's thoroughly orthodox sensibilities. Nonetheless, he insists in one of his homilies on Philippians, "Nothing rouses a great and philosophic soul to the performance of good works so much as learning that in this it is likened to God. What encouragement is equal to this? None" (*Hom. Phil.* 6.1 [*NPNF*[1] 13:206]).[10]

## Divine Condescension, Human Kindness

The core principle of patterning human conduct after the conduct and character of God is especially prominent with respect to God's "steadfast love." The precise meaning of the term *ḥesed* has been the subject of repeated scholarly analysis, the results of which can only be briefly summarized here.[11] The noun occurs nearly 250 times in Hebrew Scripture, more than half of these in fifty-four of the 150 psalms, making it the most influential of all the divine qualities enumerated in Exodus 34:6-7.[12] Such prominence is perhaps foreshadowed by the fact that *ḥesed* is the only term to appear twice within the formula: "abounding in *steadfast love* and faithfulness, keeping *steadfast love* for thousands." In essence, *ḥesed*

---

[9]See PG 64:1041. Compare the paraphrase in Gerald Bray, ed., *James, 1-2 Peter, 1-3 John, Jude* (ACCS 11; Downers Grove, IL: InterVarsity Press, 2000), 20.

[10]Treating, in Philippians 2:6, "equality with God."

[11]The major studies in English are Nelson Glueck, *Hesed in the Bible*, trans. Alfred Gottschalk (Cincinnati: Hebrew Union College, 1967); Katharine Doob Sakenfeld, *The Meaning of Hesed in the Hebrew Bible: A New Inquiry* (HSM 17; Missoula, MT: Scholars Press, 1978); Gordon R. Clark, *The Word Hesed in the Hebrew Bible* (JSOTSup 157; Sheffield: Sheffield Academic Press, 1993); for briefer and more accessible summaries, see J. S. Kselman, "Grace," *ABD* 2:1085-86; K. D. Sakenfeld, "Love," *ABD* 4:377-81.

[12]In addition, the cognate verb *ḥāsad* occurs in a single phrase, "With the loyal, you *deal loyally*" (2 Sam 22:26 // Ps 18:25), which also includes the adjective *ḥāsîd*, usually translated as "pious" or "faithful" (e.g., Ps 149:1, 5, 9). The latter occurs thirty-two times, twenty-five of these in the psalms.

describes a particular kind of relationship or way of relating, either between God and humanity, or between two or more different people. Specifically, *ḥesed* describes particular kinds of behavior in a relationship of unequals, a relationship between one who is powerful and another who is essentially powerless. It describes a way of acting, without constraint, on behalf of someone who would be lost without such help, one who cannot in any way earn or obtain or deserve so magnanimous a gesture. However grating it may be to human pride, *ḥesed* amounts to generous condescension on the part of the giver, at a moment when that precise generosity and graciousness are all that will rescue the one in need. J. S. Kselman's summary is worth repeating in full:

> (1) *ḥesed* is an action rather than simply an attitude or a psychological state, and the action involved is usually one of deliverance or protection;
>
> (2) an act of *ḥesed* is based upon and performed in an existing relationship, either explicit or implicit;
>
> (3) *ḥesed* is an action requested or expected of someone who is situationally or circumstantially superior to another who lacks power or resources to perform the desired action;
>
> (4) *ḥesed* is extralegal and cannot be coerced; the situationally superior party cannot be compelled to act and remains free not to perform the needed act of *ḥesed*; and
>
> (5) is an act which fulfills an essential need that the person in need cannot meet, and for which there is no alternative source of assistance.[13]

Of the numerous episodes that illustrate this principle in the history of Israel, we will focus initially on the stories of Ruth and Naomi, and of Mephibosheth, then turn to examine its expression in the book of Psalms.

### *Ruth and Naomi*

According to Baruch Levine,[14] Ruth reads like a parable that illustrates the meaning of *ḥesed*, even though the word itself occurs only three

---

[13]Kselman, "Grace," 1086, summarizing Sakenfeld, *The Meaning of Hesed*.

[14]Personal communication to the author, November 25, 2002. See Baruch Levine, "In Praise of the Israelite Mispaha: Legend Themes in the Book of Ruth," in *The Quest for the Kingdom of God: Studies in Honor of George E. Mendenhall*, ed. H. B. Huffmon, F. A. Spina, and A. R. W. Green (Winona Lake, IN: Eisenbrauns, 1983), 95-106.

times in the entire book. Its story is set in the time of the judges—that is, prior to the establishment of Israel's monarchy, perhaps in the eleventh or twelfth century BCE. As a result of local famine, a certain Israelite, Elimelech, is forced to leave his ancestral homeland in search of food, together with his wife, Naomi, and their two sons. The family travels south and east to the land of Moab (on the other side of the Dead Sea, in present-day Jordan). Moabites are foreigners and objects of cursing, a people with whom the Israelites are in frequent conflict (see Deut 23:3-6; Is 15:1-16:14; Jer 48:1-47). Tragically, however, Elimelech dies in exile; having married Moabite women, the sons also die within the space of ten years. Naomi has no choice but to return to the land of her birth. In a time and place in which a woman's identity and security are conveyed primarily in relation to her father or husband, she is without provision or protection. Since she is too old to marry again and bear children who will care for her in old age, her only hope is to cast herself on the mercy of a male relative.

One of the key themes of the book is announced when Naomi instructs her daughters-in-law, "Go back each of you to your mother's house. May the LORD deal kindly with you [lit., 'enact *ḥesed* with you'], as you have dealt with the dead and with me" (Ruth 1:8). Whereas one of them, Orpah, accepts the wisdom and inevitability of Naomi's assessment, the other, Ruth, insists on traveling with her mother-in-law to the land of Israel. Notwithstanding her prayer for Yahweh to enact *ḥesed* upon Orpah and Ruth, Naomi's own outlook is considerably less optimistic, for she is convinced that Israel's God has dealt harshly with her: "I went away full," is her bitter lament, "but the LORD has brought me back empty" (Ruth 1:21 [cf. Ruth 1:13, 20]).

Yet subsequent events prove that she has miscalculated, both with regard to God and concerning the people of Bethlehem, her ancestral home. As it turns out, both she and Ruth find favor (*hēn*) in the eyes of the relative, Boaz, of whom she has come in search (Ruth 2:2, 10, 13). Seeking to act after the manner of his God, Boaz takes them under his wing (the same metaphor in Hebrew as in English, in Ruth 2:12; 3:9, although in the second instance the word *kānāp* must be translated as "cloak"). Seeing the kindness with which he has treated them, Naomi declares definitively, "Blessed be he by the Lord, whose kindness [*ḥesed*] has not forsaken the living or the dead!" (Ruth 2:20). This represents a complete reversal of her earlier views. But the declaration includes an important ambiguity, for it is not entirely clear in the Hebrew whether the *ḥesed* in question is that of Boaz or of Yahweh.[15] And that, surely, is the point, for Boaz demonstrates that his gracious actions reflect the character of the God he serves.

Accordingly, the last word on this subject belongs to Boaz, who is repeatedly designated as the "redeemer" of the refugees (Ruth 2:20; 3:9, 12-13; 4:14). When Ruth comes to him at night, offering herself to him in the hope that he will care for her, he responds, "May you be blessed by the Lord, my daughter; this last instance of your *ḥesed* is better than the first; you have not gone after young men, whether poor or rich" (Ruth 3:10). At least from the reader's point of view, the statement is clearly ironic, for it is Boaz who has the upper hand in every sense, and Ruth who would be lost without his gracious generosity. She is a foreigner, a widow, and destitute—dependent and powerless in every respect. Even if Boaz himself is unwilling to acknowledge it, his actions represent the very essence of *ḥesed*, the "steadfast love" that redeems the powerless and needy, rescuing them from certain desolation.

This story finds its way into the Hebrew canon because, as we learn at the end of the book, Ruth bears a son named "Obed," Obed eventually fathers a son named "Jesse," and the youngest of Jesse's eight sons is a lad named "David." Ruth turns out, against all expectation, to be the great-grandmother of Israel's greatest king (Ruth 4:17-22). The story of Naomi and Ruth thus provides a fitting backdrop for that of King David, since the concept of *ḥesed* proves crucial both in his own experience and for the way in which David himself will be viewed by subsequent generations.

### *Mephibosheth*

In 2 Samuel 9:1-8 is recounted the fate of Mephibosheth, one of the grandsons of Saul, the deposed and disgraced king of Israel. The books of 1–2 Samuel recount the establishment of an Israelite monarchy, with

---

[15]So Katharine Doob Sakenfeld, *Ruth* (IBC; Louisville: John Knox, 1999), 47.

Saul being anointed as the nation's first king. But (largely due to his own incompetence) Saul does not reign for long; a dynastic struggle ensues in which David comes to replace him on the throne of Israel, the northern kingdom, as well as ruling the southern kingdom of Judah. Eventually Saul and several of his sons (one of whom, Jonathan, happens to be David's closest friend) are killed in fighting, not with the forces of David, but with the Philistines, another neighboring people whom the Israelites have battled for generations (1 Sam 31:1-13). When news of the deaths reaches Jonathan's family home, panic grips the household. It is not, after all, unthinkable that the remaining members of the royal family will be assassinated in order to eliminate dynastic claims on the part of Saul's descendants. This is exactly what happens to the one surviving son, Ishbaal, who (contrary to David's own wishes) is murdered in cold blood by a pair of overly zealous soldiers (2 Sam 4:5-8). Justifiably fearing that the same fate is about to overtake the child, the family nursemaid picks up Jonathan's five-year-old son, Mephibosheth, so as to flee with him to safety. But in her frantic haste she drops him, breaking the bones in his feet and leaving him permanently crippled (2 Sam 4:4).

In his case, however, the feared vengeance never comes to pass. Mephibosheth is all but forgotten. One day years later (the text does not specify how much time has now passed), David is ruminating on the events that have brought him to power:

> David asked, "Is there still anyone left of the house of Saul to whom I may show kindness [*ḥesed*] for Jonathan's sake?" Now there was a servant of the house of Saul whose name was Ziba, and he was summoned to David. The king said to him, "Are you Ziba?" And he said, "At your service!" The king said, "Is there anyone remaining of the house of Saul to whom I may show the kindness [*ḥesed*] of God?" Ziba said to the king, "There remains a son of Jonathan; he is crippled in his feet." The king said to him, "Where is he?" Ziba said to the king, "He is in the house of Machir son of Ammiel, at Lo-debar." Then King David sent and brought him from the house of Machir son of Ammiel, at Lo-debar. Mephibosheth son of Jonathan son of Saul came to David, and fell on his face and did obeisance. David said, "Mephibosheth!" He

> answered, "I am your servant." David said to him, "Do not be afraid, for I will show you kindness [*ḥesed*] for the sake of your father Jonathan; I will restore to you all the land of your grandfather Saul, and you yourself shall eat at my table always." He did obeisance and said, "What is your servant, that you should look upon a dead dog such as I?" (2 Sam 9:1-8)

Why would David act in such a way? One reason is that he is simply keeping a vow. Years earlier, when King Saul has hatched a jealous plot to murder David, the younger man is forced to escape through his bedroom window and flee to Jonathan, the king's own son, for help. Knowing the tenuousness of his situation, David pleads with Jonathan, "Deal loyally [lit., 'enact *ḥesed*'] with your servant, for you have brought your servant into a covenant of Yahweh with you" (1 Sam 20:8).[16] They appear to have sworn a solemn bond of friendship and loyalty before God (1 Sam 18:1-4), which David now has no choice but to invoke. Jonathan's response is equally telling. Rather than accepting David's need and helplessness at face value, he turns the tables, declaring (with some prescience) that David is the one who must help him: "If I am still alive, show me the faithful love [*ḥesed*] of the LORD; but if I die, never cut off your faithful love [*ḥesed*] from my house, even if the LORD were to cut off every one of the enemies of David from the face of the earth" (1 Sam 20:14-15). Thereupon Jonathan renews the covenant between them, and proceeds to rescue David from his own father's murderous jealousy. The heart of their agreement is a reciprocal assertion that each is indebted to the other: each owes the other an obligation of loyalty and protection. But lest we miss the point, what is most important about Jonathan's declaration is that it purposely equates David's *ḥesed* with the *ḥesed* of Yahweh. David, he declares, is (or one day will be) in a position to demonstrate an attitude or relationship that is characteristic of God.

This is exactly what transpires, but to the benefit of Mephibosheth rather than Jonathan. In a society where strength is not simply a social ideal but is essential for survival itself, one can hardly imagine that the life of a crippled man would have had much value. If anyone is in need

---

[16]Translation from P. Kyle McCarter, *1 Samuel: A New Translation with Introduction, Notes, and Commentary* (AB 8; Garden City, NY: Doubleday, 1980), 332.

of assistance, it is Mephibosheth, and all who share his weakness. He would have had to depend perpetually on the generosity of others, as may be implied by the fact that he has taken refuge in territory once loyal to his grandfather Saul. He therefore is a perfect candidate for unrepayable generosity, *ḥesed*. Again, David's language is striking, for it echoes that of Jonathan before him. To his own court, and to Mephibosheth himself, David declares that he is acting out of loyalty to Jonathan. But to Saul's one-time servant, Ziba, he confesses another motivation: "Is there anyone remaining of the house of Saul," he asks, "to whom I may show the *ḥesed* of God?" For he must know, as Jonathan once knew and the reader now knows with both of them, that *ḥesed* has its true source in God.

### *The Book of Psalms*

This same conviction is found throughout the book of Psalms, many of which, appropriately enough, are attributed to David himself: "The idea of חסד is one of the most characteristic features in the Psalter. . . . Out of 245 occurrences in the Old Testament, חסד is found 127 times in the Psalter. Of these, 124 occurrences are to God's חסד."[17] Why such a concentration in this specific part of the canon? Surely it has to do with the function of the psalms themselves, which represent the heartfelt prayers and praise of God's people, in the course of which no fact is more obvious than the human need of divine condescension, faithfulness, and generosity, precisely the qualities that are summed up in that single Hebrew term, *ḥesed*, for which any attempt at translation proves inadequate.[18]

[17]Hermann Spieckermann, "God's Steadfast Love: Towards a New Conception of Old Testament Theology," *Biblica* 81 (2000): 313.

[18]The difficulty of translation is evident in the different versions. Compare, for example, renderings of *ḥesed* in the opening line of Psalm 89: "great love" (NIV); "steadfast love" (NJPS, NRSV); "faithful love" (NJB); "lovingkindness" (NASB); "mercies" (KJV); and, further afield, "bonté" (Louis Segond); "misericordias" (Reina-Valera); "Gnade" (Martin Luther). This word "caused the Revised Standard Version committee so much difficulty . . . that they could not reach a satisfactory agreement throughout the many months of discussions. It became the last word on which a vote was taken by the Old Testament committee. No one English noun could reproduce *ḥesedh*, and consequently they resorted to two words: steadfast love" (Lester J. Kuyper, "Grace and Truth: An Old Testament Description of God and Its Use in the Johannine Gospel," *Interpretation* 18 [1964]: 8).

Psalm 23 surely is one of the most popular and familiar in the entire collection, perhaps in part because of its frequent use in funeral liturgies, perhaps also because it evokes for urban dwellers a pleasantly pastoral image of rolling hills, still waters, and green grass. But upon closer examination, the psalm's imagery is neither gentle nor (in the romantic sense of the word) pastoral; it has more to do with evil, enemies, and the threat of death. Yet despite appearances to the contrary, the theological center of the psalm is neither the needs and concerns of the psalmist nor the dangers that evidently confront him. Rather, the psalm declares, "Yahweh is my shepherd, I shall not want. . . . He leads me in right paths *on account of, for the sake of,* his name" (Ps 23:1, 3). In other words, God's primary concern is for his own reputation, a point that is easy to overlook given the psalm's recurrent images of consolation, rescue, and generous provision, all of which cause readers to consider their own situations of need. God's purpose in showing mercy, in caring for his people like a shepherd for sheep, is to demonstrate his own true nature and to keep them from misunderstanding what kind of God has taken charge of them. God's concern for his own name is a frequent Old Testament motif,[19] recalling for Christian readers the initial petition of the Lord's Prayer: "May your name be sanctified."

Psalm 23 ends as it has begun, again focusing on the divine name: "Surely goodness and mercy shall follow me all the days of my life, and I shall dwell in the house of the LORD whole life long" (Ps 23:6). We are liable to pass over these lines as though we had understood them long ago. Only when, for example, we encounter an alternative rendering do less obvious details begin to emerge: "Only goodness and steadfast love shall *pursue* me all the days of my life" (NJPS). As the psalmist has been speaking about enemies and threats to life itself (Ps 23:4-5), the crucial verb in this verse, *rādap* (NRSV: "follow"; NJPS: "pursue") most frequently means "to hunt, chase, persecute, harass." Yet here, in place of persecutors or enemies, it is only Yahweh's steadfast covenant love, *ḥesed*, that will hunt him down, find him out, and hold him forever captive in the very house and presence of the living God.

[19]Compare Psalm 25:11; 31:3; 106:8; 109:21; 143:11-12; Isa 48:9-11; Jer 14:7, 21; Ezek 20:9, 14, 22, 44.

This is a remarkable response to danger. Other psalms seem more true to human nature, with embattled sinners or sufferers crying out to God in desperation and fear. Yet here the psalmist seems content to wait quietly, secure in the conviction that when enemies hound him, God will beat them to their intended prey. On what is this conviction based? On the knowledge that Yahweh jealously guards the prerogative of making known the meaning of his own name, and he does so by demonstrating *ḥesed*, unfailing love, on behalf of those who put their trust in him. This was, after all, the original purpose of God's self-revelation to Moses in Exodus 34.

### Multiple Mercies

#### *Yahweh's Many Acts of Steadfast Love*

If the word *ḥesed* is difficult to render accurately in English and other Western European languages, its plural form (which occurs sixteen times in the Hebrew Bible) is even more problematic. Reading of Hezekiah or Josiah in the NIV or NRSV, one might never know from the translation what the original writer had in mind:

> Now the rest of the acts of Hezekiah, and his *good deeds*, are written in the vision of the prophet Isaiah son of Amoz in the Book of the Kings of Judah and Israel. (2 Chron 32:32 NRSV)

> The other events of Josiah's reign and his *acts of devotion* in accordance with what is written in the Law of the LORD—all the events, from beginning to end, are written in the book of the kings of Israel and Judah. (2 Chron 35:26-27 NIV)

These "good deeds" and "acts of devotion" are, in fact, multiple acts of *ḥesed*; to designate them by this term is to accord them and their doers the highest possible honor, thereby acknowledging that they have acted like the God they serve.

Elsewhere the problematic plural is similarly obscured by translation because there is no succinct way to render it into English. Psalm 25, another composition attributed to David, appears to echo the prayer of Moses in Exodus 33:13: "Make me to know your ways, O LORD; teach me your paths" (Ps 25:4). In fact, the psalmist already knows the God to whom he calls, for he is careful to recite details of the divine character:

> Be mindful of your *mercy* [*raḥămîm*], O Lord, and of your *steadfast love* [*ḥăsādîm*],
> for they have been from of old.
> Do not remember the sins of my youth or my transgressions;
> according to your *steadfast love* [*ḥesed*] remember me,
> for the sake of your goodness, O Lord! (Ps 25:6-7)

In the first line of this passage, however, both key terms are in the plural: "mercy" because that is the regular form of the word in Hebrew, "steadfast love(s)" because the Psalmist has in mind not some abstract quality or concept, but rather the many actual, concrete acts by which God has shown him a characteristically loving commitment and generosity in time of need.

The final chapters of Isaiah contain a series of poems and psalms celebrating national redemption and the restoration of Jerusalem, all the while acknowledging that many remain recalcitrant, refusing to return to the God of their ancestors. Therefore the prophet intercedes on behalf of the nation, calling to mind a historical past that is rich with evidences of God's mercy:

> I will recount the *gracious deeds* [*ḥăsādîm*] of the Lord,
> the praiseworthy acts of the Lord, because of all that the Lord has done for us,
> and the great favor to the house of Israel that he has shown them
> according to his mercy [*raḥămîm*], according to the abundance of his *steadfast love* [*ḥăsādîm*]. (Is 63:7)

Again, the first and last lines of the passage have the plural form of *ḥesed*; as seems only fitting in a context that explicitly celebrates the "praiseworthy acts" of Yahweh, the prophet sets the stage for his plea by recalling the many acts and instances of unmerited mercy that form the core of Israel's historical remembrance. The logic of such prayers, both here and throughout the biblical canon, is simple: if this is God's way with his people, if Israel's history indeed testifies that God has consistently acted in this way on their behalf, then there is no reason to think that God should do anything different in the present circumstances. As a Christian hymnist will later write, "If we are faithless, he remains faithful—for he cannot deny himself" (2 Tim 2:13).

Perhaps the clearest assurance of God's multiple mercies in the midst of calamity comes from the book of Lamentations, without doubt the gloomiest, most terrifying work in all of Hebrew Scripture. Lamentations consists of a series of dirges, laments, and prayers occasioned by the brutal destruction of God's holy city. No detail is too grim or gruesome to recount: the glee of the city's enemies (Lam 2:16); starving women eating their own children (Lam 2:20; 4:10); the wholesale slaughter of young and old alike, even of prophet, priest, and king (Lam 2:21; 4:20; 5:12). Bitterest of all is the conviction that underscores the entire work: this tragedy is a direct consequence of Israel's rebellion and sin.

The first four chapters of Lamentations are acrostic poems, with the first letter of each verse reciting in order the twenty-two letters of the Hebrew alphabet. Accordingly, chapters 1, 2, 4, and 5 each have twenty-two verses or stanzas (although chapter 5 is not an acrostic), while the book's middle chapter has sixty-six, with three stanzas for each letter of the alphabet. The writer begins this longest chapter by voicing the bleak conviction that God, not the nation's enemies, has chained and walled him in (Lam 3:7):

> He is a bear lying in wait for me, a lion in hiding;
> He led me off my way and tore me to pieces. . . .
> He has made my teeth grind on gravel,
> and made me cower in ashes. (Lam 3:10-11, 16)

But when the poet arrives at the eighth letter of the Hebrew alphabet, *ḥêt*, his dirge takes an unexpected turn. This is the first letter of the word *ḥesed*, once again in the plural:

> The *steadfast loves* [*ḥăsādîm*] of the LORD never cease,
> his *mercies* [*raḥămîm*] never come to an end;
> they are new every morning; great is your faithfulness [*ʾemûnâ*]
> "The LORD is my portion," says my soul, "therefore I will hope in
> him." (Lam 3:22-24)

In context, there is no simple way to account for this abrupt turn of thought. All evidence points to the conclusion that God has rejected his chosen nation and allowed the destruction of the city and temple, where his "name" was once said to dwell forever. Yet in the midst of unprecedented disaster God's "name" remains: personified Jerusalem confesses that she and her people have been unfaithful to Yahweh (e.g., Lam 1:18), yet Yahweh remains true to his own name. The language of Exodus 34:6 provides the anchor for this conviction and the foundation for penitential hope.[20]

Even so, might this mention of "steadfast love(s)" be merely incidental? Can we really know whether a sense of God's *ḥesed* was central to the thought of this author? One final piece of evidence points firmly in this direction. As might be expected in an extended lamentation over the disastrous consequences of Israel's rebellion against God, references both to divine "anger" and to instances of "iniquity," "transgression," and "sin," all recalling the vocabulary of Exodus 34, are frequent.[21] By contrast, just two passages reflect the more merciful aspects of God's character: the verses just cited and, a few lines later, Lamentations 3:31-33:

> For the Lord will not cast off forever,
> but, though he cause grief, he will have *compassion* [*riḥam*],
> according to the abundance of his *steadfast love* [*ḥesed*];
> for he does not willingly afflict or grieve the sons of men. (RSV)

If such language seems evocative, its location is even more so. By counting the number of verses in each chapter of Lamentations (indicated by scribal notations to the Hebrew text), and taking into consideration the acrostic pattern of the first four chapters, it is not difficult to locate the middle section of the book: it is here in this triad of verses marked by the eleventh letter of the Hebrew alphabet (*kāp*).[22] How

---

[20]So Mark J. Boda, "The Priceless Gain of Penitence: From Communal Lament to Penitential Prayer in the 'Exilic' Liturgy of Israel," *Horizons in Biblical Theology* 25 (2003): 67-69 (see also pp. 71-75). Boda notes that the poem encourages "penitential waiting upon God based on God's character of grace and justice" (ibid., 68).

[21]For "anger" (*ʾap*), see Lamentations 1:12; 2:1, 3, 6, 21, 22; 3:43, 66; 4:11; for references to "iniquity," "transgression," and "sin" (in various forms, all of which will provide the subject of chapter 6, below), see Lamentations 1:5, 8, 14, 22; 2:14; 3:39, 42; 4:6, 13, 22; 5:7, 16.

[22]Cf. Delbert R. Hillers, *Lamentations: A New Translation with Introduction and Commentary* (rev. ed.; AB 7A; New York: Doubleday, 1992), 128.

fitting, then, that Lamentations 3:33 might more literally be translated, "For [God] does not *from his heart* bring affliction or grief upon people." Given the artistry of the entire composition, the wording of this section and its final verse can hardly be accidental. For those with eyes to see, the author (or editor) has lit a beacon of hope. No matter how profound may be the failings of God's people, no matter how catastrophic the consequences or how wretched their grief, here at the very center of this tragic work lies a clear reminder of the compassionate will, character, and "heart" of the God who still loves them.

As an expression of God's covenant loyalty, *ḥesed* means quite simply that when God's people break the covenant, God does not:

> In terms of Yahweh's responsibility for Israel . . . the greatness of his *ḥesed* consists in his refusal, even in the face of rejection, to give up on his people, to set aside the responsibility which he took upon himself in choosing them as his people. It is not surprising that this usage came to fruition in the exile and later, with the amazing theological "discovery" that God did not utterly cut off his people, even in his final judgment on their apostasy, the exile, and the destruction of Jerusalem and the nation state.[23]

Just as in Exodus 33–34, where Yahweh responds with *ḥesed* to Israel's abandonment of the covenant, so in response to later rebellion God again insists, "I have loved you with an everlasting love; therefore I have continued my *ḥesed* to you" (Jer 31:3 [cf. Is 54:7-8, 10]).

### "*Keeping* Steadfast Love . . ."

There is a delightful adage in "The Sayings of the Fathers" (*Pirqe Aboth*), attributed to a rabbi with the equally delightful name "Ben Bag Bag" (said to have been a Gentile convert and disciple of Hillel), that enjoins careful examination of every detail of the biblical text: "Turn it over and over, for everything is in it" (*m. ʾAbot* 5:22). In obedience to such an admonition, it is worth pausing for a moment over the description in Exodus 34:7 of God as "*keeping* steadfast love." In Hebrew, as in English translation, the verb is cast as a participle so as to express

[23]Sakenfeld, *The Meaning of Hesed*, 120.

"the precise nuance of thought the writer desired. . . . The author of the Exodus credo wished it to be understood that God's action in this respect is not occasional, or merely habitual, but is the result of the uniform direction of His will and purpose—or, in other words, is of the essence of His nature."[24] In this context the word means something like "maintaining" (NIV) or even "extending" (NJPS), although this particular verb, נצר (*nṣr*), is more often translated, "to guard, to watch over," and therefore, "to preserve."

That the Hebrew verb entails such a wide range of meanings allows subsequent writers to create word plays incorporating all three key terms from Exodus 34 ("keeping," "steadfast love," "faithfulness") that fail to survive even the most skillful translation. Hence we must resort to italics to point them out. If Exodus 34:7 describes Yahweh as "*keeping* steadfast love," the psalmist responds with a prayer that employs identical vocabulary: "Do not, O LORD, withhold your compassion from me; let your steadfast love and your faithfulness *keep* me safe forever" (Ps 40:11). If Yahweh indeed maintains steadfast love for thousands, surely that very steadfast love—and faithfulness—will maintain the petitioner. Psalm 61:7 repeats the same entreaty on behalf of God's anointed king: "May he be enthroned forever before God; appoint steadfast love and faithfulness to *watch over* him." Similarly, a proverb attributed to King Solomon declares, "Steadfast love and faithfulness *preserve* the king" (Prov 20:28). Perhaps the most artful play on words is that of Psalm 31:23, which turns the two nouns ("steadfast love" and "faithfulness") into adjectives: "Love the LORD, all you his loyal servants [*ḥăsādîm*]; the LORD *protects* the faithful [*ʾĕmûnîm*]" (NEB).[25] All four passages take God at his word, as it were, for all four are intent on specifying the particular sphere or manner in which God indeed "preserves" or "maintains" steadfast love and fidelity for particular individuals and their specific situations.

[24]Robert C. Dentan, "The Literary Affinities of Exodus XXXIV 6f," *Vetus Testamentum* 13 (1963): 44-45.

[25]As we will see shortly, the word *ʾemûnâ* ("faithfulness") and the adjective derived from it (which appears here) are closely related to *ʾemet* ("fidelity, trustworthiness, truth"), the noun used in Exodus 34:6b.

### ". . . FOR *THOUSANDS*"

Continuing in the spirit of Ben Bag Bag, we now have to ask what is meant by the description of God as "keeping steadfast love *unto thousands*," which is how the verse literally reads. Why, then, the translation in some Bibles, "for the thousandth *generation*" (so NJPS, NRSV)? Or, for that matter, at the end of the verse, why translate "to the third and the fourth *generation(s)*" (JB, NJPS, NASB, NIV, NRSV) when the Hebrew literally reads, "to (the ones) third and to (the ones) fourth"? The latter is less problematic: if the text speaks of extending parental culpability "upon the children and the children's children," then the phrase "to those third and fourth" must refer to subsequent generations. But interpretation of the first example, "thousands," is complicated by the fact that with Hebrew numerals greater than ten, one must rely on context to determine whether it is a cardinal (one, two, three, etc.) or an ordinal (first, second, third, etc.), since the form of the word itself remains unchanged. Thus in all four occurrences of this formula (Ex 20:6; 34:7; Deut 5:10; Jer 32:18) the phrase can be translated either "keeping steadfast love unto *thousands*" or "keeping steadfast love unto (the) *thousandth*."

The problem of proper interpretation is not new: the book of Deuteronomy, recapitulating the terms of the covenant for a later audience, summarizes as follows:

> Know therefore that the LORD your God is God, the faithful God who maintains covenant loyalty with those who love him and keep his commandments, to *a thousand generations* [or, *a thousandth generation*], and who repays in their own person those who reject him. He does not delay but repays in their own person those who reject him. (Deut 7:9-10)

Recapitulating the essence of Exodus 34:6-7, the writer seeks to clarify two possible misconceptions that could arise on the basis of the original formula. First, he inserts the Hebrew word for "generation" and, second, he emphasizes that the extension of culpability to subsequent generations does not mean that children and grandchildren will be punished instead of those who are actually guilty of rebellion or disobedience. The latter assertion raises significant theological questions of its own and will be discussed in the next chapter. But in the meantime, it seems clear that reference to a thousand "generations" has long been viewed as the intended sense of Exodus 34:7, a reading confirmed by a number of other ancient renderings (LXX; *Tg.* Ex 20:6; *Tg. Onq.* Ex 34:7; *L.A.B.* 11:6).[26]

But is this really what Scripture implies? One later interpretation notes that the text refers not to a "thousand" generations but rather to "thousands" in the plural, implying two thousand generations at a minimum. In *Exodus Rabbah* Moses uses this detail to intercede with God on behalf of the Israelites:

> Moses then said: "They have nullified the beginning of the commandments, namely, 'You shall have no other gods before Me' (Ex. 20:3), and by making the Golden Calf they have transgressed this command, but You want to destroy the concluding part of that commandment which says, "And showing mercy unto the thousandth generation of them that love Me and keep my commandments' [Ex 20:6]; and it also says, 'The seed of Abraham my friend' (Isa. 41:8). You promised Abraham: 'I will keep lovingkindness for your children for two thousand generations,' as it says, 'And showing mercy unto the thousands' [Ex 20:6]. How many generations have passed from the time of Abraham till now?—Seven; namely, Abraham, Isaac, Jacob, Levi, Kohath, Amram, Moses. Well, if You do not show any mercy to the seventh generation, how can You be merciful to the thousandth generation?" (*Exod. Rab.* 44:9)[27]

It is an audacious interpretation, to be sure, with any number of unexpected turns. First, although Moses initially quotes the text of Exodus 20:6, the sentence "I will keep lovingkindness *for your children* . . . " appears to paraphrase Exodus 34:7. But—in addition to quoting Isaiah!—Moses takes these words as though they had originally been addressed to Abraham, seven generations previously (cf. Gen 24:12). Most importantly, Moses' recitation of Scripture represents a daring

---

[26]The various texts are set out in greater detail in James L. Kugel, *The Bible as It Was* (Cambridge, MA: Belknap Press, 1997), 431-32, and in the expanded edition of this work, *Traditions of the Bible: A Guide to the Bible as It Was at the Start of the Common Era* (Cambridge, MA: Harvard University Press, 1998), 724-25.

[27]Quoted from Karla R. Suomala, *Moses and God in Dialogue: Exodus 32-34 in Postbiblical Literature* (SBL 61; New York: Peter Lang, 2004), 119-20.

challenge. God has promised to keep faith with two thousand generations: since only seven generations have now passed and God's patience already seems to be wearing thin, how will his mercy last even half that long? Another rabbi supplies the conclusion: "R. Isaac said: Then [God] could give no reply, but could only say, 'You have argued well.'"[28]

James Kugel draws attention to an interpretation of the "thousand generations" developed much earlier among members of the Qumran community. Although scholars initially had doubted whether the separatists of Qumran held to the doctrine of resurrection, more recently examined texts indicate this to have indeed been the case. This observation may help to clarify the following passage from the so-called Damascus Document, one of several texts that set out rules for community life:

> For all those who walk according to these matters in perfect holiness, in accordance with his teaching, God's covenant is a guarantee for them that they shall live a thousand generations. As it is written: "He keeps the covenant and favor for those who love him and keep his precepts for a thousand generations" [Deut 7:9]. (CD 19:1-2)[29]

On this reading, the combination of a belief in resurrection and the conviction that God's favor endures for a thousand generations suggests that this is how long the righteous will prevail.

The second-century BCE book of *Jubilees* suggests two additional interpretations.[30] Describing the judgment that will ultimately descend upon sinners and the glory that awaits the faithful, *Jubilees* 23:27 explains that

> the days will begin to increase and grow longer
> among those sons of men, generation by generation,
> and year by year, until their days approach *a thousand years*,
> and to a greater number of years than days.

---

[28]Ibid., 120-21.

[29]With the missing introductory lines restored from CD 7:4-5, quoted from Florentino García Martínez, trans., *The Dead Sea Scrolls Translated: The Qumran Texts in English* (Leiden: Brill, 1994), 37, 45. The same passage is quoted in a different translation by Kugel, *Bible*, 434; *Traditions*, 726, with discussion of a possible reference to resurrection in *Traditions*, 740.

[30]"The Book of Jubilees is an account of matters revealed to Moses during the forty days that he spent on Mount Sinai (Ex 24:18) . . . [following] the outline of Israel's history that is given in Genesis and the early chapters of Exodus" (O. S. Wintermute, "Jubilees: A New Translation and Introduction," *OTP* 2:35).

As for those who have already died, declares the author,

> their bones will rest in the earth,
> and their spirits will increase [in?] joy,
> and they will know that the Lord is an executor of judgment;
> but he will show mercy *to hundreds and thousands*,
> to all who love him. (*Jub.* 23:31)[31]

That God's mercy is reserved for "all who love him" (and not, by implication, those who fail to do so) recalls the conditions stipulated by Exodus 20:6 and Deuteronomy 7:9-10. In this context, therefore, "thousands" may mean either "thousands of individuals" or, a few verses earlier, "a thousand years." This passage offers early evidence for the conviction, prevalent among Jewish and Christian writers of the Second Temple period and well beyond, that God's faithful will reign for a thousand years or more (e.g., Rev 20:4-7).[32] And, if we are correct in interpreting *Jubilees* 23:27 together with *Jubilees* 23:31, it seems that reflection on Exodus 34:7 provides the ultimate source for this idea. Certainly the wording of 2 Peter 3:8-9 suggests such a link: "With the Lord one day is like *a thousand years*, and *a thousand years* are like one day. The Lord is not slow about his promise, as some think of slowness, but is *forbearing* [*makrothymeō*] with you, not wanting any to perish, but all to come to repentance."

Kugel notes several further possibilities. First, "keeping steadfast love *unto thousands*" could be taken to mean "that God does not count up or reckon each and every sin, but forgives them by the thousands, without strict accounting."[33] The texts that he cites in favor of this reading (*T. Zeb.* 9:7; Pr Man 7-9; *1 Clem.* 60:1-2) refer to multitudes of sins in general, but without mentioning any specific number. The Jerusalem Talmud pursues a similar logic on the basis of Job 33:23-24, which refers to God's judgment of the faithful in the present life: "If

---

[31]Translation from Wintermute, "Jubilees," 102. My discussion of these passages is indebted in part to an interpretation offered by Philip Burggraff.

[32]See G. R. Beasley-Murray, *Revelation* (NCB; Grand Rapids: Eerdmans, 1981), 288-89; J. Massyngberde Ford, *Revelation: A New Translation with Introduction and Commentary* (AB 38; Garden City, NY: Doubleday, 1982), 350-53.

[33]Kugel, *Bible*, 434; *Traditions*, 726-27.

there should be for one of them an angel, a mediator, *one of a thousand*, one who declares a person upright, [God] is gracious to that person, and says, 'Deliver him from going down into the Pit; I have found a ransom.'" In the Talmud Rabbi Yoḥanan recounts the following tradition in the name of a teacher who flourished in the middle of the second century CE, then adds his own commentary. In view here are not a thousand generations, individuals, or sins, but rather a thousand angels offering (as may be suggested by Job 9:3) a thousand arguments for or against an individual sinner:

> R. Eliezer, son of R. Yosé the Galilean, says, "Even if 999 angels argue against a person, and a single angel argues in his favor, the Holy One, blessed be he, still inclines the scales in his favor." And that is not the end of the matter. . . . Even if 999 aspects of the argument of that single angel argue against a man, but a single aspect of his case of that single angel argues in favor, the Holy One, blessed be he, still inclines the scales in favor of the accused." (*y. Qidd.* 1:9 [cf. *b. Šabb.* 32a])

Discussion of how God balances the scales of judgment then turns to consider what transpires if an individual's good and bad deeds are of equal weight. Here too Exodus 34:6 breaks the deadlock:

> What does the Holy One, blessed be he, do? He snatches one of his bad deeds, so that his good deeds outweigh the balance. . . . That is the opinion of R. Eleazar, for R. Eleazar said, "'Abundant in mercy' [i.e., steadfast love] teaches that he inclines the scale in favor of mercy." (*y. Qidd.* 1:9)

The parallel passage in *y. Pe*ʾ*ah* is more imaginative, as well as more specific, seizing on a detail of the biblical text in order to make a point about the way in which "steadfast love" prevails even at the moment of final judgment:

> Rebbi Yose ben Ḥanina said: It does not say "He lifts sins," but rather "He lifts sin." The Holy One, praise to Him, seizes one document from the sins and the merits tilt. Rebbi Eleazar said (Ps 62:13): "Kindness [*ḥesed*] is Yours, O Master, because You repay everyone according to his deeds," and if he has none, You give him from Yours. (*y. Pe*ʾ*ah* 1:1)[34]

---

[34]Quoted from Heinrich W. Guggenheimer, ed. and trans., *The Jerusalem Talmud: First Order: Zeraim, Tractates Peah and Demay* (SJ 19; Berlin: de Gruyter, 2000), 57. Cf. *t. Sanh.* 13:4;

Still more attentive to details in the text is the reading offered by *Midrash Tanḥuma* to Exodus, which takes careful note of the contrast between the "thousands" blessed by God's "steadfast love" and the "children and children's children" who (at the end of the same verse) are said to reap the consequences of parental sin:

> It is also written (concerning the Holy One in Exod. 34:7) "preserving steadfast love *for thousands*." And it is written (ibid.): "Visiting the iniquity of parents *upon children and children's children*. . . ." From here it is shown that a good measure is five hundred times greater than a measure of divine punishment. (*Tanḥ*. Exod. 16:4ff., Part II; Parashah 4.21; italics added)

Since the logic of this passage is far from obvious, the translator comes to our rescue with the following explanation. The biblical text is understood as referring not to angels or arguments, but to numbers of individuals: "The plural of 'thousand' denotes at least two thousand with reference to steadfast love, while children and children's children denote at least four. Therefore, steadfast love is five hundredfold greater than the punishment for iniquity."[35] However much it delights in splitting the finest of exegetical hairs, this interpretation nonetheless remains faithful to the spirit of the biblical text, with its insistence that God's mercy and graciousness overwhelmingly outweigh divine judgment or condemnation.

Perhaps, then, we should read the passage as referring not to individuals, their sins, or judgment, but rather to the character and ways of God. Just so, *Tosefta Soṭah* 4:1 ponders the meaning of a phrase in the Mishnah, "With the same measure a man metes out it will be measured to him again" (*m. Soṭah* 1:7 [cf. Mk 4:24 par.]).[36] But the principle of equivalent recompense does not apply in relation to God, who (to

*b. Roš. Haš.* 17a. The reference in the opening sentence is to the wording of Exodus 34:7, more commonly translated as "forgiving iniquity"; chapter 6, below, will explore various interpretations of the verb in question.

[35]John T. Townsend, *Midrash Tanhuma: Translated into English with Indices and Brief Notes (S. Buber Recension)*, vol. 2, *Exodus and Leviticus* (Hoboken, NJ: Ktav, 1997), 92n72.

[36]The Tosefta ("addition, supplement" [i.e., to the Mishnah]) dates perhaps from "the late third or fourth centuries" (H. L. Strack and G. Stemberger, *Introduction to the Talmud and Midrash*, trans. Markus Bockmuehl [Edinburgh: T & T Clark, 1991], 176), although its origins and dating are controverted.

borrow the words of Ps 103:10) "does not . . . repay us according to our iniquities." Far from it, God visits retribution only "to the third and fourth generation" (Ex 20:5), yet has "mercy upon thousands" (Ex 20:6). The conclusion, according to the Tosefta, is inescapable: "You must therefore conclude that the measure of [divine] goodness is five hundred times greater than the measure of retribution."[37]

So which is it? Thousands of people? A thousand generations or a thousand years? A thousand angels or a thousand sins? The millennia of the resurrected life? Some of these may be the products of an overly pious imagination. From another perspective, however, all of them attempt to answer the simple question "How long, how far, does God extend his steadfast love?" While some proposals may be closer than others to the intent of the biblical text, all of them are consistent with the basic thrust of the original, which is that God's *ḥesed* is abundant and its scope vast, not as something incidental or occasional—a divine whim—but as the consistent, enduring expression of the very essence of God's character.

*Praise the LORD, all you nations!*
*Extol him, all you peoples!*
*For great is his steadfast love toward us,*
*and the faithfulness of the LORD endures forever.*
*Praise the LORD!*

**PSALM 117**

[37]Jacob Neusner, trans., *The Tosefta, Translated from the Hebrew: Third Division: Nashim (The Order of Women)* (New York: Ktav, 1979), 160.

# 5

# A God Trustworthy and True

*And the* LORD *passed before him and proclaimed,*
*"The* LORD*, the* LORD*, a God compassionate and gracious,*
*slow to anger, and abounding in steadfast love* and faithfulness,
*keeping steadfast love for thousands,*
*forgiving iniquity and transgression and sin,*
*but who will by no means clear the guilty. . . ."*

EXODUS 34:6-7

## Truth and Trusting

At the beginning of the preceding chapter we encountered the teaching of Simeon the Just: "By three things is the world sustained: by the law, by worship, and by deeds of loving-kindness [*ḥesed*]" (*m. ʾAbot* 1:2). But only a few verses later the Mishnah notes the rejoinder offered by another Simeon—Simeon ben Gamaliel II, who lived around 130-160 CE: "By three things is the world sustained: by truth [*ʾemet*], by judgment, and by peace" (*m. ʾAbot* 1:18). At least two elements of this second triad appear reasonably straightforward: righteous judgment marks the reign of a just God, who thereby creates *shalom*—peace, harmony, and reconciliation—both in heaven and on earth (see *y. Taʿan.* 4:2). But in what sense is the world sustained "by truth"? Answering this question will require careful attention to the many dimensions of the Hebrew term *ʾemet*.

Throughout the Hebrew Bible *ḥesed* is often paired with *ʾemet* (as in Ex 34:6), the latter typically translated either as "truth" or as "faithfulness." Thus the attention of the two Simeons to *ḥesed* and *ʾemet*, respectively, and the juxtaposition of their teaching in the opening and closing verses of the first chapter of *ʾAbot* hardly seem accidental. Since the compilation of the Mishnah is traditionally attributed to ben Gamaliel's son, Judah ha-Nasi, perhaps Rabbi Judah strategically inserted the proverb concerning *ʾemet* as both a complement to the wisdom of the earlier Simeon and a compliment to the piety of his own father. What, then, did Rabbi Judah have in mind? Is the world sustained by truth, by faithfulness, or by some combination of the two?

The word *ʾemet* belongs to a larger group of words that derive from a Hebrew root transliterated into Roman characters as *ʾmn*.[1] Its various forms, appearing more than 275 times in the Hebrew Bible, include a verb, *ʾāman*, meaning "to be true, consistent, faithful"; nouns such as *ʾemet*, and several others (e.g., *ʾēmûn*, *ʾemûnâ*, *ʾōmen*) that more directly convey the idea of fidelity or steadfastness; an adverb, *ʾāmēn* ("truly"), that we employ as a conclusion to prayer; and an adjective, *ʾamûn*, meaning "faithful." Far more than a simple grammar lesson, these terms together explain the nature of faith. At least in Western Christendom, "faith" often is understood as consisting primarily of intellectual assent, "belief" that something is in fact so. This appears obvious from a text such as Hebrews 11:1: "Faith is the assurance of things hoped for, the conviction of things not seen"; even more so, Hebrews 11:6: "Without faith it is impossible to please God, for whoever would approach him must believe that he exists and that he rewards those who seek him." On this view, to have faith consists of believing (agreeing with, giving mental assent to) the facts of God's existence and willingness to respond to human piety. But what is it about God that makes such assent possible?

One answer emerges from God's declaration to Moses that he is "abounding in [lit., 'great of'] *ʾemet*." Sometimes this word refers to "truth" in the abstract sense. King Zedekiah of Israel complains to the

---

[1]The initial letter, *ʾālep*, has no equivalent in the Roman alphabet, and so it either is omitted in transliteration or represented by a superscript right half-ring.

prophet, "How many times must I make you swear to tell me nothing but the *truth* in the name of the LORD?" (1 Kings 22:16), and Jeremiah complains about the people of Jerusalem, "No one speaks the *truth*; they have taught their tongues to speak lies" (Jer 9:5). Yet the usual meaning of ʾ*emet* is more concrete and personal, indicating "reliability," "certainty," and therefore "faithfulness." Thus Jethro advises his son-in-law Moses, swamped with the burdens of administration, "You should look for able men among all the people, men who fear God, are *trustworthy*, and hate dishonest gain; set such men over them as officers over thousands, hundreds, fifties and tens" (Ex 18:21 NRSV [similarly NJPS, NIV]). Or when Isaiah declares that he will die of his illness, King Hezekiah cries out, "Remember now, O LORD, I implore you, how I have walked before you in *faithfulness*" (2 Kings 20:3; Is 38:3), and that is indeed the later historian's assessment of him: "Hezekiah . . . did what was good and right and *faithful* before the LORD his God" (2 Chron 31:20).[2] Above all, when it refers to Israel's God, ʾ*emet* is less an abstract quality than a relational one: "The 'God of truth' (Jer. 10:10) is not the God who reveals eternal truth, but the God who can be trusted to keep His covenant."[3] God's "faithfulness" is thus a matter of being true to his name, his word, and his covenant promises. That God is faithful to his name and covenant makes faith possible. That is, the first and most essential component of faith lies not in the believer, the one who exercises trust, but rather in the God who has proven trustworthy and who therefore can be trusted. Fittingly, Jewish tradition observes that the three letters of this word, ʾ*alēp*, *mêm*, and *tāw*, are in turn the first, middle, and last letters of the Hebrew alphabet, suggesting that God's ʾ*emet*—divine truth and trustworthiness—encapsulates the whole meaning of Scripture.[4]

Such observations help to clarify the many instances, beginning with Exodus 34:6, in which *ḥesed* occurs in tandem with ʾ*emet* or one

---

[2]Although in two of these instances the English sense requires an adjective, the Hebrew text consistently employs nouns.

[3]George E. Ladd, *A Commentary on the Revelation of John* (Grand Rapids: Eerdmans, 1971), 253.

[4]This interpretation is cited in *Genesis Rabbah* 81:2 (and elsewhere) as originating with Simeon ben Laqish, a famous Palestinian rabbi of the early third century CE. See André Chouraqui, *L'univers de la Bible*, vol. 1, *Genèse, Exode* (Paris: Éditions Lidis, 1982), 447-48.

of its cognates. According to one interpreter, "The phrase is a hendiadys, in which the second noun is to be taken as modifying the first. The meaning is something like '*enduring* love, kindness, or loyalty.'"[5] Thus each term interprets the other: the *ḥesed* of Yahweh is manifested in covenant *faithfulness*; divine *fidelity* is an expression of *steadfast love*. The combination implies that in being loyal to his covenant and covenant people, Israel's God is by nature disposed to steadfast loyalty (*ḥesed*) and, as an extension of that love, is reliable and can be relied on. Deuteronomy 7:9 suggests as much (using a cognate verb): "Know therefore that the LORD your God is God, the faithful [*ʾāman*] God who maintains covenant loyalty [*ḥesed*] with those who love him and keep his commandments, to a thousand generations." Still, the two terms cannot simply be merged; later biblical literature personifies them as separate divine attributes: "Appoint steadfast love [*ḥesed*] and faithfulness [*ʾemet*] to watch over him" (Ps 61:7); "Righteousness and justice are the foundation of your throne; steadfast love [*ḥesed*] and faithfulness [*ʾemet*] go before you" (Ps 89:14 [cf. Ps 85:10]).[6]

This sense of divine fidelity emerges clearly in the account of Abraham's servant and his mission in the land of his master's ancestors. Already in his hundredth year at the time of Isaac's birth (Gen 21:5), Abraham has begun to worry that the family line will die out. So he sends his servant back, laden with gifts, to seek a bride for his son in Haran, the family's ancestral home on the upper reaches of the Euphrates River system. Upon his arrival, the servant's fervent prayer for success begins and ends on an important note:

> O Lord, God of my master Abraham, please grant me success today and show steadfast love [*ḥesed*] to my master Abraham. I am standing here by the spring of water, and the daughters of the townspeople are coming out to draw water. Let the girl to whom I shall say, "Please offer your jar

---

[5]Robert C. Dentan, "The Literary Affinities of Exodus XXXIV 6f," *Vetus Testamentum* 13 (1963): 43n3.

[6]LXX Ex 34:6-7 renders "abounding in steadfast love and faithfulness, keeping steadfast love for thousands" into Greek as "very merciful and truthful [in the sense of real and genuine], *preserving righteousness* and practicing mercy for thousands" (cf. LXX Prov 20:28; see Hermann Spieckermann, "God's Steadfast Love: Towards a New Conception of Old Testament Theology," *Biblica* 81 [2000]: 311n10).

> that I may drink," and who shall say, "Drink, and I will water your camels"—let her be the one whom you have appointed for your servant Isaac. By this I shall know that you have shown steadfast love [*ḥesed*] to my master." (Gen 24:12-14)

Then, when events transpire in full accordance with his prayers, the servant's response includes one further, crucial detail:

> The man bowed his head and worshiped the LORD and said, "Blessed be the LORD, the God of my master Abraham, who has not forsaken his steadfast love and his faithfulness [*ʾemet*] toward my master." (Gen 24:26-27)

The mention of the name "Yahweh" is no more accidental than is the added reference to God's *ʾemet*, for the latter clarifies more fully what the former implies: Yahweh has demonstrated "steadfast love" precisely by remaining faithful and true to his covenant and promises. Believing the match to be "made in heaven," the servant relates these convictions to the girl's family and asks whether they, like God, will respond to Abraham's quest with *ḥesed* and *ʾemet* of their own: "Now if you will show *kindness* and *faithfulness* to my master, tell me; and if not, tell me, so I may know which way to turn" (Gen 24:49 NIV).

### *Rahab in the Land of Promise*

Much as God's *ḥesed* and *ʾemet* are essential to the survival of the patriarchs, they are no less critical to the eventual fulfillment of God's promise of a homeland for his people (Gen 13:13-17). In essence, the book of Joshua relates the Israelite conquest of Canaan: having wandered rather longer than they had planned in the wilderness, the Israelites finally cross the Jordan River to wage war against Canaan's current inhabitants. The campaign begins with espionage: Joshua sends a pair of unnamed spies across the river into Jericho to ascertain the strength of the enemy. Their task complete, presumably, the men retire for the night to a house of ill repute. But word reaches the king of Jericho regarding the two unwelcome guests and their unorthodox accommodation. When challenged, the mistress of the house insists that the men have already departed, and then she conceals them on the roof in case the search party should return for a closer look. The following exchange takes place between her and the spies:

> She said to the men: "I know that the Lord has given you the land, and that dread of you has fallen on us, and that all the inhabitants of the land melt in fear before you. . . . The Lord your God is God indeed in heaven above and on earth below. Now then, since I have enacted *ḥesed* with you, swear to me by the Lord that you in turn will enact *ḥesed* with my family. Give me a sign of good faith [*ʾemet*] that you will spare my father and mother, my brothers and sisters, and all who belong to them, and deliver our lives from death." The men said to her, "Our life for yours! If you do not tell this business of ours, then we will deal kindly and faithfully [or, 'enact *ḥesed* and *ʾemet*'] with you when the Lord gives us the land." (Josh 2:9, 11-14)

The story is a study in the unexpected. The men, on a mission from God, choose lodging that raises questions about their fidelity as much as their judgment (the word translated "prostitute" in Josh 2:1 has overtones of covenant unfaithfulness as well as of sexual misconduct).[7] The prostitute in question is worried about her family (notwithstanding the shame that her profession must bring). A Canaanite and worshiper of foreign gods, she nonetheless clearly knows and fears the God of Israel, for it is she who first cites the name of Yahweh. Most striking of all, she enacts *ḥesed*, saving magnanimity, on behalf of the two Israelite "guests," whom she could more easily have betrayed to death. Then, just as she has freely offered *ḥesed*, she seeks *ḥesed* and a sign of fidelity (*ʾemet*) in return. But whereas her own actions were unbidden and unconditional, the Israelites respond only conditionally: "*If* you do not tell this business of ours, *then* we will do *ḥesed* and *ʾemet* with you when the Lord gives us the land."

It is fitting that of all the characters in this story only the prostitute, Rahab, is given a name. Christian tradition knows her both as an ancestor of the Messiah (Mt 1:5) and as a model of trusting faith (Heb 11:31). But already in the context of Israelite history the story has pro-

---

[7]Her name suggests both connotations: "Rahab" means "broad" (i.e., "wide" [a similar sexual connotation may be present in Ezek 23:32; cf. Song 7:2]) and is also the name of the chaos serpent in Job 9:13, 26:12; Psalm 89:10; Isaiah 51:9.

found implications: a Canaanite prostitute, one who symbolizes everything that Israel abhors, is the first person to enact Yahweh's steadfast love and fidelity within the borders of the promised land. The episode constitutes a powerful counternarrative to the nationalistic hubris by which the Israelites will subsequently be tempted, and against which the law of Moses must frequently warn (e.g., Ex 22:21; 23:9; Lev 19:10, 33-34; Deut 23:7). Here as elsewhere the biblical writers have few illusions about the worthiness of the people through whom God has chosen to demonstrate his saving character.

The people of Israel are only the first of many who will claim that they alone are faithful to Yahweh. Yet Rahab's greater faithfulness indicates that true service of God is less about words, less about ethnic, political, or even religious identity, than it is about acting the way God acts. Jesus' parable of the Samaritan, a religious pariah, who shows "mercy" to a man robbed and beaten (Lk 10:30-37), offers a close parallel. The parable of the sheep and the goats (Mt 25:31-46) contains a similarly unexpected outcome, this one set in the context of final judgment. The parable portrays Jesus' beleaguered "brothers" as those in need of *gĕmilût ḥăsādîm*, "deeds of loving-kindness," such as feeding the hungry, clothing the naked, caring for the sick, and visiting the imprisoned. The quality and character of their "steadfast love" is clear, yet those responsible for them are astonished to discover both the implications of their actions and who it is they have been serving. The unexpected outcome of their *ḥesed* is that they receive *ḥesed* in turn and find themselves welcomed, not into the promised land of Canaan, but into "eternal life" in the kingdom of the compassionate Father (Mt 25:46). Stated simply, these illustrations together suggest that the life of "faith" is as much about concrete actions as about convictions or words, and that sometimes—at least according to Jesus—the most truly "faithful" are not those who think themselves so.

## Faith and Good Works in the Letter of James

Such was his reforming zeal that Martin Luther (1483-1546) took a particularly dim view of the Letter of James, fearing that it counseled reliance on the very "works righteousness" that had blinded the church of his day to the imperative of grace. In the preface to his 1522 translation of the New Testament into German, Luther famously called James "an epistle of straw," with "nothing of the nature of the gospel about it."[8] Following his lead, many Protestant interpreters have wrestled with the apparent contradiction between what James advocates and Paul's emphatic insistence that one "is justified not by the works of the law but through faith in Jesus Christ" (Gal 2:16 [similarly Rom 3:28]). Yet faith alone, says James with equal conviction, is insufficient, even deficient:

> What good is it, my brothers and sisters, if you say you have faith but do not have works? Can faith save you? If a brother or sister is naked and lacks daily food, and one of you says to them, "Go in peace; keep warm and eat your fill," and yet you do not supply their bodily needs, what is the good of that? So faith by itself, if it has no works, is dead. (Jas 2:14-17)

It is no accident that James refers to the same "works" described by his brother Jesus in the parable of the sheep and the goats: feeding the hungry, clothing the naked, and exercising hospitality toward strangers (so also Jas 2:2-4; cf. Mt 25:35-36). These are not just any acts; they are *gĕmilût ḥăsādîm*, "deeds of loving-kindness" in particular. We saw in chapter 3 that James clearly has in mind the language and traditions of Exodus 34:6-7 as he writes his letter. Understood within a Jewish context, then, far from representing an attempt to earn favor with God, the "works" to which he refers are nothing other than a faithful, grateful response on the part of those who have experienced the unrepayable mercy and staggering generosity—the *ḥesed*—of God. They are simply acts and actions by which the saints treat others as God has treated them. Not to act in such a manner, James insists, offers compelling proof that one's so-called faith is in fact fruitless, "barren," even "dead" (Jas 2:17, 20), indicating that one has not yet encountered the revolutionary, radically transforming power of God's love. Jesus makes the same point in equally

[8]E. Theodore Bachman, ed., *Luther's Works*, vol. 35, *Word and Sacrament* (Philadelphia: Muhlenberg, 1960), 362. Luther removed these comments, however, from subsequent editions of the preface.

unambiguous terms: "You will know them by their fruits. Not everyone who says to me, 'Lord, Lord,' will enter the kingdom of heaven, but only the one who does the will of my Father in heaven" (Mt 7:20-21).

## Faith, Faithfulness, and the Fidelity of God

In contrast to the broader semantic range of *ʾemet*, the cognate term *ʾemûnâ* more narrowly refers to "faithfulness." In particular, Psalm 89 describes the divine faithfulness that gives rise to faith. The poem begins with an exultant declaration of God's *ḥesed* and covenant fidelity:

> I will sing of your *steadfast love*, O Lord, forever;
> with my mouth I will proclaim your faithfulness [*ʾemûnâ*] to all
> generations.
> I declare that your *steadfast love* is established forever;
> your faithfulness [*ʾemûnâ*] is as firm as the heavens. (Ps 89:1-2)

Such faithfulness is evident, first, in the covenant itself, the significance of which is so great that even the heavenly council rejoices: "Let the heavens praise your wonders, O Lord, your faithfulness [*ʾemûnâ*] in the assembly of the holy ones" (Ps 89:5). Second, says the psalmist, it is there in Yahweh's reign over the might of creation, for "Who is mighty as you, O Lord? Your faithfulness [*ʾemûnâ*] surrounds you. You rule the raging of the sea; when its waves rise, you still them" (Ps 89:8-9). Third, as we saw earlier, faithfulness is central to the character and ways of Israel's God: "Righteousness and justice are the foundation of your throne; steadfast love and faithfulness [*ʾemet*] go before you" (Ps 89:14). Moreover, Yahweh bestows the same qualities to his regent, the one who rules in his stead: "My faithfulness [*ʾemûnâ*] and steadfast love shall be with him" (Ps 89:24); likewise, with a verbal form of the same root, "Forever I will keep my steadfast love for him, and my covenant with him will *stand firm*" (Ps 89:28). Even should the nation fail and prove unfaithful, God cannot reverse his favor: Yahweh may choose to punish the nation, "but I will not remove from him my steadfast love, or be false to my faithfulness [*ʾemûnâ*]" (Ps 89:33). Yet because of the people's infidelity, the throne and city of David now appear in grave danger, broken and trampled by triumphant enemies. All this leads to an obvious question, which provides the climax of the poem: if God's fidelity is established in creation, evident in the covenant, and essential to the life of the nation, what has become of it now? "Lord, where is your *steadfast love* of old, which by your faithfulness [*ʾemûnâ*] you swore to David?" (Ps 89:49). The answer is already there in the language of the question itself; this heartfelt plea intentionally names the grounds on which the psalmist expects it to be answered: despite everything, Israel's God will indeed prove both faithful and true, for that is his unchangeable character.

The dynamics of faith, then, can be traced in the various forms of this one word, as long as we keep in mind the overarching context of God's covenant. Because God is by nature faithful and true (*ʾemet*, *ʾemûnâ*), so too are God's ways: "The works of his hands are faithful and just; all his precepts are trustworthy [*ʾāman*]" (Ps 111:7). The saving works of Yahweh thus provide the source and content of testimony among the faithful:

> I have not hidden your saving help within my heart,
> I have spoken of your *faithfulness* and your salvation;
> I have not concealed your steadfast love and your *faithfulness* from the great congregation. (Ps 40:10)

The same dynamic emerges in God's establishment of David and his house to reign over Israel. In 2 Samuel David prays,

> And now, O Lord God, as for the word that you have spoken concerning your servant and concerning his house, confirm it forever; do as you have promised. Thus your name will be magnified forever in the saying, "The Lord of hosts is God over Israel"; and the house of your servant David will be established before you. . . . And now, O Lord God, you are God, and your words are *true* [*ʾemet*], and you have promised this good thing to your servant; now therefore may it please you to bless the house of your servant, so that it may continue forever before you. (2 Sam 7:25-29 [cf. 1 Chron 17:23-27])

In his dedication of the temple that he, rather than David, has built, King Solomon echoes the language of his father's prayer:

> Now LORD, God of Israel, keep for your servant David my father the promises you made to him when you said, "You shall never fail to have a man sit before me on the throne of Israel, if only your sons are careful in all they do to walk before me as you have done." And now, O God of Israel, let your word that you promised your servant David my father *come true* [ʾāman]. (1 Kings 8:25-26 // 2 Chron 6:16-17 NIV [cf. 2 Chron 1:9])

David's noun becomes Solomon's verb: because God's words are true, God will make true all that he has promised.

If one form of the verb ʾ*mn* (the Niphal, which has a passive or reflexive sense as in the passage above) means "to be verified, established, or made true," another form (the Hiphil, typically indicating causation) means "to place trust in, to believe." That is, the proper human response to divine trustworthiness is to place one's trust in God, as does, for example, Abraham, in the first such appearance of this form in the Hebrew Bible: "And he *believed* the LORD; and the LORD reckoned it to him as righteousness" (Gen 15:6). It can mean "to believe a thing to be true," as with the Queen of Sheba's response to the vast wealth of King Solomon ("The report was *true* that I heard in my own land of your accomplishments and of your wisdom, but I did not *believe* the reports until I came and my own eyes had seen it" [1 Kings 10:6-7 // 2 Chron 9:5-6]). But the element of active trust is frequently to the fore, as with the careful word play in King Jehoshaphat's challenge on the eve of battle: "Listen to me, O Judah and inhabitants of Jerusalem! *Believe* in the LORD your God and you will *be established*; *believe* his prophets" (2 Chron 20:20).[9] When the same verb applies to God, it indicates God (reciprocally) putting trust in his servants or entrusting them with some responsibility: "My servant Moses . . . is *entrusted* with all my house. With him I speak face to face" (Num 12:7-8). Faithful execution of such responsibilities means that they, like God, are considered "trustworthy" in turn, as is Samuel (1 Sam 3:20), or as in Ezra's estimation of his ancestor Abraham: "You found his heart *faithful* before you" (Neh 9:8).

The relevance of this analysis for students of the New Testament lies

---

[9]Compare Isaiah 7:9: "If you will not *believe*, surely, you shall not *be established*" (NJPS mg.); Psalm 78:22: "They did not *put their trust* in God, did not rely on His deliverance" (NJPS).

in the fact that many of these passages translate such terms into Greek using the same language (the noun *pistis* and the verb *pisteuō*) that New Testament writers later employ to indicate saving "faith." True, the respective Hebrew and Greek terms are not exact equivalents, in addition to which language evolves over time, and the sense of a given word often differs according to context. Nonetheless, the foregoing study of *ʾemet*, *ʾemûnâ*, and various forms of the verb *ʾmn* has shown that there is a fundamental connection between God's "truth," God's "trustworthiness," and the human response of "faith" and "faithfulness" to which they give rise. It therefore is appropriate to understand Paul's language concerning faith (in Greek) not only in light of the Septuagint, but also in terms of its ultimate Hebrew background.

In fact, the precise nuance implied by the word *pistis* when it refers to Christ has sparked intense academic debate. Specifically, does it indicate "*faith in* Christ," as exercised by the faithful (which is the traditional reading of the phrase), the "*faithfulness of* Christ," which gives rise to saving trust, or even Christ's own faith in God (i.e., in texts such as Rom 3:22, 26; Gal 2:16; 3:22; Phil 3:9; Jas 2:1; Rev 14:12)?[10] The Hebrew antecedents can accommodate the full range of possibilities. And what of "faith" on the part of God's servants? We saw earlier that Ezra is said to have interpreted Abraham's "belief" (from Gen 15:6) in terms of "faithfulness": "You found his heart *faithful* before you, and made with him a covenant" (Neh 9:8 [cf. 1 Macc 2:52; 2 Macc 1:2]). Paul, on the other hand, quotes the Septuagintal (Greek) text of Genesis 15:6 twice (Rom 4:3, 9; Gal 3:6), both times appealing to Abraham as an example of saving faith in God. Yet even here the different dimensions of the various Greek terms overlap. New Testament writers repeatedly declare both God (1 Cor 1:9; 10:13; 2 Cor 1:18; 1 Thess 5:24) and Christ (2 Thess 3:3; 2 Tim 2:13; Heb 2:17; 3:1-2) to be "faithful": those who serve them are therefore said to be "faithful" in turn, both in the sense of believing or "trusting" (Jn 20:7; 1 Tim 6:2) and in the sense

[10]For a brief summary of the debate, see Paul Pollard, "The Faith of Christ in Current Discussion," *Concordia Journal* 23 (1997): 213-28; for a more comprehensive treatment, see Ian G. Wallis, *The Faith of Christ in Early Christian Traditions* (SNTSMS 84; Cambridge: Cambridge University Press, 1995).

of being "trustworthy" (1 Cor 4:2; Eph 1:1; Col 1:2). Abraham, for example, is said to have had faith in God's fidelity: "By *faith* he received power of procreation, even though he was too old—and Sarah herself was barren—because he considered him *faithful* who had promised" (Heb 11:11). This is what makes him a model for believers: "so those who are 'of faith' are blessed together with Abraham the faithful one [or, 'the man of faith']" (Gal 3:9 [my translation]). Thus in the New Testament, as much as in the Hebrew Bible, to believe or have "faith" in God is not simply an act of intellectual assent or a single, determinative act of will; rather, it involves an ongoing relationship of trusting dependence on a dependable God, matched by faithfulness in conduct that mirrors God's own fidelity. In short, to live by faith means putting faith in a faithful God and acting faithfully in turn. Attitude and action, divine initiative and human response are each essential to and inseparable from one another.

Jesus himself makes this principle into the touchstone of true piety, declaring that certain religious authorities in his own day have failed to meet its standard: "Woe to you, teachers of the law and Pharisees, you hypocrites! For you give a tenth of your spices—mint, dill and cummin. But you have neglected the more important matters of the law—justice, mercy and faithfulness. You should have practiced the latter, without neglecting the former" (Mt 23:23 TNIV). The tragedy is that in their zeal for uncompromising obedience, obedience that extends to the smallest detail of human affairs, those whom Jesus criticizes evidently have lost sight of the deeper principles on which God's commandments are based. True piety, Jesus insists, is characterized by "justice" or "judgment" (*krisis*), "mercy" (*eleos*), and "faithfulness" (*pistis*). In the Septuagint *eleos* typically translates *ḥesed*, while *pistis*, although rarely used to translate *ʾemet*, nonetheless conveys the sense of covenant fidelity implied by the Hebrew term. Thus Jesus' choice of vocabulary, according to Matthew, directly recalls the *ḥesed* and *ʾemet* of Exodus 34, together with the tradition of interpretation it has inspired, according to which faithful human conduct reflect the character of a faithful God. With the addition of *krisis* ("judgment"), Jesus' three foundational principles, serving to guide the implementation of Mosaic law, embrace the respective emphases of both Simeon the Just before him and Simeon ben Gamaliel II in the century following.[11]

## The Christ of Grace and Truth

Further New Testament echoes of the phrase "steadfast love and faithfulness" reveal the conviction of the early church that Jesus himself most fully reveals these characteristically divine qualities. Four examples will serve to illustrate the point—two from Johannine literature (the Gospel of John and the book of Revelation), one from Paul, and one more from the letter to the Hebrews.

In philosophical terms, the depiction in John's prologue (Jn 1:1-18) of the "Word," or the Logos, that came from God into the world offers a careful balance between Jewish concepts (echoing Gen 1:1 in particular) and themes from Hellenistic philosophy.[12] But the advent of the Logos is concrete and material rather than merely conceptual:

> And the Word became flesh and lived among us, and we have seen his glory, the glory as of the Father's only son, full of *grace and truth*. . . . From his fullness we have all received, grace upon grace. The law indeed was given through Moses; *grace and truth* came through Jesus Christ. (Jn 1:14-17)

This passage echoes the Exodus tradition in a number of ways. First, the Greek verb *skēnoō* in the phrase "lived among us" apparently alludes to the "tabernacle" in which God dwelt with Israel, since its etymological sense is "to live in a tent." Second, the concept of "glory" recalls the glory revealed to Moses both on Sinai (Ex 24:16-17; 33:18-22) and in the tent of meeting (Ex 40:34-35). Third, the phrase "grace and truth" appears to be John's rendering of the phrase "steadfast love and faithfulness" from Exodus 34:6b and subsequent reiterations.[13] Al-

---

[11]The Greek word *krisis*, which often has the sense of "judgment" rather than the more abstract "justice," is frequently used to translate *dîn*, the second of three principles attributed to Simeon ben Gamaliel II in *m. ʾAbot* 1:18.

[12]For representative discussions, see C. K. Barrett, *The Gospel According to St. John: An Introduction with Commentary and Notes on the Greek Text* (London: SPCK, 1972), 28-30, 127-30; Raymond E. Brown, *The Gospel According to John I-XII: A New Translation with Introduction and Commentary* (AB 29; Garden City, NY: Doubleday, 1981), 519-24.

[13]This summary is indebted to Barrett, *St. John*, 139-40; Brown, *John I-XII*, 14; George R.

though the evangelist's language is not that of the Septuagint, he appears to offer an independent, imaginative, and no less accurate rendering of the Hebrew original.

John's assertion is momentous: evidence of God's character (specifically, God's *ḥesed* and *ʾemet*) is no longer found primarily in creation, the Mosaic covenant, or the life of God's people; rather, the "glory" of God, which is also the "grace" and fidelity of God, has now "taken flesh and lived among us." This leads to the triumphant conclusion that just as the law was given through Moses, so also grace and truth (which the Mosaic revelation initiates) have now been revealed through Christ. Where rabbinic exegesis would later understand the law of Moses to be a revelation of God's *ʾemet*, "truth" (so *Midr. Pss.* 25 §11, on Ps 25:10), that revelation comes to full expression already in the person of the incarnate Word.[14] In short, says John, Jesus is the fulfillment of the divine name revealed to Moses on Sinai and celebrated throughout Jewish history: "the only Son, who is close to the Father's heart, . . . has made him known" (Jn 1:18). Jesus is thus the full expression of God's unmeritable covenant loyalty and steadfast love.

The apostle Paul concurs. Near the conclusion of his letter to the Romans he addresses Jews and Gentiles in the Christian community, bidding them to embrace one another despite their different backgrounds (Rom 15:7-13). Earlier, in his discussion of disagreements over what kinds of food were acceptable for followers of Christ, Paul had argued that the believers were to take their cue from God. If God had welcomed a particular member of the community, whatever that person's eating habits, other members ought to follow suit (Rom 14:3-4). In this subsequent passage, he says, they are to welcome one another as Christ has welcomed them.[15] By way of explanation, Paul reminds both groups that Christ's ministry had three basic purposes. He explains,

---

Beasley-Murray, *John* (WBC 36; Dallas: Word, 1991), 14-15; and especially A. T. Hanson, *The New Testament Interpretation of Scripture* (London: SPCK, 1980), 97-109.

[14]See Barnabas Lindars, *The Gospel of John* (NCB; Grand Rapids: Eerdmans, 1972), 97-98.

[15]Joseph A. Fitzmyer, *Romans: A New Translation with Introduction and Commentary* (AB 33; New York: Doubleday, 1993), 705-6.

Christ has become a servant of the 'circumcision,'
for the vindication of God's *truth* [*alētheia*; RSV: "truthfulness"],
so as to confirm the promises made to the fathers,
and that the Gentiles may glorify God for his *mercy*. (Rom 15:8-9)[16]

Paul's reasoning is, at one level, that the Christians are to base their conduct on that of Christ and, at a deeper level, that Christ's own conduct reveals the *ḥesed* and *ʾemet*—here understood as mercy and truth—of God. The way in which he uses these terms, however, does not single them out for particular attention: as one well versed in the sacred text, he simply calls upon the foundational language of Jewish faith and piety. What is novel here, to be sure, is the application of such language to the Messiah.

In similar fashion, the second chapter of Hebrews explains why it was necessary for Jesus, as God's Son, to take on flesh and share in the suffering of humanity:

> Therefore he had to become like his brothers and sisters in every respect, so that he might be a merciful [*eleēmōn*] and faithful [*pistos*] high priest in the service of God, to make a sacrifice of atonement for the sins of the people. Because he himself was tested by what he suffered, he is able to help those who are being tested. (Heb 2:17-18)

According to Ceslas Spicq, Hebrews 2:17 sums up the content and message of the entire Letter to the Hebrews.[17] The letter contends that in order for Jesus to offer a perfect sacrifice for the sins of humankind, he had to be made like us. The traditional Christian position is that this "likeness" consists of his sharing our physical human nature, which provides the actual substance of the sin offering that Jesus makes. But this writer offers a slightly different emphasis: it was Jesus' actual participation in human suffering and temptation that qualified him for this task. More specifically, says the author, it was through having to experience such crippling weakness that he became both "compas-

[16]Translation, with alterations, from C. K. Barrett, *The Epistle to the Romans* (HNTC; New York: Harper & Row, 1957), 268.

[17]Ceslas Spicq, *L'Épitre aux Hébreux* (SB; Paris: Gabalda, 1977), 77. Spicq suggests that the notion of a compassionate high priest is altogether novel, insofar as total consecration to God was thought to preclude concern for human weakness.

sionate" and "trustworthy" with regard to human need.[18]

From the viewpoint of a "high" Christology, orthodox Christianity might contend that, being already fully divine, Jesus had no need to learn anything. But again, the author is very clear on this point, that Jesus, "*although* he was a Son, learned obedience through what he suffered; and having been made perfect, became the source of eternal salvation for all who obey him" (Heb 5:8-9). The implication of such assertions is breathtaking: the purpose of the incarnation was for Jesus to learn empathy and thereby to demonstrate the divine character. Again, whereas Paul and John understand Jesus to be the full expression of God's mercy and faithfulness, the author of Hebrews proposes something more startling: in sharing the human condition, the Messiah came to more fully resemble God. The paradox could hardly be more delicious.

For the final example we return to the Johannine corpus. The book of Revelation describes a terrifying figure who leads the white-clad armies of heaven into battle:

> Then I saw heaven opened, and there was a white horse! Its rider is called Faithful and True, and in righteousness he judges and makes war. His eyes are like a flame of fire, and on his head are many diadems; and he has a name inscribed that no one knows but himself. (Rev 19:11-12)

The names by which others know him are "The Word of God" (Rev 19:13), "King of Kings and Lord of Lords" (Rev 19:16), and, in an earlier, only slightly less fearsome manifestation, "the *Amen*, the *faithful* and *true* witness" (Rev 3:14).

This last phrase, the opening salutation to the church of Laodicea, is particularly instructive because it clearly reveals that the author thinks in two languages: "amen" is a Hebrew loanword; "faithful" and "true" are Greek equivalents for various other words from this same group. But in Revelation 19 such familiar language appears in an unfamiliar setting. Without exception, the passages reviewed thus far have understood God's *ḥesed* and *ʾemet* or *emûnâ* in a positive sense, as expressions of God's enduringly favorable regard toward his people, recurrent sin

[18]In Hebrews 2:17, "so that he might *be* a merciful and faithful high priest," the crucial verb *ginomai* can be translated either "to be" (NRSV) or "to become" (NIV, NASB).

and apostasy notwithstanding. Here, however, not only has a divine attribute once more been transferred to Jesus—for that is indeed the rider's real name—but the task of "Faithfulness" and "Truth" is "to strike down the nations, and he will rule them with a rod of iron; he will tread the wine press of the fury of the wrath of God the Almighty" (Rev 19:15). Such an unexpected reversal raises an important question: what are the limits of divine "faithfulness" toward those who are obstinately unfaithful? By the same token, what are the limits of God's "mercy," "steadfast love," or, for that matter, "forgiveness"? The vivid imagery of Revelation provides at least an implicit response, for it describes the thousand-year reign of Christ's followers (Rev 20:4), followed by God's ultimate judgment of all creation (Rev 20:10-15) and the emergence of "a new heaven and a new earth" (Rev 21:1). The author of Revelation is equally confident that in this matter too the exalted Jesus fully expresses God's purpose and identity.

Other biblical authors likewise wrestle with issues of justice, divine judgment, and forgiveness as they apply to our temporal existence. In considering God's response to "iniquity and transgression and sin," it is to these questions that our discussion now turns.

*O God, who art faithful and true, who "hast mercy on thousands and*
*ten thousands of them that love Thee," the lover of the humble,*
*and the protector of the needy, of whom all things stand in need,*
*for all things are subject to Thee; look down upon this*
*Thy people, who bow down their heads to Thee,*
*and bless them with spiritual blessing.*

*Apostolic Constitutions* 8.39.3-4
(FOURTH CENTURY CE)[19]

[19]*ANF* 7:497. See David A. Fiensy, *Prayers Alleged to Be Jewish: An Examination of the Constitutiones Apostolorum* (BJS 65; Chico, CA: Scholars Press, 1985), 121.

# 6

# A God of Forgiveness and Justice

*And the Lord passed before him and proclaimed,*
*"The Lord, the Lord, a God compassionate and gracious,*
*slow to anger, and abounding in steadfast love and faithfulness,*
*keeping steadfast love for thousands,*
forgiving iniquity and transgression and sin,
but who will by no means clear the guilty,
visiting the iniquity of the parents upon the children
and the children's children,
to the third and fourth generation."

**Exodus 34:6-7**

## The Scapegoat

On the Day of Atonement, the most sacred day of the ancient Jewish calendar, the high priest took two unblemished male goats and cast lots over them. Depending on how the lots fell, one goat was designated "for the Lord" and ritually slaughtered as a sin offering to purify the temple and its precincts (Lev 16:9, 16-17). The other goat was designated "for Azazel," referring either to a demonic figure associated with wrath or the wilderness destination, itself considered the abode of demons, to which the goat was sent (Lev 16:8, 10). We have William Tyndale's 1530 translation of the Pentateuch to thank for the erroneous rendering of "Azazel" as "scapegoat" (i.e., the goat that "escapes" into the wilderness), which gained wide currency through its repetition in the King James Version.[1] Before sending the goat away to Azazel, the high priest would, according to the Mosaic legislation,

> lay both his hands on the head of the live goat, and confess over it all the *iniquities* of the people of Israel, and all their *transgressions*, all their *sins*, putting them on the head of the goat, and sending it away into the wilderness by means of someone designated for the task. (Lev 16:21)[2]

Not specified in the book of Leviticus, but nonetheless an essential aspect of the ritual according to the Mishnah, was the stipulation that after confession the high priest should recite Leviticus 16:30 ("For on this day atonement shall be made for you, to cleanse you; from all your sins you shall be clean before the LORD [*yhwh*]"), pronouncing the sacred and terrifying name "Yahweh" in its full and original form (*m. Yoma* 6:2). The goat was then driven out of the temple over a specially constructed causeway, directed a considerable distance into the wild, then finally pushed to its death over a rocky precipice (*m. Yoma* 6:4-6).

Although no rationale appears for pronouncing God's full name, the specification that the goat atones for iniquity, transgression, and sin suggests a possible explanation. These three terms cover the widest possible range of offenses:

> It is actually difficult to determine the distinction between the three synonyms *iniquity* (עָוֹן *ʿāwōn* from the root עָוָה *ʿāwā*, which signifies to turn actions aside from the straight course), *transgression* (פֶּשַׁע *pešaʿ*: essentially an expression of 'rebellion'), and *sin* (חַטָּאָה *ḥaṭṭāʾā*: etymologically an act that misses the desired mark). Possibly, however, it was not intended here to differentiate between three varieties of sin, but to mention various synonyms in order to cover the entire range of wrongdoing.[3]

---

[1]Camille R. Bossière, "Scapegoat," in *A Dictionary of Biblical Tradition in English Literature*, ed. David Lyle Jeffrey (Grand Rapids: Eerdmans, 1992), 684.

[2]As previously noted, the term used here (and subsequently) is a close cognate with a slightly different spelling (*ḥaṭṭāʾt*), since *ḥaṭṭāʾâ* is a rare form that occurs only in Exodus 34:7 and Isaiah 5:18. Their close equivalence is indicated by Moses' use of the more common word immediately following, in Exodus 34:9 ("pardon our iniquity and our *sin*").

[3]Umberto Cassuto, *A Commentary on the Book of Exodus*, trans. Israel Abrahams (Jerusalem: Magnes, 1967), 440.

Definitions offered by the sages differ only slightly from this more recent view: "'Wrongs' [or '*iniquities*'] are deliberate misdeeds . . . 'transgressions' are rebellious deeds . . . 'sins' are inadvertent omissions" (*b. Yoma* 36b [cf. *t. Yoma* 2:1]). Of all the sacrifices provided for in biblical legislation and practice, only the goat driven into the wilderness was deemed sufficient to atone for all three categories. Within the Pentateuch, only the ritual of the "scapegoat" and the revelation to Moses on Sinai mention all three forms of wrongdoing together. Perhaps it seemed fitting to utter the unspeakable name of Yahweh on the Day of Atonement because Exodus 34:7 expounds the sacred name as an expression of God's willingness to forgive the entire range of human wrongdoing: "iniquity and transgression and sin." Alternatively, Rabbi Yose (probably ben Ḥalafta, from Sepphoris during the mid-second century CE) takes the three terms not as a means of distinguishing between categories or kinds of sin, but rather as a reference to the number of sins in question. Thus he understands Exodus 34:7 to mean that one may be forgiven two or three misdeeds, but not four: "forgiving iniquity and transgression and sin" refers to the first three, he says, "but he will by no means clear the guilty" refers to the fourth (*t. Yoma* 4:13).[4]

Outside the Pentateuch, the same threefold listing indicates profound or extensive wrongdoing.[5] Thus Psalm 51, which (as we recalled earlier) the Psalter identifies as David's confession after Nathan has confronted him regarding Bathsheba, begins with confession:

> Have mercy [*ḥānan*] on me, O God, according to your steadfast love
> [*ḥesed*];
> according to your abundant mercy [*raḥămîm*] blot out my *transgressions*.
> Wash me thoroughly from my *iniquity*, and cleanse me from my *sin*.
> (Ps 51:1-2)

Perhaps wisely, David's confession of manifold wickedness appeals to precisely the divine characteristics that make such for-

[4]Cited in James L. Kugel, *Traditions of the Bible: A Guide to the Bible as It Was at the Start of the Common Era* (Cambridge, MA: Harvard University Press, 1998), 740-41.

[5]In addition to the examples cited here, see Job 13:23; 14:16-17; Psalm 59:3-4; Isaiah 43:24-25; 59:12; Ezekiel 21:23-24; 33:9-10; Daniel 9:24.

giveness possible. Another psalm, also attributed to King David, reflects the consequences of confession:

> Happy are those whose *transgression* is forgiven,
> whose *sin* is covered.
> Happy are those to whom the LORD imputes no *iniquity*,
> and in whose spirit there is no deceit. . . .
> Then I acknowledged my *sin* to you,
> and I did not hide my *iniquity*;
> I said, "I will confess my *transgressions* to the LORD,"
> and you forgave the *iniquity*[6] of my *sin*. (Ps 32:1-2, 5)

An even richer use of such language appears in Micah, one of the earliest of the so-called Minor Prophets whose ministry dates from the fall of the northern kingdom in the late eighth century BCE. The book that bears his name consists of three main sections, each juxtaposing oracles of divine judgment and doom, on the one hand, with promises of glorious hope and a restored future, on the other.[7] The vocabulary of "transgression" and "sin" recurs as a constant refrain at the beginning of each section. The book opens with Micah warning that a judgment of fire and destruction hangs over Jerusalem: "All this," he says, "is for the transgression of Jacob and for the sins of the house of Israel" (Mic 1:5). Next he inveighs against other cities of Judah: "You were the beginning of sin to the Daughter of Zion, for the transgressions of Israel were found in you" (Mic 1:13). Then at the outset of the second section Micah proclaims his own prophetic anointing: "As for me, I am filled with power, with the spirit of the LORD . . . to declare to Jacob his transgression and to Israel his sin" (Mic 3:8). The book's third and final section begins with God calling on his people to plead their case and defend their conduct, as in a court of law. Micah responds by asking what possible sacrifice could replace Yahweh's demand for justice, *ḥesed*, and humility: "Shall I give my firstborn for my transgression, the fruit of my body for the sin of my soul?" (Mic 6:7).

---

[6]The NRSV has "guilt" here, and I have amended the translation to indicate the presence of the Hebrew term rendered in the previous lines (and consistently elsewhere) as "iniquity."

[7]See Leslie C. Allen, *The Books of Joel, Obadiah, Jonah and Micah* (NICOT; Grand Rapids: Eerdmans, 1976), 260-61.

The offenses that Micah describes are so extensive, and the promised judgment is so devastating, that his repeated references to "transgression" and "sin" (to this point only in combination, but see also Mic 7:9, 19) makes one wonder why there is no corresponding mention of "iniquity," the third member of the set. In fact, *ʿāwōn* occurs only twice in the entire book, and then only at its very conclusion, in a passage fairly bursting with echoes of Exodus 34:

> Who is a God like you, forgiving *iniquity* [*ʿāwōn*] and passing over the *transgression* [*pešaʿ*] of the remnant of your possession? He does not retain his *anger* [*ʾap*] forever, because he delights in showing *steadfast love* [*ḥesed*]. He will again *have compassion* [*rāḥam*] upon us; he will tread our *iniquities* [*ʿāwōn*] under foot. You will cast all our *sins* into the depths of the sea. You will show *faithfulness* [*ʾemet*] to Jacob and unswerving *loyalty* [*ḥesed*] to Abraham, as you have sworn to our ancestors from the days of old. (Mic 7:18-20)

With a deft rhetorical flourish, the fullness of Israel's disobedience—in a threefold formula repeatedly anticipated but not finally articulated until this point—comes to expression only in the recitation of God's saving mercy. Despite the frequently menacing tone of Micah's message, and despite the actual devastation that followed upon it historically, there could hardly be a more graphic way of demonstrating that even "iniquity and transgression and sin" in all their various manifestations would ultimately be overcome by the promises of mercy, compassion, and forgiveness "sworn to our ancestors from the days of old."

To this end, Micah's conclusion entails a multilayered word play on the meaning of names. Micah 7:18 poses the question "Who is a God [or, 'god,' *ʾēl*] like you?" The answer is implicit in the prophet's own name, the longer form of which (as we saw in chapter 1) is not "Michael" ("Who is like God?"), but "Micaiah" ("Who is like Yah[weh]?"). The name "Yahweh" is not actually mentioned in these final three verses, yet its meaning is evident throughout, for the recitation of forgiveness, forbearance, steadfast love, compassion, and faithfulness expounds in full the identity of Israel's God. Accordingly, Rabbi Abbahu, head of the academy at Caesarea in the third-century CE, finds in these verses an apt summary of the divine character:

> The Holy One, blessed be he—before him there [truly] is no such thing as forgetting. But it is as if, on account of Israel, he becomes forgetful, for it is said, "Who is a God like thee, forgiving sin, and passing over transgression, for the remnant of his inheritance?" (Mic. 7:18). (*y. Qidd.* 1:9 [cf. *y. Sanh.*10:1])

## Exonerating Yet Not Exonerating

Exodus 34:7 illustrates the way in which acquaintance with a biblical language can initially prove more confusing than helpful. In this case, the phrase translated as "yet by no means clearing the guilty" (NRSV), or "he does not leave the guilty unpunished" (NIV), or "He does not remit all punishment" (NJPS) consists of only three words in the original. Taken literally, the Hebrew reads, "and to exonerate he will not exonerate" or "to leave unpunished he will not leave unpunished." So which is it? Does God acquit or not?

From the perspective of grammatical structure, the explanation is straightforward enough: "The word translated 'by no means' is the infinitive absolute of 'to clear' and serves to emphasize the finite verb."[8] Restated for nongrammarians, this means that repetition of the same verb in a different form adds force to the idea that the writer seeks to convey. Since this particular verb (*nāqâ*) is expressed in the negative ("he will *not* clear"), the addition of an infinitive ("*to clear* he will not clear") further emphasizes the negation, conveying the idea that God "in no way" or "by no means" acquits the guilty. Still, pious interpreters found more creative ways to read this text.

The first appearance in the Hebrew Bible of *nāqâ* with this specific sense is highly prominent and, like its occurrence in Exodus 34, also concerns the divine name:

---

[8]E. P. Sanders, *Paul and Palestinian Judaism* (Philadelphia: Fortress, 1983), 160. For further occurrences of this construction, see Numbers 14:18; Jeremiah 30:11; 46:28; Nahum 1:3 (repeating Ex 34:7 exactly); cf. Joel 3:21. See Robert C. Dentan, "The Literary Affinities of Exodus XXXIV 6f," *Vetus Testamentum* 13 (1963): 46.

> You shall not misuse the name of the LORD your God, for the LORD will not *hold guiltless* [*nāqâ*] anyone who misuses his name. (Ex 20:7 // Deut 5:11)

According to an ancient principle of interpreting one verse by analogy to another verse containing similar language, the appearance of the same verb in both passages meant that Exodus 20:7 could be read in light of Exodus 34:7. According to their strict grammatical sense, the two texts say essentially the same thing: some offenses are unpardonable. But what if, on the assumption that nothing in Scripture is extraneous, we read the two verbs in Exodus 34 ("to clear he will not clear") not as an infinitive and a finite form, but rather as two finite verbs, each describing a separate divine action? The second-century Rabbi Eleazar proposes just such a strategy. Eleazar takes issue with the warning that God "will not clear" those who take the divine name in vain:

> It is impossible to say: "He will not clear," since it is also said, "And that will clear" (Ex. 34.7). But it is just as impossible to say: "He will clear," since it is also said: "He will not clear" (ibid.). You must therefore say: He clears those who repent, but does not clear those who do not repent. (*Mek. Baḥodesh* 7)[9]

With a single bold stroke, Eleazar solves two difficulties, one exegetical and the other practical. The first is the apparent contradiction between Exodus 34:7 (God will forgive) and Exodus 20:7 (God will not forgive); the second is the identification of which particular sins are indeed beyond forgiveness. On his reading of the text, even blasphemy or misuse of God's name may be forgiven, provided that the miscreant repents. Thus the larger principle emerges: Yahweh's explanation of his own name teaches that he acquits the penitent but does not acquit the impenitent. Or as *Targum Onqelos* to Exodus 34:7 paraphrases, "He forgives those who return to His Torah; but those who do not return, He does not acquit."

Although *Targum Onqelos* is among the earliest of the Aramaic para-

---

[9]Quoted from Jacob Z. Lauterbach, trans., *Mekilta de-Rabbi Ishmael. A Critical Edition on the Basis of the Manuscripts and Early Editions with an English Translation, Introduction, and Notes* (3 vols., repr., Philadelphia: Jewish Publication Society of America, 1976 [1933]), 2:249; also cited in Sanders, *Paul and Palestinian Judaism*, 158. See, similarly, *b. Yoma* 86a, *t. Yoma* 4:9. *Mekilta* likely dates from "the second half of the third century [CE]" (H. L. Strack and G. Stemberger, *Introduction to the Talmud and Midrash*, trans. Markus Bockmuehl [Edinburgh: T & T Clark, 1991], 279).

phrases, having likely originated in Palestine in the first or early second centuries CE, it is not the only one.[10] *Targum Neofiti*, also from Palestine but dated some two centuries later, offers a more expansive interpretation of Exodus 34:7:

> forgiving and remitting sins and passing over rebellions and atoning for transgressions and *acquitting*; but He will *not acquit* on the great day of judgment, recalling the sins of wicked fathers upon rebellious sons and grandsons, until the third and fourth generation.[11]

Here the distinction appears more subtle. Forgiveness is said to be withheld from the persistently disobedient, which implies the opposite for those who relent. More importantly, final reckoning may be withheld altogether until the "day of judgment," when all creatures must give an account before their righteous Creator (similarly *Tg. Ps.-J.* and *Tg. Neof.* Num 14:18). At that point, the translator is certain, justice will be done, and the true measure of God's "acquitting" and "not acquitting" will be revealed. If *Targum Neofiti* locates the meaning of the passage in the world to come, Rashi in the eleventh century CE sees an application in the present age: according to him, the dual reference to acquittal and nonacquittal "implies that He does not overlook a sin completely, but punishes it little by little."[12] Taking a different tack altogether, Jerome's translation into vernacular Latin (ca. 398-405 CE) avoids grammatical and theological difficulties entirely by rendering the problematic Hebrew phrase as a reference not to God's forgiveness but rather to human need of it: *nullusque apud te per se innocens est* ("and no man of himself is innocent before thee").[13]

---

[10]For this date, see Philip S. Alexander, "Targum, Targumim," *ABD* 6:321; cf. the slightly later estimate (positing composition in the beginning to middle of the second century CE) in Bernard Grossfeld, trans., *The Targum Onqelos to Genesis, with a Critical Introduction, Apparatus, and Notes* (ArBib 6; Wilmington, DE: Michael Glazier, 1988), 30-35.

[11]Cited in James L. Kugel, *The Bible as It Was* (Cambridge, MA: Belknap Press, 1997), 433; idem, *Traditions*, 725.

[12]Cited in Israel Drazin, trans., *Targum Onkelos to Exodus: An English Translation of the Text with Analysis and Commentary (Based on the A. Sperber and A. Berliner Editions)* (New York: Ktav, 1990), 313-14n11.

[13]Karla R. Suomala, *Moses and God in Dialogue: Exodus 32-34 in Postbiblical Literature* (SBL 61; New York: Peter Lang, 2004), 58, 63. The English translation of Jerome's Latin, widely known as the Vulgate Bible, is from the Douay-Rheims Bible of 1609-1610.

Each of these examples seeks to clarify the conditions and limitations of divine forgiveness: the third commandment applies "not acquitting" to blasphemy in particular; *Targum Onqelos* and rabbinic interpreters see the distinction between conviction and acquittal as hinging on contrition; *Targum Neofiti* and Rashi interpret the phrase in terms of its application over time, either in the course of human life or at life's ultimate end. But *Targum Neofiti* brings into focus an even more thorny problem: who (if anyone) should bear responsibility for the sins of another, and for how long? Beyond simpler matters of guilt and forgiveness, why should any son or daughter have the consequences of their parents' sin visited upon them?

## The Sins of the Fathers

The book of Lamentations offers a simple explanation for the destruction of God's holy city: "Our fathers sinned and are no more; and we must bear their guilt" (Lam 5:7 NJPS). The notion of parental sin being visited upon children apparently was a common motif in the ancient Near East, as indicated by a similar declaration on the part of the Hittite ruler Mursilis II (ca. 1300 BCE): "The sins of the father come upon the son; and so my father's sins have come upon me."[14] But even if the dynamic of intergenerational culpability might have been more obvious three thousand years ago, it still fails to account for the precise stipulation of "the third and fourth generation." From a sociological point of view, it could be argued that three or four represents the maximum number of generations likely to be living in a given household at any one time.[15] The only problem with this otherwise appealing interpretation is that not a single ancient commentator understands the passage in this way. If anything, the link between generations is interpreted in terms of an in-

[14]Cited in Brevard S. Childs, *Exodus: A Commentary* (OTL; London: SCM, 1974), 619. A similar view is also present in Homer's *Iliad* (20.288-308), which had something approaching "biblical" status in ancient Greece; see also Origen, *Against Celsus* 8.40. For a survey of recent discussion of intergenerational culpability in biblical literature, see Mark J. Boda, "Confession as Theological Expression: Ideological Origins of Penitential Prayer," in *Seeking the Favor of God*, vol. 1, *The Origin of Penitential Prayer in Second Temple Judaism*, ed. Mark J. Boda, Daniel K. Falk, and Rodney A. Werline (SBLEJL 21; Atlanta: Society of Biblical Literature, 2006), 34-39.

[15]So Ronald E. Clements, *Exodus* (CBC; Cambridge: Cambridge University Press, 1972), 124.

herited propensity for wickedness. What we see here has less to do with sociology or household structure than with ancient notions of corporate personality. In the original setting of Moses' day and for generations thereafter, parents and children were not viewed as entirely distinct entities, but rather as sharing an extended or joint identity. Even amidst the radical individualism of contemporary Western cultures, our own folk wisdom acknowledges as much: "Like father, like son," we say, "Like mother, like daughter," or, more obliquely, "The apple never falls far from the tree." The principle of corporate solidarity is all the more familiar (although in broader terms) for Christians, whose doctrine hinges at critical points on both corporate guilt (that of Adam) and corporate merit (that of Christ) (Rom 5:12-21).[16] In each instance the actions of particular individuals are seen to be determinative for those who subsequently share in their identity.

What, then, does it mean to say that God visits "the iniquity of the parents upon the children and the children's children, to the third and fourth generation" (Ex 34:7)? One answer may be found by returning to the Ten Commandments of Exodus 20 and finding there a further expansion of the conditions for and against divine forgiveness. The commandment prohibiting idolatry in Exodus 20 expands on Exodus 34:7 in combination with language from Exodus 34:14 ("you shall worship no other god, because the LORD, whose name is Jealous, is a jealous God"):

> You shall not make for yourself an idol, whether in the form of anything that is in heaven above, or that is on the earth beneath, or that is in the water under the earth. You shall not bow down to them or worship them; for I the LORD your God am a jealous God, punishing children for the iniquity of parents, to the third and the fourth generation *of those who reject me*, but showing steadfast love to the thousandth generation *of those who love me and keep my commandments*. (Ex 20:4-6 // Deut 5:8-10)

On this view, Exodus 20 and Deuteronomy 5 qualify and clarify the meaning of Exodus 34. Because there is no reference here to pun-

[16]Augustine, for example, cites Exodus 20:5 and Ezekiel 18:2 in support of the doctrine of original sin (*Enchir.* 46).

ishment of the actual wrongdoers, the implication seems to be that God forbears punishing sinners in the hope that they will eventually repent. Only when the parents teach their children to act in the same way, and the children comply, does judgment descend (hence "punishing children for the iniquity of parents").

In the context of a culture that viewed the punishment of offspring for the sins of their ancestors as normal, what the biblical legislation emphasizes is not the principle itself, but rather its limitation to a maximum of three or four generations. The legislation, in other words, appears to function in precisely the same manner as the more familiar notion of "an eye for an eye, and a tooth for a tooth" (Ex 21:23-25; Lev 24:19-20; Deut 19:21), not encouraging retribution (already an accepted practice) but instead emphasizing its limitation according to principles of justice. In this instance, the limited extent of intergenerational liability is emphasized yet further by the obvious contrast between the three or four generations to which culpability might extend and the "thousands of generations" over which God's "steadfast love" would reign.

But it is equally possible, perhaps even preferable, to read the two texts in canonical order, taking the language of Exodus 34:7 not as the source for, but instead as a subsequent comment on, the provisions of the second commandment in Exodus 20.[17] Read in this way, the context of Exodus 34 is all-important, for the people of Israel have by this point descended into the very idolatry and apostasy that the commandment expressly forbids. Just when we expect God to reiterate the gravity of their offense and the justice of the penalty they have earned, the opposite sense emerges. In Exodus 20 God's response seems dependent on the conduct of his people, with punishment or unfailing love elicited, respectively, either by rejection or by loving obedience: "punishing . . . the third and fourth generation of those who reject me, but showing steadfast love to the thousandth generation of those who love me and keep my commandments." Yet now these stipulations are strangely absent: precisely because it reiterates God's self-sufficient character—"I will be who I will be"—Exodus 34:7 omits any sense of contingency or

[17]Following R. W. L. Moberly, "How May We Speak of God? A Reconsideration of the Nature of Biblical Theology," *Tyndale Bulletin* 53 (2002): 199.

response. In the face of grave provocation, Yahweh chooses not to restate the terms and conditions that have already failed to deter sin, but rather, by omitting them, to emphasize instead the overwhelming abundance of his love.

Still, the possibility that God's justice could be delayed a generation or more might seem problematic.[18] Accordingly, Deuteronomy 7:9-10 sets out to correct any possible misunderstanding:

> Know therefore that the LORD your God is God, the *faithful* God who maintains *covenant loyalty* [*ḥesed*] with those who love him and keep his commandments, to a thousand generations, and who repays in their own person those who reject him. He does not delay but repays in their own person those who reject him.

Here the writer emphatically denies any possibility of delay: either that punishment might be suspended, even for a generation, or (as the Targumim will later assert) that justice is done only on the day of judgment. But in common with both the second and third commandments (Ex 20:4-7), retention or remission of sins, whether for two, three, or a thousand generations, is once more said to depend on human fidelity to the fidelity of Yahweh: the crucial factor is whether parents and children alike adhere in the long run to God's covenant.

The implications of this debate are significant. Such is our individualism that "teenage rebellion" (a phrase we employ with no hint of irony) is taken to be the norm, as much for religious as for nonreligious families. Children are expected, sometimes even encouraged, to challenge the values of their parents' generation. Conversely, the fifth commandment famously asserts, "Honor your father and mother" (Ex 20:12); lest the point be somehow overlooked, the parallel passage in Deuteronomy 5:16 adds, "as the LORD your God commanded you." Yet

[18]This principle is known as "cross-generational" or "trans-generational" retribution: "Trans-generational retribution is a form of corporate retribution in which the guilt of a sinful generation and its consequent punishment are stored for a generation or more and then released against a later generation. It does not exclude the idea that the recipient may also be somewhat deserving of punishment" (J. S. Kaminsky, *Corporate Responsibility in the Hebrew Bible* [JSOT-Sup 196; Sheffield: Sheffield Academic, 1995], 44). On the avoidance of "double jeopardy" in rabbinic thought (i.e. that two generations should not suffer punishment for the sins of only one), see Sanders, *Paul and Palestinian Judaism*, 192-94.

this all-important precept is nonetheless subject to a prior principle: fidelity to Yahweh takes precedence even over fidelity to parents. Taken together, the commandments imply that one is bound to walk in the ways of the previous generation only to the extent that one's parents themselves have walked in the ways of Yahweh.

### *Manasseh*

Apart from the Pentateuch itself, biblical tradition includes a variety of reflections on intergenerational sin, not all of which are in complete agreement with one another. The story of King Manasseh provides an excellent example of the conservative view.[19] According to 2 Kings 21:1-18, Manasseh was one of the most evil kings ever to reign in Jerusalem. Not only did he repudiate the worship of Yahweh and embrace the Canaanite "host of heaven," he also apparently sacrificed his own son by fire, practiced divination and witchcraft, and "filled Jerusalem from one end to another" with the innocent blood of murdered victims. Yet, strangely, Manasseh managed to remain on the throne a full fifty-five years (longer than King David or his own, more faithful father, Hezekiah), at the end of which he died unopposed and "slept with his ancestors" (2 Kings 21:1, 18). In other words, 2 Kings has him getting off scot-free, without ever being called to account for or bearing the consequences of his sins—a deeply problematic notion for any doctrine of immediate divine retribution.

The writer of 2 Chronicles, in a later and largely parallel account, solves this difficulty rather neatly.[20] In 2 Chronicles 33:12-13 is added the helpful detail that the king of Assyria defeated Manasseh and held him captive in Babylon: "While he was in distress he entreated the favor of the Lord his God and humbled himself greatly before the God of his ancestors. He prayed to him, and God received his entreaty, heard his plea, and restored him again to Jerusalem and to his kingdom. Then Manasseh knew that the Lord indeed was God." Still, one detail remained missing. Although 2 Chronicles 33:18 specifies that "the acts of

---

[19]Compare also the examples of King David (2 Sam 12:11-14) and King Ahab (1 Kings 21:19-29).

[20]See further discussion in J. H. Charlesworth, "Prayer of Manasseh," *OTP* 2:630-31; on the date of Prayer of Manasseh, see ibid., 627. Compare *m. Sanh.* 10:2.

Manasseh, his prayer to his God, and the words of the seers who spoke to him in the name of the LORD God of Israel . . . are in the Annals of the Kings of Israel," the prayer itself was no longer to be found. Accordingly, some time prior to the second destruction of Jerusalem, likely in the first or second century BCE, a pious (and anonymous) writer undertook to supply this lack. The resulting composition, the deuterocanonical Prayer of Manasseh, is a brief but profoundly eloquent and sensitive evocation of the divine mercy that leads to repentance.

Not surprisingly, Manasseh's prayer focuses on the qualities of God's name as cause for hope in the face of judgment, even for those guilty of great wrongdoing:

> The wrath of your threat to sinners is unendurable;
> yet immeasurable and unsearchable is your promised mercy,
> for you are the Lord Most High, of great compassion, long-suffering,
> and very merciful, and *you relent at human suffering.*
> O Lord, according to your great goodness you have promised repentance
> and forgiveness to those who have sinned against you,
> and in the multitude of your mercies you have appointed repentance
> for sinners,
> so that they may be saved. (Pr Man 5-7)

This, at least, is the NRSV translation. But there is more than one way to render the italicized line: the RSV has "[thou] repentest over the evils of men," while James Charlesworth translates more literally, "you feel sorry over the evils of men." Whichever version we choose, it is clear that the poet no longer envisages God relenting or repenting over of the "evils" and calamities that divine judgment will visit upon the wicked. Rather, God is said to regret human evils, in much the same way that the sins of Noah's generation cause God to be remorseful for having created humankind (Gen 6:5-6). In other words, so great is the poet's conviction that the God of Manasseh will forbear condemnation that he literally writes it out of his paraphrase of the divine name. Not only do humans lament their sin, but so too does God!

Returning to Manasseh and his terrifying legacy, the author of 2 Kings is very specific as to when and how divine retribution takes place. While the (presumably prerepentant) king is still on his throne, Yahweh promises by means of unnamed prophets to bring upon "Jerusalem and Judah such evil that the ears of everyone who hears of it will tingle. . . . I will wipe Jerusalem as one wipes a dish, wiping it and turning it upside down" (2 Kings 21:12-13). But disaster ensues neither in the king's lifetime, nor in that of his son Amon, nor in that of his grandson Josiah. Josiah, we recall, is wholly faithful to Yahweh and does all in his power to undo the sins of his forefathers. The biblical account is unstinting in its praise of him: "Before him there was no king like him, who turned to the Lord with all his heart, with all his soul, and with all his might, according to all the law of Moses; nor did any like him arise after him" (2 Kings 23:25). Yet not even this is sufficient to turn aside the promised retribution; on the contrary, it is reiterated (2 Kings 23:26-27).

Josiah is killed by the Pharaoh Neco, but this fate is not said to indicate divine displeasure (2 Kings 23:29). His son, Jehoahaz, ascends the throne, and when the latter proves unacceptable to his Egyptian overlords, he is replaced in turn by his more pliable brother, Jehoiakim (2 Kings 23:31-35). Neither does this turn of events evoke theological commentary. In the course of Jehoiakim's reign the Babylonian Empire takes over as the regional superpower, although the international balance of power is sufficiently tenuous that Jehoiakim is willing to risk rebellion against his new masters. His son and successor, Jehoiachin, pursues a similar policy, the eventual outcome of which is utter defeat and exile for Jerusalem and the people of Judah (2 Kings 24:10-16). The prophet Jeremiah concludes, not unreasonably, that destruction and captivity at the hands of the Babylonians are the (somewhat delayed) consequence of Manasseh's sins (Jer 15:4). Not so the author of 2 Kings. This is because Jehoiachin, during whose reign these events commence, is the great-great-grandson of Manasseh, making him a *fifth*-generation descendant of the author of iniquity. Because that would place retribution beyond the range of its divinely appointed limits, 2 Kings specifies instead that God's judgment upon Manasseh had already taken effect one generation earlier, during the reign of Jehoiakim:

> The LORD sent against him bands of the Chaldeans, bands of the Arameans, bands of the Moabites, and bands of the Ammonites; he sent them against Judah to destroy it, according to the word of the LORD that he spoke by his servants the prophets. Surely this came upon Judah at the command of the LORD, to remove them out of his sight, for the sins of Manasseh, for all that he had committed, and also for the innocent blood that he had shed; for he filled Jerusalem with innocent blood, and the LORD was not willing to pardon. (2 Kings 24:2-4)

Here, then, is a clear example of how Yahweh visits "the iniquity of the parents upon the children and the children's children," even as far as the third or, as in this case, the fourth generation.[21] At least for this writer, Exodus 34:7 need not be taken to mean that every subsequent generation, to a possible maximum of four, must suffer for ancestral sin, but only that divine retribution may be delayed this long and no longer. Indeed, the Talmud explicitly affirms such a view: "With reference to all transgressions in the Torah, if [one] has merit, punishment is suspended for two or three generations" (*b. Šebu.* 39a).

## JOB

What, then, of Job? Although his actions are blameless and his piety is unblemished, an unthinkable catastrophe befalls him: on a single day his camels and his cattle, his servants, his seven sons and his three daughters are carried off by enemies or killed outright. Whereas the reader is granted a behind-the-scenes view of the heavenly court, and of the diabolic chicanery that produces this disaster, Job's three friends offer a simpler explanation. Since God is inalterably just, Job's predicament surely is a straightforward matter of moral cause and effect. God rewards righteousness and punishes iniquity; therefore, one or more of Job and his family must have sinned.

[21]Jeremiah 15:4 and 2 Kings 23:3-4 may reflect different ways of reckoning generations: a great-great-grandson is a fifth-generation descendant, but only four generations removed from his great-great-grandfather. Whether "to the . . . fourth generation" applies to Jehoiakim or Jehoiachin depends on where one starts counting. On the other hand, the final defeat of Jerusalem takes place during the reign of Jehoiachin's successor, Zedekiah (2 Kings 24:18-25:12; cf. Jer 52:1-16), who is Jehoiachin's uncle (2 Kings 24:17) and thus of the previous generation (with Jehoahaz and Jehoiakim)!

The first to speak is Eliphaz the Temanite:

Think now, who that was innocent ever perished?
Or where were the upright cut off?
As I have seen, those who plow *iniquity*
and sow trouble reap the same.
By the breath of God they perish,
and by the blast of his *anger* they are consumed. (Job 4:7-9)

Job, he insists, should submit patiently to the discipline of God. Job's rebuttal, directed less to Eliphaz than at God, employs a comprehensive vocabulary of "wickedness":

"If I *sin*, what do I do to you, you watcher of humanity?
Why have you made me your target?
Why have I become a burden to you?
Why do you not *pardon* my *transgression*
and take away my *iniquity*?" (Job 7:20-21)

Next to weigh in is Bildad the Shuhite: "If your children *sinned* against [God Almighty], he delivered them into the power of their *transgression*" (Job 8:4). All Job need do is repent, says Bildad, and God will restore him. Yet Job steadfastly maintains that he is blameless and innocent (Job 9:15, 20; 10:7). This brings a third friend, Zophar the Naamathite, into the theological fray. He retorts, "God exacts of you less than your *iniquity* deserves" (Job 11:6). Zophar too insists that Job's only recourse is humble repentance, along with submission to God's sovereign will.

Job agrees that God is to blame for the misfortunes that have befallen him, but he bitterly laments the injustice of his situation, since he has no way of knowing what (if anything) he has done to cause offense. Since his life and conduct are irreproachable, says Job, it is obvious that God neither rewards nor punishes human deeds in this present life. So the argument continues, with the three friends insisting in turn that Job has only himself to blame: "Is not your wickedness great?" demands Eliphaz. "There is no end to your *iniquities*" (Job 22:5).

The language of human "iniquity," "transgression," and "sin," and of the divine "anger" to which they give rise, figures prominently throughout the debate.[22] This observation leads to intriguing questions. Might this be a case in which punishment is suspended for two or three generations? Might his descendants have later been made to bear the consequences of some hidden misdeed? Whoever wrote the book of Job clearly has anticipated such concerns. When God finally chooses to speak, he rebukes the theological ignorance that characterizes Job and his friends alike. Who, demands the sovereign God, can argue with divine wisdom, knowledge, and might? So they all repent, and Job prays for his companions. Then "the LORD restored the fortunes of Job when he had prayed for his friends; and the LORD gave Job twice as much as he had before" (Job 42:10). As a result, Job ends up with twice as many sheep, camels, oxen, and donkeys as were his before disaster struck (Job 42:12). Another seven sons and three daughters are born to him (Job 42:13).

But the text adds one final detail before this remarkable tale of righteous suffering comes to an end:

> After this Job lived one hundred and forty years, and saw *his children, and his children's children, four generations*. And Job died, old and full of days. (Job 42:16-17)

Strictly speaking, the reference to "sons, and sons of sons" (the exact meaning of the Hebrew text) indicates only two additional generations, for a total of three if we include Job himself. But the text specifies unmistakably that Job lives to see precisely four generations. Why? Surely it is to prevent pious readers from speculating that whereas Job himself had been spared the punishment due his sins, his descendants might have suffered in his stead. This, then, represents the final refutation of all Job's accusers: not among his "children and his children's children"—three generations—nor even to the fourth generation, the absolute limit of transgenerational retribution, is there any evidence of God requiting "iniquity," "transgression," or "sin." As God is truly just, so Job is truly innocent; by alluding to Exodus 34:7, the conclusion of his story vindicates both.[23]

---

[22]For the vocabulary of "iniquity," "transgression," and "sin," see Job 10:6-7, 14-15; 13:23; 14:16-17; 20:27-28; 22:5; 31:33; 33:9; 34:6, 31-32, 37; 35:3, 6; 36:9-10; concerning God's anger, see Job 9:5, 13; 14:13; 16:9; 19:11; 21:17; 35:15; 36:33; 42:7.

[23]Both at Qumran and in rabbinic exegesis the restoration of Job was interpreted as an expres-

Incidentally, Job's conclusion sheds an interesting light on the opening of Joel. As we saw earlier, the prophet Joel pronounces divine judgment on Judah in the form of drought and locusts, yet midway through his thundering rebuke he calls for national repentance on the basis of God's gracious mercy, forbearance, and steadfast love (Joel 2:13). But from the outset of his work he warns that the consequences of present disaster threaten not only his immediate hearers, but also generations yet to come:

> The word of the LORD that came to Joel son of Pethuel:
> Hear this, O elders, give ear, all inhabitants of the land!
> Has such a thing happened in your days, or in the days of your ancestors?
> Tell your children of it,
> and let your children tell their children,
> and their children another generation. (Joel 1:1-3)

As with the book of Job, Joel's count is intentional and precise, for here he specifies that (should repentance not be forthcoming) the judgment of which he speaks will reverberate to the full extent of its biblically mandated scope, even to the third and the fourth generations yet to come.

### *Jeremiah, Ezekiel, and God's Answer to Moses*

On the other side of the equation, Jeremiah and Ezekiel join the author of Deuteronomy in offering voices of respectful, yet unequivocal dissent.[24] Jeremiah 31, for instance, articulates the prophet's vision of restoration following judgment and of a new relationship between God and his people. The passage in question is structured in three parts, each of which begins, "The days are surely coming, says the LORD, when I will . . ." (so Jer 31:27, 31, 38). The second of these sections is especially prominent in the theology of the early church because it promises a new covenant marked by knowledge of God and forgiveness of sins (Jer 31:31-34, quoted in, e.g., Heb 8:8-12; 10:16-17). The third section looks forward to the rebuilding of Jerusalem (Jer 31:38-40). But

sion of the divine attribute of mercy or compassion (Aramaic *rḥmyn* in 11Q10 38:3), so prominent in Exodus 34:6 and subsequent tradition. See Kenneth Numfor Ngwa, *The Hermeneutics of the "Happy" Ending in Job 42:7-17* (BZAW 354; Berlin: de Gruyter, 2005), 33, 44-47.

[24]For a fuller treatment of this question, see Michael A. Fishbane, *Biblical Interpretation in Ancient Israel* (Oxford: Clarendon Press, 1985), 335-45.

the threefold prophecy as a whole begins with a reiteration of Jeremiah's own prophetic call (first articulated in Jer 1:9-10):

> Just as I have watched over them to pluck up and break down, to overthrow, destroy, and bring evil, so I will watch over them to build and to plant, says the Lord.
> In those days they shall no longer say: "The parents have eaten sour grapes, and the children's teeth are set on edge."
> But all shall die for their own sins; the teeth of everyone who eats sour grapes shall be set on edge. (Jer 31:28-30)

In other words, the first defining feature of Israel's restoration is neither the renewal of the covenant nor the rebuilding of Jerusalem, but rather that each individual will be required to answer for his or her own sins—an explicit refutation of the intergenerational responsibility set out in Exodus 34:7. Ironically, Jeremiah's own prayer in the chapter immediately following—"You show steadfast love to the thousandth generation, but repay the guilt of parents into the laps of their children after them" (Jer 32:18)—acknowledges that these conditions have not yet come into force. First comes punishment, apparently, and only later come restoration and renewal.

Ezekiel, the other prophet who speaks of covenant renewal, expands at length upon the same principle:

> The word of the Lord came to me: "What do you mean by repeating this proverb concerning the land of Israel, 'The parents have eaten sour grapes, and the children's teeth are set on edge'? As I live, says the Lord God, this proverb shall no more be used by you in Israel. Know that all lives are mine; the life of the parent as well as the life of the child is mine: it is only the person who sins that shall die." (Ezek 18:1-4)

The chapter goes on to spell out the various cases to which this new principle applies: those of a righteous father, a wicked son, or the righteous son of a wicked father. Such deliberations lead to the general conclusion that neither the merit of the righteous nor the guilt of the unrighteous may accrue from one generation to the next: "the righteousness of the righteous will be his own, and the wickedness of the wicked shall be his own" (Ezek 18:20). Nor even, insists the prophet, need the individual's own iniquities remain upon his or her own head, precisely because Yahweh delights above all in forgiveness. "Turn, then," he pleads, "and live" (Ezek 18:32).

The difficulty, of course, is that whereas a guilty parent might interpret delay of punishment as an expression of God's mercy, their children or grandchildren would be likely to take the opposite view.[25] Accordingly, the authors of Deuteronomy, Jeremiah, and Ezekiel each apply a principle already normative in matters of civil or criminal liability to matters of covenant faithfulness and the divine-human relationship. This principle is succinctly expressed in Deuteronomy 24:16: "Parents [lit., 'fathers'] shall not be put to death for their children, nor shall children be put to death for their parents [fathers]; only for their own crimes may persons be put to death." The biblical record includes several instances of corporate punishment in cases of grave sacrilege or blasphemy (Num 16:1-50; Josh 7:10-26; 1 Sam 2:27-34; Is 65:6-7). But apart from direct offenses against God, not even regicide is deemed sufficiently grievous as to warrant the punishment of a subsequent generation (so 2 Kings 14:5-6, directly citing Deut 24:16). On the other hand, the principle was not always observed. Psalm 109 represents David calling down a divine curse upon an unidentified enemy, his wife, children, and parents—three generations in all (Ps 109:6-14).[26] And the idea evidently remained popular in the time of Jesus, as is clear from the question the disciples pose to their teacher upon seeing a man blind from birth: "Rabbi, who sinned, this man or his parents, that he was born blind?" (Jn 9:2).

Likewise in the pages of the Talmud, pious interpreters continued to wrestle with the notion of inherited culpability, and with the apparently contradictory directives of the sacred text. Yet their solution to this problem was singularly elegant. For example, tractate *Sanhedrin* of the Babylonian Talmud, in a discussion of who may testify or give evidence before a court, first discusses Deuteronomy 24:16 ("Fathers shall not be put to death for their children," etc.), then says,

---

[25]Ibid., 342-43.

[26]Further examples are included in the excellent discussion by André Chouraqui, *L'univers de la Bible*, vol. 1, *Genèse, Exode* (Paris: Éditions Lidis, 1982), 447, to which much of the present treatment is indebted.

> Are not children then to be put to death for the sins committed by their parents? Is it not written, *Visiting the iniquities of the fathers upon the children*?—There the reference is to children who hold in their [own] hands the deeds of their parents (*b. Sanh.* 27b).[27]

That is, only if the children willfully continue in wickedness learned from their parents will the younger generation be held accountable for the sins of their elders. They are held accountable, in other words, only for "parental" sins that they themselves have committed.

Discussion of the three favors for which Moses is said to have asked God, recounted in the name of Rabbi Yose of Sepphoris, represents a more complex response. According to this account, Moses asked, first, that the divine presence rest upon Israel; second, that it not rest upon "the idolaters" (presumably meaning everyone else); and, third, that he be shown God's "ways" (Ex 33:13). According to Rabbi Yose, all three requests were granted, the final one in the following manner:

> Moses said before Him: "Lord of the Universe, why is it that some righteous men prosper and others are in adversity, [while] some wicked men prosper and others are in adversity?" He replied to him, "Moses, the righteous man who prospers is [a] righteous man, the son of a righteous man; the righteous man who is in adversity is a righteous man [but] the son of a wicked man. The wicked man who prospers is a wicked man [but the] son of a righteous man; the wicked man who is in adversity is a wicked man, son of a wicked man." (*b. Ber.* 7a)

On this view, neither the wicked nor the righteous reap the rewards of their actions; all consequences, be they for good or ill, accrue only to the following generation. "But this is not so!" retorts an anonymous commentator, "For, lo, one verse says: *Visiting the iniquity of the fathers upon the children*, and another verse says: *Neither shall the children be put to death for the fathers*." As we might expect, the apparent contradiction is again resolved by reference to the actual deeds of the younger generation. But it also leads to the requirement that God's words be emended as follows:

[27]Following the literal sense provided by the footnote in the Soncino edition: the text reads, "children who follow their parents' footsteps." Compare *Pesiqta de Rab Kahana* 167ab.

> [You must] therefore [say that] the Lord said thus to Moses: "A righteous man who prospers is a perfectly righteous man; the righteous man who is in adversity is not a perfectly righteous man. The wicked man who prospers is not a perfectly wicked man; the wicked man who is in adversity is a perfectly wicked man."

But whether the notion of moral character being revealed by the circumstances of one's life succeeds in resolving the matter is highly debatable, for it eliminates any possibility of truly unmerited suffering and would declare Job guilty simply on the evidence of his suffering—precisely the position for which his uncomprehending friends are ultimately rebuked.

With profound wisdom, therefore, the Talmud gives the last word to a second-century contemporary of Yose, Rabbi Meir of Tiberias, according to whom God granted only the first two of Moses' requests and declined the third:

> For it is said: *And I will be gracious to whom I will be gracious*, although he may not deserve it, *And I will show mercy on whom I will show mercy*, although he may not deserve it.[28]

This response implies at least three things. First, Rabbi Meir takes God's answer to Moses in Exodus 33:19 to mean that in any given case God acts independently of what an individual may or may not deserve. In other words (to use the example of Jn 9), a man's blindness betrays neither his own nor his parents' sin. Second, insofar as Rabbi Meir takes these words to be a *non*-answer, then the ways of God are ultimately inscrutable, beyond the comprehension of mere mortals. Yet, third, the one overriding assurance that remains is that although neither mercy nor divine graciousness may be deserved, God at least reveals this much, and this much his servants understand. Even according to the minimalist view of Rabbi Meir, the intricacies and apparent inconsistencies of divine justice in particular situations can only be resolved by appeal to the divine character as a whole. In terms of the revelation to Moses in

---

[28]Compare the stricter view of *Targum Neofiti* and *Targum Pseudo-Jonathan* to Exodus 33:19: "I will pity the one who *is worthy of* pity, and I will have mercy on the one who *is worthy of* mercy." As Karla Suomala comments, "God in both Tg. Neof. and Ps.-J. is not . . . ready to disperse grace as freely as the God of the Hebrew Bible" (*Moses and God in Dialogue*, 176).

Exodus 34:6-7, the end of the passage ("visiting the iniquity of the parents upon the children and the children's children") makes sense only in light of its beginning ("a God gracious and merciful").

## Bearing and Forbearing

Still, the problem with forgiveness is that it frequently creates the appearance of injustice. Much as the guilty are likely to favor leniency, their victims may be understandably less enthusiastic. Even "victimless" crimes represent an offense against divine justice. The language of Exodus 34:7—"*forgiving* [*nāśā*ʾ] iniquity and transgression and sin"—acknowledges this sobering reality, for in Hebrew the verb *nāśā*ʾ ("to forgive") has an original sense of "to carry" or "to bear." If this connotation is retained in subsequent usage, the nuance of the Hebrew idiom seems to be that in order to forgive, God must "bear" the sin of his people and the cost of wrongdoing. In the view of one Jewish interpreter, "The correct sense is that God forbears to act (carries the debit item on the books, refrains from foreclosure)."[29] Of course, God cannot exactly be "repaid," for there is no currency with which to satisfy the debt. To ask God for forgiveness, then, as does Moses by using this language after the episode of the golden calf (Ex 32:31-32), expects God not only to forgo retribution, but also to absorb a cost or consequences that should rightly fall on the shoulders of the guilty. This reality is neatly summed up in the words of Micah, more a statement of awe and worship than a true question: "Who is a God like you, *bearing* [*nāśā*ʾ] iniquity and passing over the transgression of the remnant of your possession?" (Mic 7:18).

Christians should be familiar with this notion, for at the heart of their faith lies the conviction that the one who is Messiah and Son of God "bore our sins in his body on the cross, so that, free from sins, we might live for righteousness" (1 Pet 2:24 [similarly Heb 7:27; 9:28]). But pious Jews were no less aware that it is God who pays the price for sin. In almost identical terms, *Targum Neofiti* (quoted earlier) and *Targum*

[29]Herbert Chanan Brichto, *Toward a Grammar of Biblical Poetics: Tales of the Prophets* (New York: Oxford University Press, 1992), 84n26.

*Pseudo-Jonathan* (cited here) expound this passage from Exodus as "remitting and forgiving sins, passing over the rebellious, and *making atonement* for sins, pardoning those who return to the Law." Already in the Second Temple period (and apart from the theology of the early church), the idea that God, rather than wrongdoers, should make atonement for sins is current at Qumran, where the same reading of Exodus 34:7 occurs in the hymns of the community:

[You have purified] your servant from all his sins
[by the abundance of your great co]mpassion [*raḥămîm*]
[as y]ou said through the hand of Moses,
[forgiving rebellion], iniquity, sin,
*atoning* for [failings] and disloyalty. . . .
For you have supported me by your kindnesses [*ḥesed*]
and by your abundant compassion [*raḥămîm*]
Because you *atone for sin*
and cle[anse man] of his fault through your justice.
(1QH[a] 4:11-12; 12:37)[30]

In a similar vein, the hymnist goes on to exult:

I will chant your kindness,
I will ponder your might the whole day,
I will bless your name continually,
I will declare your glory among the sons of man,
and in your abundant goodness my soul will delight. . . .
For your glory, *you have purified man from sin*,
so that he can make himself holy for you. (1QH[a] 19:5-7, 10-11)[31]

Our recognition of this principle among all the heirs of Abraham provides a final insight into the place of forgiveness within the multifaceted formulation of divine characteristics from Exodus 34. For the propensity to forgive is not simply another in a long list of God's "character traits"; rather, forgiveness is itself an integral expression of divine

[30]Translation from Florentino García Martínez, trans., *The Dead Sea Scrolls Translated: The Qumran Texts in English* (Leiden: Brill, 1994), 317, 336 (italics added). The first of these two passages is also quoted (in a different translation, and cited as 1QH[a] 17:12-13) in Kugel, *Bible*, 430; *Traditions*, 723.

[31]Translation from García Martínez, *Dead Sea Scrolls*, 353 (italics added).

"compassion," "mercy," and "steadfast love" by virtue of the fact that it too is something that only God can accomplish, and is a burden that, ultimately, only God can bear. The choice of this particular verb (*nāśāʾ*) acknowledges the immense cost of injustice and wrongdoing, not only to the wrongdoers themselves and those who suffer from their misdeeds, but even to God.

This, then, is the final conundrum to be faced. If it is true (at least according to Exodus 34) that God forgives all degrees and categories of sin, balances a preference for acquittal against the demands of justice, and considers the sins of one generation in light of previous generations, how is the cost that God bears to be weighed against the price that its human victims must bear? The example of Jonah and the Ninevites, together with Jesus' parable of the ungracious debtor, provide important test cases in the application of divine forgiveness.

### *Jonah, Nahum, and Joel*

The story of Jonah resembles that of Rahab in a number of important respects. Unlike other prophetic books, the book of Jonah weaves a narrative rather than pronouncing judgment or announcing restoration. Jonah presents a "Tale of Two Cities"—Tarshish and Nineveh. Although Nineveh is well known, the identity of Tarshish is no longer certain; it may represent Tartessos, a Phoenician colony on the Atlantic coast of southwestern Spain, or perhaps a location on the island of Sardinia. Frequently associated with shipping and commerce (e.g., 1 Kings 10:22; 22:48; Ps 48:7; Is 2:16; Ezek 27:25), Tarshish represents the "ends of the earth," the very farthest point to which one might travel if one were setting out from Israel at the opposite end of the Mediterranean. "Because of ambiguity regarding the identification of Tarshish, we are not able to say with confidence where Jonah was heading when he set sail from Joppa. All we can be sure of is that he was going west, and that he thought he would be leaving his God behind."[32] That is precisely what Jonah, son of Amittai, intends to do, when "the word of the LORD" comes to him with a command to preach against the wickedness of Nineveh (Jon 1:1-3). He and his readers know that great city only too

[32]David W. Baker, "Tarshish [Place]," *ABD* 6:333.

well: Nineveh is the capital of the mighty Assyrian Empire, which crushed Samaria and the northern kingdom of Judah in 722-721 BCE, leading its inhabitants into exile (2 Kings 17:1-6, 22-23).

To gain a sense of how God's people viewed Nineveh, we need only turn to the prophet Nahum, whose words, inveighing bitterly against cruelty and treachery of the Assyrians, proclaim the ultimate triumph of divine justice over this hated city: "Ah! City of bloodshed, utterly deceitful, full of booty—no end to the plunder! . . . Because of the countless debaucheries of the prostitute, gracefully alluring, mistress of sorcery, who enslaves nations through her debaucheries, and peoples through her sorcery, I am against you, says the LORD of hosts, and will lift up your skirts over your face; and I will let nations look on your nakedness and kingdoms on your shame. I will throw filth at you and treat you with contempt, and make you a spectacle. Then all who see you will shrink from you and say, 'Nineveh is devastated; who will bemoan her?'" (Nah 3:1, 4-7). Nahum's invective is enough to make readers blush, even today! And what faithful prophet would not leap at the chance to add to it? The opportunity of announcing divine judgment against Nineveh, of all places, seems too good to be true, making Jonah's flight in the opposite direction almost incomprehensible.

The opening verses of the book thus establish a dramatic tension that will not be resolved until its final chapter. In the meantime, however, we learn of Jonah's adventures on the high seas. The sailors who take him on board turn out to be more pious than their passenger by far. When a mighty storm blows up around the ship, we are told, each of them "cried to his god" (Jon 1:5). Jonah, by contrast, has chosen this moment for a nap, and he must be roused and browbeaten into following the sailors' lead. When these efforts fail (although we are never actually told that Jonah did as he was bidden), the sailors cast lots of their own, only to discover that Jonah himself is the cause of their current peril. Intense questioning elicits from him a reluctant confession: "I am a Hebrew. I worship [or, 'fear'] the LORD, the God of heaven, who made the sea and the dry land" (Jon 1:9). This creates even greater "fear" among the sailors (Jon 1:10); indeed, it is the pagans who turn out to be God-fearing in every sense. They refuse Jonah's initial suggestion of sacrificing a human being—himself!—to appease the angry god (Jon 1:11-13); when faced with no other option, they pray eloquently to Jonah's God for forgiveness (Jon 1:14); and when the awful deed is finally accomplished, they offer other, presumably less lethal, sacrifices, apparently binding themselves to Israel's God with vows of personal consecration (Jon 1:16).

Rescued and returned to land by a novel means of conveyance, Jonah prudently reconsiders his earlier position; then, having been given a second chance, he proceeds with his original task. "Yet forty days," he cries out, "and Nineveh shall be overthrown!" (Jon 3:4). The irony of the story is that, exactly like the sailors before them, and in a manner reminiscent of the Canaanite Rahab, the Ninevites likewise emerge as scrupulously pious and God-fearing. They immediately believe God, repent, and proclaim a fast that prohibits both food and water, and applies not only to human inhabitants of the city, but also to their livestock.

The unique name "YHWH" occurs twenty-six times in this book, twenty of these prior to the moment when Jonah finally sets foot within Nineveh. Yet what we are told of Jonah's preaching to the Ninevites does not mention the divine name, nor does it occur in any of the narrative having to do with the city's inhabitants. Instead, the narrative employs only the more generic term for God, "Elohim":

> And the people of Nineveh believed *God*; they proclaimed a fast, and everyone, great and small, put on sackcloth. . . .
> "By the decree of the king and his nobles. . . . Human beings and animals . . . shall cry mightily to *God*. . . . Who knows? *God* may relent and change his mind; he may turn from his fierce anger, so that we do not perish."
> When *God* saw what they did, how they turned from their evil ways, *God* changed his mind about the calamity that he had said he would bring upon them; and he did not do it. (Jon 3:5, 7-10)

Whereas the pious sailors both learned of and called upon the name of Yahweh, the Ninevites have no such knowledge. All they know is that Jonah's God shows fierce, or burning, "anger" (*ʾap*). Yet that alone is sufficient to inspire thoroughgoing repentance on their part.

All of this serves to focus attention on Jonah's astonishing response, which takes up the name of Yahweh once more and explains the stubborn reluctance that has caused this unwilling prophet so much turmoil:

> He prayed to the LORD and said, "O LORD! Is not this what I said while I was still in my own country? That is why I fled to Tarshish at the beginning; for I knew that you are a gracious God and merciful, slow to anger, and abounding in steadfast love, and *ready to relent from punishing*. And now, O LORD, please take my life from me, for it is better for me to die than to live." (Jon 4:2-3)

So deep are his anger and his desire for vengeance that he cannot even bear to mention "forgiveness." Instead, he manages to paraphrase the remainder of Exodus 34:7 in such a way as to refer to punishment rather than grace. Once more, comparison with the oracles of Nahum proves instructive, for the work of that prophet opens with another meditation on Exodus 34:

> An oracle concerning Nineveh. The book of the vision of Nahum of Elkosh.
> A jealous and avenging God is the LORD, the LORD is avenging and wrathful;
> the LORD takes vengeance on his adversaries and rages against his enemies.
> The LORD is *slow to anger* but great in power, and the LORD will *by no means clear the guilty*. His way is in whirlwind and storm, and the clouds are the dust of his feet. (Nah 1:1-3)

Jonah, it seems, is a prophet after Nahum's own heart, for neither of them is keen on extending forgiveness to their enemies. It is no accident that Jonah omits mention of "Yahweh" in his dealings with the Ninevites. He knows of God's mercy, but he is unwilling to be bound by it. The pagans and the prophet are of one mind that this God is "ready to relent from punishing" (Jon 4:2), but whereas the Ninevites seek forgiveness, Jonah does not wish to allow it.

Joel, on the other hand, acknowledges that God's chosen people also have much to repent of. He makes this point by applying the language of Jonah to the sins of Judah:[33]

---

[33]T. B. Dozeman argues that the paraphrases of Exodus 34:6-7 in Joel 2:1-17 and Jonah 3:1-4:11

Yet even now, says the Lord, return to me with all your heart, with fasting, with weeping, and with mourning; rend your hearts and not your clothing.
Return to the Lord, your God, for he is gracious and merciful, slow to anger, and abounding in steadfast love, and relents from punishing.
Who knows whether he will not turn and relent, and leave a blessing behind him. (Joel 2:12-14)

Even if God's ultimate intention is to restore Zion and satisfy his people with good things, they themselves are as much in need of forgiveness as the nations that have wronged them. Placed side by side, the messages of Joel and Jonah are like two sides of the same coin: however much they have suffered, God's people must allow others the same forgiveness that they expect for themselves; the sins of other nations, however great, do not make their own sins any less grave.

In much the same way, Jesus of Nazareth teaches his disciples to pray, "Forgive us our sins, as we also forgive those who sin against us," and then goes on to explain, "For . . . if you do not forgive others, neither will your Father forgive you your sins" (Mt 6:12, 14-15). Or in the words of Raba (d. 352 CE), "He who forgoes his right [to exact punishment] is forgiven all his iniquities, as it says, *Forgiving iniquity and passing by transgression.* Who is forgiven iniquity? One who passes by transgression [against himself]" (*b. Roš. Haš.* 17a). No less relevant is the saying attributed to Muhammad by another of his companions: "Allah will not be merciful to those who are not merciful to mankind."[34] The principle is well illustrated by a story said to have made Muhammad both laugh and weep as he related it. Two men knelt before God, one of whom had wronged the other. Whereas the victim demanded restitution, the wrongdoer lamented that he had nothing with which to repay and thus make good his debt.

are interrelated, each capable of being read in light of the other, each exploring the motif of covenant renewal from Exodus 32–34 as it applies to Israel and the nations alike ("Inner-Biblical Interpretation of Yahweh's Gracious and Compassionate Character," *JBL* 108 [1989]: 207-23). See also Fishbane, *Biblical Interpretation*, 345-47.

[34]Related by Jārir bin ʿAbdullāh, quoted from Muhammad Muhsin Khan, trans., *Ṣaḥīḥ al-Bukhārī: The Translation of the Meanings of Sahih al-Bukhari* (rev. ed.; 9 vols.; Chicago: Kazi, 1979]), vol. 9, book 93, no. 473 (p. 350). Compare no. 474 (p. 352): "Allah bestows His mercy only on those of His slaves who are merciful (to others)."

> So God—great and glorious—said to the one who had been wronged: "Lift your eyes and look into paradise." And he said: "O Lord, I see cities of silver and palaces of gold decorated with pearls. For which prophet, righteous one, or martyr is this?" The Lord . . . said: "This belongs to whomever pays the price." And he said "O Lord, who can come up with such a sum?" But He said: "It is in your power." "But how, O Lord?" And He answered: "By forgiving your brother." And he said: "O Lord, I have already forgiven him." So God—great and glorious—said: "Take your brother by the hand and lead him into paradise."[35]

Even so, the message of Jonah and Jesus, of Raba and Muhammad, is not simply that God's people should forgive their enemies and oppressors, much as that is true. In any number of circumstances, not least those of Nahum and Jonah, forgiveness may seem humanly impossible, for any number of legitimate reasons. The message of Jonah, rather, is that those who know and name the God of Israel are bound by the full reality that the name implies, however challenging or difficult it may prove. The greater faithfulness of the sailors and Ninevites consists in their willingness to act on what they know, whereas Jonah will not, even to the very last verse of the book. Storms and sea creatures can (eventually) transport his body, but to the end his heart appears unmoved. The same turns out to be true for the central character in Jesus' parable of the ungracious debtor, to which we now turn.

### *The Ungracious Debtor*

Rather than citing the example of Jonah, Jesus' famous parable on the subject of forgiveness alludes to a far more sinister figure from the book of Esther. Recorded in Matthew 18:23-35, the parable hinges on the contrast between the enormous debt forgiven a certain royal servant, and the comparatively trivial debt that he himself refuses to forgive. When the king calls in his accounts, the man in question is found to owe the unthinkable sum of ten thousand talents. Because he is unable to come up with the cash, the king orders that his courtier be sold into

[35]David B. Burrell and Nazih Daher, trans., *The Ninety-Nine Beautiful Names of God: al-Maqṣad al-asnā fī s̲harḥ asmāʾ Allāh al-ḥusnā* (Cambridge: Islamic Texts Society, 1995), 141 (and p. 192n94, noting that al-Ghazālī is here citing al-Ḥākim al-Naysābūrī [ca. 933-1014 CE])

slavery together with his wife and children, and all of their property is to be liquidated to satisfy the debt. Aghast, the man falls to his knees, pleading with the ruler, "Have patience [*makrothymeō*] with me, and I will pay you everything!" (Mt 18:26). Not content with mere patience, however, the ruler is moved to compassion (or, in most translations, "pity" [*splanchnizomai*]), and forgives the entire amount (Mt 18:27). But on his way out of the royal chambers, the same man encounters a fellow servant who owes him a mere hundred denarii. Likewise unable to pay, the fellow servant pleads for patience with almost the exact words that the first servant has just employed before the king. But to no avail. The newly liberated debtor refuses to treat his fellow servant as he himself has been treated, and he has the man jailed. Outraged, other members of the court complain to the king, who promptly reinstates the original debt and flings the ungracious servant into prison until the full amount should be repaid. As with several other key terms, the language of the king's rebuke is both familiar and significant: "Should you not have had mercy [*eleeō*] on your fellow slave, as I had mercy [*eleeō*] on you?" (Mt 18:33).

How much money is at stake? For Jesus and his contemporaries, a denarius was the standard day's wage for a laborer; based on a six-day work week, a debt of one hundred denarii would represent almost seventeen weeks' worth, or about four months' wages. This would have been a sizable sum, given that few people had any savings or liquid assets. Even so, it pales beside the figure of ten thousand talents. Although the value of a talent has been variously estimated, ten thousand talents would have represented between sixty million and one hundred million denarii, which (again allowing for a six-day work week and various annual festivals) works out to somewhere between 200,000 and 325,000 years of day labor![36] According to Josephus, the annual taxes of Perea and Galilee around the time of Jesus' birth amounted to a mere two hundred talents (*Ant.* 17.318); those of Judea, Samaria, and Idumea combined were six hundred

[36]On these sums, see Craig S. Keener, *A Commentary on the Gospel of Matthew* (Grand Rapids: Eerdmans, 1999), 458-59; cf. Joachim Jeremias, *The Parables of Jesus* (NTL; London: SCM, 1972), 210-11n6.

talents (*Ant.* 17.320). Jerome relates that the revenue of all Egypt in the time of Ptolemy Philadelphus (282-246 BCE) was 14,800 talents; Cicero (106-43 BCE) estimates it in the time of Ptolemy Auletes (ca. 80-51 BCE) at 12,500 talents.[37] The servant's debt, in other words, is many times the annual economy of Jesus' homeland, but it approaches that of populous and wealthy Egypt, the breadbasket of the Mediterranean world.

In Jesus' day, the only "servant" who could possibly have incurred such astronomical indebtedness would have been the king's chief financial officer, charged with collecting tax revenues throughout the realm. A peasant audience surely would have rejoiced at the thought of such a hated figure ensnaring himself in crushing obligation. By the same token, the king's easy remission of the debt would have seemed shocking, considering that the man's task was to extort this sum from the poor of the land through a series of equally rapacious middlemen, each of whom would have lined his own pockets in the process. But in the end, the CFO is not forgiven after all: because his avaricious nature is unaffected by generosity, the king ultimately decides to hold him to the same unyielding standard that he has used against his fellow retainer, and for a considerably smaller debt.

In addition to these contemporary resonances, however, the parable recalls another high official who once owed exactly ten thousand talents to a king: Haman, one of the most universally despised and hated figures in all of Jewish folklore. To this day, Jewish children celebrate the downfall of the wicked Haman during the annual festival of Purim. Set in Persia during the reign of Xerxes the Great (485-465 BCE), the book of Esther relates the fortunes of Mordecai, an exiled Jew, and his beautiful adopted niece, Esther, whom King Xerxes takes as his wife.[38] When Mordecai makes the mistake of failing to demonstrate an appropriate obeisance before Haman, the king's highest official, Haman plots revenge against the entire Jewish community:

---

[37]W. D. Davies and Dale C. Allison Jr., *The Gospel According to Saint Matthew* (3 vols.; ICC; Edinburgh: T & T Clark, 1988-1997), 2:798n48.

[38]For a discussion of the date (between 400 and 114 BCE) and canonicity of the book of Esther, see Carey A. Moore, *Esther: A New Translation with Introduction and Commentary* (AB 7B; Garden City, NY: Doubleday, 1971), xxi-xxxi, lvii-lx.

> Then Haman said to King Xerxes, "There is a certain people scattered, yet unassimilated, among the peoples throughout the provinces of your kingdom whose statutes are different from every other people's. They do not observe even the king's statutes! Therefore, it is not appropriate for the king to tolerate them. If it please the king, let it be recorded that they are to be destroyed; and I shall pay *ten thousand silver talents* to the proper officials to deposit in the king's treasury." So the king took his signet ring from off his hand and gave it to Haman, son of Hammedatha, the Agagite, the enemy of the Jews. "Well, it's your money," said the king to Haman, "do what you like with the people." (Esther 3:8-10)[39]

Fortunately for the future of Judaism, Haman's stratagem backfires. Although there are many additional twists and turns to the story, Haman, after begging unsuccessfully to be spared, is hanged on the same gallows that he erected for Mordecai, and the Jews successfully defend themselves against those who would have done them harm.

If Haman is the very embodiment of human evil, the reputation of tax collectors in Jesus' day was little better: the fact that this one in Jesus' parable owes his king ten thousand talents suggests a particular resemblance to the hated enemy of Mordecai, Esther, and the Jewish people. Thus it comes as no surprise that his vicious inclinations prevail, and that ultimately he is made to suffer the very fate that he, in turn, had intended for his fellow courtier. He deserves as much. Yet Jesus' conclusion to the parable is nothing short of astonishing: "So my heavenly Father will also do to every one of you, if you do not forgive your brother or sister from your heart" (Mt 18:35). The lesson is straightforward, if uncompromising: just as the King of heaven is forbearing, compassionate, and merciful in forgiving his servants, so must those servants be willing to forgive lesser wrongs suffered at one another's hands. Not to do so is conduct worthy of Haman, the archetypal enemy of God's people. The real sin here is not simply lack of forgiveness, but refusal to imitate God. Yet the implication of the parable, troubling though it may be, is that a truly evil character is incapable of change, no matter how much mercy he may be shown, no matter how much he is forgiven. For that reason, the example of the ungracious

---

[39]Translation from ibid., 34 (italics added).

debtor surely is one that any pious listener would be keen to avoid imitating. The price of forgiveness is loss, both moral and material. Yet it is a loss that God's servants share in common with their King.

Jonah and Jesus implicitly acknowledge the difficulty of forgiveness, both for those who have suffered injustice and for those who have caused it. For this reason, the ultimate resolution of sin, wrongdoing, and our common guilt is found not in the realm of human relations alone, but rather by entering together into the presence of Israel's God. For according to Exodus 34:7, it is ultimately God who bears sins, and whose compassion, mercy, and enduring faithfulness are sufficient to restore what has been broken. In the last analysis, therefore, because God is the first to forgive, it is God who makes possible even the most humanly impossible forgiveness.

*O Merciful and Compassionate One, forgive us our iniquities*
*and offences and transgressions and trespasses.*
*Reckon not every sin of your servants and handmaidens,*
*but cleanse us with the cleansing of your truth,*
*and direct our steps that we may walk in holiness of heart*
*and do what is good and well-pleasing in your sight.*

*1 Clement* 60:1-2 (ca. 96 CE)[40]

[40]Cited in part in Kugel, *Bible*, 434; *Traditions*, 727; this translation follows J. Manning Potts, ed., *Prayers of the Early Church* (Nashville: Upper Room, 1953), 18 (revised).

# 7

# Conclusions

## God in Our Midst

*For now we see in a mirror, dimly, but then we will see face to face.*
*Now I know only in part; then I will know fully,*
*even as I have been fully known.*

1 Corinthians 13:12

### Joseph

#### *A Man After God's Own Heart*

In the entire corpus of Jewish and Christian Scripture no single story illustrates the character of God and its consequences for human conduct better than that of Joseph, the pampered son betrayed by jealous brothers.[1] Indeed, the authors or editors of the Joseph cycle construct the account of his life with an eye to the vocabulary of the divine character. To see how this is so requires a brief detour through several other passages that draw attention to the inner logic of the narrative of Genesis as a whole. After recounting the universal origins of humankind, Genesis relates the adventures of several generations of the family of Abraham and Sarah, newcomers from the region of the Fertile Crescent, as they take up residence in the land that they believe God has given them as an inheritance. The various episodes that make up this larger story depict more than the simple expansion of a particular

[1]The Joseph cycle has inspired a rich history of interpretation and expansion. See, for example, Alan Jacobs, "Joseph the Patriarch," in *A Dictionary of Biblical Tradition in English Literature*, ed. David Lyle Jeffrey (Grand Rapids: Eerdmans, 1992), 414-16; James L. Kugel, *In Potiphar's House: The Interpretive Life of Biblical Texts* (2nd ed.; Cambridge, MA: Harvard University Press, 1994); Maren Niehoff, *The Figure of Joseph in Post-Biblical Jewish Literature* (AGJU 16; Leiden: Brill, 1992).

Near Eastern clan. Their deeper theological purpose is to describe a series of obstacles and reversals that challenge the fulfillment of God's promises to Abraham. If Abraham and Sarah are well past the age of childbearing, how can God make of them a "great nation" (Gen 12:2)? Where are they to find an appropriate wife for their son, Isaac? Which of Isaac's sons will inherit the ancestral blessings? How is the family line to be carried on when the wife of Jacob, Isaac's youngest, is unable to conceive? These and a host of other impediments, resulting variously from periodic famine, tribal politics, or internecine strife, threaten to derail the divine plan. At key moments in the patriarchal history familiar vocabulary appears.

When Abraham sets out from his family home in response to God's call, he brings with him a nephew, Lot, whose actions are of critical importance for the destiny of the larger clan. Lot has the misfortune to settle in Sodom, but he has the good sense to act hospitably toward two heavenly messengers who are on their way to destroy the city. They return the favor by warning Lot of impending doom, and they urge him to flee into the hills. Although he quibbles about exactly how lengthy a flight is required to put him beyond danger, Lot clearly is grateful: "Your servant has found favor [*ḥēn*] with you," he declares, "and you have shown me great kindness [*ḥesed*] in saving my life" (Gen 19:19). The point of such language is that it reflects the characteristic mercy of Yahweh, whom the angels explicitly represent, even in the face of judgment.

We have already examined (in chapter 5) the account of how Abraham's servant finds a wife for Isaac by relying on the "steadfast love" (*ḥesed*) and "faithfulness (*ʾemet*) of his master's God (Gen 24:27). Success in finding a wife to carry on Abraham's family line is essential if God's promises are to prove true. Such language makes it clear that this is not merely a matter of human ingenuity or perseverance; rather, Yahweh must act to maintain the covenant that he has made. Only then do the human actors know to respond in kind. Eventually, Isaac and Rebekah (the young woman at the well) have two sons, Jacob and Esau, who over time become estranged, largely because Jacob is a swindler and a thief. Esau plots revenge; Jacob must flee for his life. Fortunately for the future of the nation, advancing years bring Jacob a measure of wisdom and penitence, motivated in no small part by news of his brother's imminent and unexpected arrival. Fear inspires newfound piety, as Jacob prays to the God of Abraham and Isaac,

> O Lord . . . , I am not worthy of the least of all the [acts of] *steadfast love* [pl., *ḥăsādîm*] and all the *faithfulness* [*ʾemet*] that you have shown to your servant. . . . Deliver me, please, from the hand of my brother, from the hand of Esau, for I am afraid of him. (Gen 32:9-11)

Then, for good measure, Jacob reminds God of the covenant promises made to Abraham and subsequently reiterated both to Isaac and to himself. As in previous instances, his prayers are answered, but the narrative has again underscored the need for divine intervention in keeping with the character of Israel's God.

The language of the brothers' actual meeting drives home the point even further. Esau is puzzled that Jacob (still afraid for his own skin) has sent family members and gifts first, with Jacob himself timidly bringing up the rear:

> Esau said, "What do you mean by all this company that I met?" Jacob answered, "To find favor [*ḥēn*] with my lord." But Esau said, "I have enough, my brother; keep what you have for yourself." Jacob said, "No, please; if I find favor [*ḥēn*] with you, then accept my present from my hand; for truly to see your face is like seeing the face of God—since you have received me with such favor. Please accept my gift that is brought to you, because God has dealt graciously [*ḥānan*] with me, and because I have everything I want." So he urged him, and he took it. (Gen 33:8-11 [cf. Gen 33:5, 15])

God (here the narrative uses "Elohim") has dealt "graciously" with Jacob, who, in a gesture of extravagant flattery, proposes that seeing Esau is like seeing God's own face. At least, Jacob hopes that Esau will be like God. As we will see shortly, the narrator may have a specific reason for avoiding the name of Yahweh for the time being. Still, readers know that Jacob has already called upon the specific name of his grandfather's God, the one who is described not only in terms of steadfast love (*ḥesed*) and faithfulness (*ʾemet*) but as being gracious (*ḥannûn*) as well.

Viewed simplistically, there is no way for Abraham, Isaac, or Jacob to have known these divine qualities, for they will only be revealed to Moses hundreds of years later as an exposition of the name "YHWH." But patriarchal narratives may have more in common with modern narrative than they do with modern historiography. They are tales artfully told, in which the reiteration of key terms from Exodus 34:6-7 indicates an underlying theological orientation. The stories of the patriarchs—Abraham, Isaac, and Jacob alike—are not recounted simply out of historical interest, relating the family origins of later Judaism. Rather, they are told with an eye to the identity, character, and characteristics of the God who keeps covenant with every generation of Abraham's descendants. This foundational theological concern is even more important for the rags-to-riches story of Joseph, the luckless Hebrew slave who rises to a position of unparalleled power and authority in ancient Egypt.

From the nineteenth century onward, Western scholars have contended that the stories contained in the Pentateuch are derived from four main literary sources, sources whose individual contributions have been woven together to form the traditional biblical narrative that has come down to us.[2] Two of these sources are distinguished by their use, respectively, of either "YHWH" or "Elohim" for God. The divine name "Elohim," for instance, occurs 219 times in Genesis, but not once in Genesis 10–16. The name "YHWH," on the other hand, occurs 165 times, with 153 of these in Genesis 1–32. As for the remaining twelve occurrences, "YHWH" appears three times in Genesis 38, eight times in Genesis 39, and once more in Genesis 49:18. Although the documentary hypothesis provides a simple and elegant explanation for stylistic differences in the respective sections of text, it does not offer a satisfactory explanation for the narratives concerning Joseph.[3] Insofar as the Joseph cycle occupies Genesis 37; 39–47; 50, the name "YHWH" figures prominently in the first full account of Joseph's captivity in

---

[2]For a brief survey, see Richard Elliott Friedman, "Torah (Pentateuch)," *ABD* 6:609-19.

[3]According to George W. Coats, although "the Joseph story has served OT scholars as a showcase for evidence that can be used to support identification of the classical pentateuchal sources," subsequent analysis "concludes that the story is fundamentally a unit, the work of one hand" ("Joseph, Son of Jacob," *ABD* 3:979).

Egypt (Gen 39) but nowhere else in his story. Has an author or editor simply cobbled together different parts of the story from different sources? Careful reading indicates that, whatever previous versions may or may not be involved, literary and theological strategies are also at play.

## A Brother Betrayed

Although Joseph is not an entirely sympathetic character (he slanders his brothers and lacks the good sense to keep his self-aggrandizing dreams to himself [Gen 37:2-8]), nothing justifies the hate-filled treachery of his elder siblings. Jealous at the favoritism shown him by their father, the other brothers stage his death (an actual fate that he barely escapes [Gen 37:18-20]) and sell him into slavery, consoling themselves with cash for the trouble that Joseph has caused them (Gen 37:26-28). But the narrator's first remarks upon Joseph's arrival in the household of an Egyptian military official are theologically instructive:

> The LORD was with Joseph, and he became a successful man; he was in the house of his Egyptian master. His master saw that the LORD was with him, and that the LORD caused all that he did to prosper in his hands. So Joseph found favor [*ḥēn*] in his sight and attended him; he made him overseer of his house and put him in charge of all that he had. From the time that he made him overseer in his house and over all that he had, the LORD blessed the Egyptian's house for Joseph's sake; the blessing of the LORD was on all that he had, in house and field. (Gen 39:2-5)

Given the relative scarcity of the name "YHWH" ("the LORD") in recent chapters (it has appeared only three times in the previous 213 verses), this fivefold repetition is immediately obvious to readers of Hebrew. Although it is in the eyes of his master that Joseph finds "favor," the implication of the story is that Yahweh too has favored him.[4] For when, in a manner quite unlike Joseph's God, his master's

[4]"Both places where *yhwh* occurs are at the darkest moments of Joseph's life. Here in this episode Joseph, rudely rejected by his brothers and callously sold by them, finds himself abandoned in Egypt. 'But YHWH was with him'—not just *God*, but God in his more involved, particularistic, and covenant-keeping aspects" (Robert E. Longacre, *Joseph: A Story of Divine Providence; A Text Theoretical and Textlinguistic Analysis of Genesis 37 and 39–48* [Winona Lake, IN: Eisenbrauns, 1989], 45).

anger (ʾ*ap* [Gen 39:19]) results in Joseph being imprisoned for a sin he has not committed, the divine attributes come once more to the fore:

> But the Lord was with Joseph and showed him steadfast love [*ḥesed*]; he gave him favor [*ḥēn*] in the sight of the chief jailer. The chief jailer committed to Joseph's care all the prisoners who were in the prison, and whatever was done there, he was the one who did it. The chief jailer paid no heed to anything that was in Joseph's care, because the Lord was with him; and whatever he did, the Lord made it prosper. (Gen 39:21-23)

As in this instance, the vocabulary of Exodus 34 is placed strategically within the remainder of the narrative, even though the actual divine name is not mentioned again.

The narrative repeatedly implies the question "Where are grace, faithfulness, and steadfast love to be found?" Certainly they are not characteristic of Joseph's fellow prisoners. Thrown into the guardhouse with him are Pharaoh's wine steward ("cupbearer") and baker, the two servants who provide Egypt's supreme ruler with food and drink. Both have offended (lit., "sinned against" [*ḥāṭāʾ*]) their master (Gen 40:1), and both must pay the price. By interpreting their dreams, Joseph foresees that the cupbearer is about to be released and restored to prominence, but that the baker will not be so fortunate. Joseph therefore pleads with the cupbearer, "Remember me when it is well with you; please do me the kindness [*ḥesed*] to make mention of me to Pharaoh, and so get me out of this place" (Gen 40:14). The choice of language is appropriate; after all, Joseph is powerless to help himself. There is no sense that he is waiting out a ten- or twenty-year sentence. Rather, he is entirely at the mercy of others, and he will languish in prison until someone higher up decides either to execute him (the fate of the baker) or to set him free. The newly liberated servant, however, has either a poor memory or a poor grasp of *ḥesed*, or both. Not until the Pharaoh has a dream of his own, a full two years later, does the cupbearer recall his fellow prisoner and exclaim, "I remember my faults [lit., 'my sins,' *ḥăṭāʾay*] today" (Gen 41:9).

Nor are such qualities to be found among Joseph's brothers. As the story unfolds, Joseph is called before Pharaoh to interpret a series of troubling dreams. Joseph understands these dreams to mean that a great famine will soon envelop the land and proposes measures to remedy the situation. Quite unexpectedly, the former slave and prisoner is given responsibility for implementing his plan. Eventually, severe famine indeed develops, extending to the land of Canaan and "throughout the world" (Gen 41:57). Hearing that grain can be purchased in Egypt, Joseph's brothers make the journey south, only to appear before Joseph himself—although they do not recognize him. Joseph's response, now that the tables are turned, is psychologically plausible: rather than acceding to their request, he accuses them of spying, and puts them to the test.

> But Joseph said to them, "It is just as I have said to you; you are spies! Here is how you shall be tested: as Pharaoh lives, you shall not leave this place unless your youngest brother comes here! Let one of you go and bring your brother, while the rest of you remain in prison, in order that your words may be tested, whether there is truth [*ʾemet*] in you; or else, as Pharaoh lives, surely you are spies." (Gen 42:14-16)

Is there "truth" in them? Joseph knows that there is not, at least not in the sense of fidelity to covenant, for if there had been, they would not have sold their own brother into slavery. Joseph throws them into prison for three days, just to give them a taste of their own medicine. The brothers' own interpretation of the situation is no less perceptive:

> They said to one another, "Surely we are being punished because of our brother. We saw how distressed he was *when he pleaded with us* for his life, but we would not listen; that's why this distress has come upon us." Reuben replied, "Didn't I tell you not to *sin against* the boy? But you wouldn't listen. Now we must give an accounting for his blood." (Gen 42:21-22 NIV)

The implications of their language ("when he pleaded with us") are entirely obscured by translation: this phrase translates a form of the verb *ḥnn* that means "to seek grace or favor." Reuben's answer, on the other hand, is quite clear, for it acknowledges that the brothers have "sinned" (*ḥāṭāʾ*). Their sin is precisely in having failed to show mercy or favor to Joseph when he was in their power. As they see it, the vengeance of a righteous God has at last caught up with them.

### *"Am I in the Place of God?"*

Joseph, by contrast, turns out to be the very opposite of his brothers, notwithstanding the ungracious nature of his initial response. To make a long story short, the brothers return home to their father leaving one of their number, Simeon, behind as a hostage. No less troubling than the loss of another brother is the fact that Joseph has secretly returned to each the money with which they had paid for their provisions. Upon learning all this, their father expresses hope that God will nonetheless sort things out, and he sends them back with a heartfelt prayer: "May God Almighty grant you compassion [*raḥămîm*] in the man's sight" (Gen 43:14). When they arrive once more in Egypt, not only is Joseph indeed compassionate ("Do not be afraid," he says, "your God and the God of your father must have put treasure in your sacks" [Gen 43:23]), but also he declares to Benjamin, his only full brother (the rest are half-brothers), "God be gracious [*ḥānan*] to you, my son" (Gen 43:29):

> With that, Joseph hurried out, because he was overcome with *compassion* [*raḥămîm*] for his brother, and he was about to weep. So he went into a private room and wept there. (Gen 43:30)

Their father's prayer has been answered in the character and conduct of the lost son, so clearly evocative of the God they both serve. Or from another perspective, the brothers who so feared divine vengeance now discover their God to be unexpectedly gracious and forgiving, for their crimes have not been requited as they deserve.

These are the only two occurrences of the word *raḥămîm* in Genesis. Even so, this and similarly strategic language elsewhere in the narrative might seem accidental were it not for the way in which Joseph's story concludes. In sum, Joseph eventually reveals his true identity, forgives his astonished siblings, and invites the entire family to live with him in Egypt. But after a number of years of life in comfortable exile, the elderly Jacob senses that his time is at last coming to an end. The father issues a theologically pregnant challenge to the son on whom he has latterly come to depend:

> When the time drew near for Israel [Jacob] to die, he called for Joseph his son and said to him, "If I have found favor [*ḥēn*] in your eyes, put your hand under my thigh and promise that you will show me *kindness* and *faithfulness*. Do not bury me in Egypt, but when I rest with my fathers, carry me out of Egypt and bury me where they are buried." (Gen 47:29-30 NIV)

Jacob's request is, literally, "Do unto me steadfast love [*ḥesed*] and faithfulness [*ʾemet*]," an exact citation of the phrase from Exodus 34:6 and elsewhere. True to form, Joseph swears to do all that his father has asked, and the old man promptly expires.

The remaining brothers, by contrast, have somewhat less confidence in Joseph's good graces. Now that their father is dead, they reason, Joseph will finally seize the opportunity to repay their betrayal of him. So they (also true to form) invent a deathbed vow of their own:

> So they approached Joseph, saying, "Your father gave this instruction before he died, 'Say to Joseph: I beg you, forgive [*nāśāʾ*] the crime [*pešaʿ*] of your brothers and the wrong [*ḥaṭṭāʾt*] they did in harming you.' Now therefore please forgive [*nāśāʾ*] the crime [*pešaʿ*] of the servants of the God of your father." (Gen 50:16-17)

Again, the language explicitly recalls that of Exodus 34; the brothers are asking Joseph to be forgiving precisely after the manner of Israel's God.[5] Joseph's tearful reply, however, is not to be taken entirely at face value:

> But Joseph said to them, "Do not be afraid! Am I in the place of God? Even though you intended to do harm to me, God intended it for good, in order to preserve a numerous people, as he is doing today. So have no fear; I myself will provide for you and your little ones." In this way he reassured them, speaking kindly to them. (Gen 50:19-21)

"Am I in the place of God [Elohim]?" With this telling response, the

---

[5]Here the noun *ḥaṭṭāʾt* corresponds to *ḥaṭṭāʾâ* from Exodus 34:7. Genesis 50:16-17 thus directly echoes the verb and two of the three terms for sin from Exodus 34. To complete the picture, Judah has already confessed his "iniquity" (*ʿăwōn*) in Genesis 44:16.

entire narrative comes to its intended climax. For as discerning readers will have recognized, Joseph may not be "in the place of Elohim," but there is no question that he has consistently acted in the manner of Yahweh, Israel's Lord. In contrast to Potiphar (and in keeping with Judah's own explicit plea at Gen 44:18), Joseph is not liable to anger; unlike the cupbearer, he demonstrates "steadfast love"; as opposed to his brothers, he proves to be a man of mercy and graciousness—all this in addition to showing compassion and truthfulness/fidelity, even to the point of forgiving their "iniquity and transgression and sin." In a final rhetorical flourish, Joseph even promises to care for the next generation, lest we imagine the sins of these fathers being visited upon *their* children. Much earlier in the patriarchal accounts Jacob had been exceedingly angry with his wife, Rachel (Joseph's mother), demanding, "Am I in the place of God [Elohim], who has withheld from you the fruit of the womb?" (Gen 30:2). Likewise we recall Jacob's flattery of Esau: "Truly to see your face is like seeing the face of God [Elohim]" (Gen 33:10). Whether Jacob or Esau is in the place of God, the honor of representing and resembling Yahweh, the one true God known to Israel alone, is reserved above all for their son and nephew, Joseph. The cycle that concerns him began with eight references to the divine name in Genesis 39, implying that Joseph learns the meaning of steadfast love, favor, and the like, on the basis of the care and blessing that he receives from the God of his ancestors—not any god, but Yahweh. From that point onward, although the divine name is not mentioned again within his story, Joseph himself becomes the embodiment of the divine attributes.

In addition to providing a model of pious conduct, the theological relevance of this strategy likely relates to the location of Joseph's exile in Egypt. There is no way of knowing with certainty which Pharaoh the Joseph cycle refers to: the name "Pharaoh" itself means "Great House," applied to the Egyptian ruler in much the same way that "the White House," "10 Downing Street," or "Buckingham Palace" might refer to the opinions of a president, prime minister, or queen. One prominent opinion notes the parallels between Joseph's story and Egyptian texts dating from the Nineteenth Dynasty (ca. 1320-

1200 BCE), although other scholars have suggested that the story may originate several centuries earlier or later.[6] The fact is not made explicit in the text of Genesis (its authors would have considered the notion blasphemous), but throughout the patriarchal period and for generations to come the Egyptian monarch was considered to be the embodiment and image, even the "son," of the gods.[7] "Ramesses," for instance (the name of several rulers of the Eighteenth Dynasty and later ones, perhaps even the name of the Pharaoh of the Exodus), means "Ra [the Egyptian sun god] is the one who begot him." In the end, however, it is Joseph, not the unnamed Pharaoh of the story, who most resembles God. Or perhaps we should say that whereas a Pharaoh might reflect the glory of Ra or claim to be the embodiment of Horus the sky god, Joseph alone exemplifies the righteousness, mercy, forbearance, and fidelity of Yahweh, the one true God, whom he and all Israel worship. If, as the Egyptians believed, their rulers personified the gods they serve, how much more so, through testing and adversity, does Joseph come to resemble the God he serves. He is, in the last analysis, the very expression of the divine character in human conduct.

## The Imitation of God

The story of Joseph, though the most comprehensive example, is only the first of many instances in which the divine character determines the core values of godly conduct in Judeo-Christian tradition (and on into Islamic practice). Following Mosaic legislation, the admonitions of Hebrew prophets, the teaching of Jesus, and the exegetical wisdom of Maimonides, God's people are bidden to demonstrate compassion, mercy, and graciousness to one another, their actions reflecting the way in which God has dealt with them. The books of *2 Baruch* and 2 Maccabees, the Letter of James, and Augustine counsel patience and long-suffering in imitation of God and in light of God's ultimate justice.

[6]See the discussion in J. Alberto Soggin, *A History of Israel: From the Beginnings to the Bar Kochba Revolt, AD 135*, trans. John Bowden (London: SCM, 1985), 115-17.

[7]A full treatment is provided by Georges Posenor, *De la divinité du pharaon* (Paris: Imprimérie nationale, 1960); for a briefer summary, see J. Richard Middleton, *The Liberating Image: The Imago Dei in Genesis 1* (Grand Rapids: Brazos, 2005), 108-11.

Rabbis from Simeon the Just, Jesus, and James onward insist that "deeds of loving-kindness" are the highest expression of piety. And the example of Jonah epitomizes the need for the godly to be Godlike even to the point of forgiving their enemies and persecutors, however difficult that may be. Here we have a final opportunity to reflect on ways in which the formula of the divine name and character provided the ultimate model for a life of faith and faithfulness. We will look at examples from three different settings: postbiblical Judaism, the New Testament, and the early centuries of the Christian church.[8]

At Qumran, a messianic community roughly contemporary with Jesus and his disciples, imitation of God's character provided a core standard for godly conduct. To this end, the Qumran *Rule of the Community*, a document setting out requirements for membership in this strict sectarian group, describes the starkly differing paths followed by the "sons of truth," on the one hand, and those who "walk in all the paths of darkness and evil cunning," on the other. It lists key virtues manifested by those who walk in the light, describing them as "the counsels of the spirit for the sons of truth in the world":

> a spirit of meekness, of patience [*ʾerek ʾappayim*], generous compassion [*raḥămîm*], eternal goodness, intelligence, understanding, potent wisdom which trusts in all the deeds of God and depends on his abundant mercy [*ḥesed*]; a spirit of knowledge in all the plans of action, of enthusiasm for the decrees of justice, of holy plans with firm purpose, of generous compassion [pl., *ḥăsādîm*] with all the sons of truth [*ʾemet*]. (1QS 4:3-6)[9]

In its own way, the description of the "wayward" is also fascinating: "to the spirit of deceit belong greed, frailty of hands in the service of justice, irreverence, deceit, pride and haughtiness of heart" (1QS 4:9). But the previous passage holds our attention because of its language, the biblical origins of which we recognize at once. Indeed, the language

[8]The goal of achieving likeness to the gods was also common in Greco-Roman thought. See L. Ann Jervis, "Becoming Like God through Christ: Discipleship in Romans," in *Patterns of Discipleship in the New Testament*, ed. Richard N. Longenecker (Grand Rapids: Eerdmans, 1996), 145-47 (with discussion of Jewish contexts, pp. 148-50).

[9]Translation from Florentino García Martínez, trans., *The Dead Sea Scrolls Translated: The Qumran Texts in English* (Leiden: Brill, 1994), 6.

is used in such a proverbial and unobtrusive manner as to suggest that these terms have already been fully incorporated into the sectarians' vocabulary and are for them an almost instinctive way of describing the life of piety. For the Qumran community, a godly life is evidently one that reflects the character of God.

Within the New Testament, perhaps the closest we come to the broad terms of the Qumran ideal is in the paired letters to the Ephesians and Colossians, the first of which instructs members of that congregation:

> Be towards one another
> kind, compassionate [*eusplanchnos*], forgiving each other,
> just as God in Christ forgave you.
> So be *imitators of God*
> as beloved children, and walk in love,
> just as Christ loved us and gave himself for us. (Eph 4:32–5:1 [my translation])

Paul not infrequently exhorts his congregants to imitate him, particularly in regard to his own imitation of Christ (1 Cor 4:16; 11:1; 2 Thess 3:7-9). Likewise, he tells the Thessalonian believers, "You became imitators of us *and* of the Lord" (1 Thess 1:6). But here in Ephesians the saints are instructed to imitate God directly: they are to exhibit kindness, compassion, forgiveness, and love, on the grounds that these are the divine qualities modeled by Christ. This is in line with Jesus' own instructions that his followers should emulate their heavenly Father in demonstrating mercy, generous forgiveness, and moral perfection (Mt 5:45-48 // Lk 6:32-36).

In similar terms, the believers at Colossae are said to have already "put on the new nature, which is being renewed in knowledge after the image of its creator" (Col 3:10 RSV). But resemblance to God is by no means automatic; rather, it involves profound moral responsibility:

> Put on then, as God's chosen ones, holy and beloved, compassion, kindness [*splanchna oiktirmou*], lowliness, meekness, and patience [*makrothymia*], forbearing one another and, if one has a complaint against another, forgiving each other; as the Lord has forgiven you, so

> you also must forgive. And above all these put on love, which binds everything together in perfect harmony. (Col 3:12-14 RSV)

As in the letter to the Ephesians, resemblance to the Creator and renewal "in knowledge" has to do with practical matters of reconciliation, humility, and compassion toward others. This is what it means to be both "holy" and "beloved." Far from being the product either of personal piety or of individual asceticism, it is in the simple kindness and relative harmony of a reconciled community that the image of God comes to the fore.

Here, as throughout the New Testament, the distinctive feature of Christian ethics (when compared to the outlook of Qumran or other streams of Judaism) is the role of Jesus as the one in whom the divine character has been most fully expressed. For his followers, the devout life consists of imitating Jesus himself as much as, perhaps even more than, his heavenly Father (see Jn 13:15; Heb 6:12; 12:2-3; 13:7; 1 Pet 2:21). Or at the very least, Jesus is the one through whom imitation of God becomes possible. This dual focus on Jesus and the God of Israel is particularly evident in the Eastern Orthodox concept of "theosis."[10] Theosis, which refers to divinization or participation in the divine nature and is a long-standing cornerstone of Eastern Orthodox spirituality, is the process of devotion, self-surrender, and moral exertion by which the faithful are drawn into and transformed by the life of Christ. According to this tradition, just as Adam was made "in the image and likeness of God" (Gen 1:26), so Christ, himself "the image of the invisible God" (Col 1:15), enables humankind to approach once more what Adam and Eve lost through sin. The resemblance is quite specific. In the words of Maximus the Confessor (ca. 580-662 CE), "The one is by nature, the other by grace. Every rational nature [i.e., every human being] is made to the image of God, but only the good and the wise to His likeness" (*The Four Hundred Chapters on Love* 3.25).[11] Or as

[10]I am grateful to James R. Payton of Redeemer College for helping to clarify many aspects of this tradition; see further idem, *Light from the Christian East: An Introduction to the Orthodox Tradition* (Downers Grove: IVP Academic, 2007), 132-54, esp. 142-46; and Robert L. Wilken, *The Spirit of Early Christian Thought: Seeking the Face of God* (New Haven: Yale University Press, 2003), 262-90.

[11]Quoted from Polycarp Sherwood, trans., *St. Maximus the Confessor: The Ascetic Life; The Four Centuries on Charity* (ACW 21; New York: Newman, 1955), 177.

John of Damascus explains, "'According to his image' means the intellect and free will, while . . . 'according to his likeness' means such likeness in virtue as is possible" (*An Exact Exposition of the Orthodox Faith* 2.12).[12] Thus, whereas intellect and will are qualities exhibited by the righteous and the wicked alike, only the exercise of moral virtue is said to reflect God's own "love of humanity" (*philanthrōpia*). This kind of transformation—by grace—was in fact the purpose of the incarnation, according to the famous dictum of Athanasius (ca. 296-373 CE): "He was made man that we might be made God" (*Inc.* 54.3 [*NPNF*² 4:65]).

Already in the Greek world, says Robert Wilken, "the goal of the moral life was 'likeness to God'"—above all in terms of the cardinal Hellenistic virtues of prudence, justice, courage, and temperance.[13] But while they sought to interpret biblical virtues in light of this cultural ideal, Christian writers from the second century onwards recognized that "biblical saints fit uncomfortably in the classical categories."[14] For what has always been distinctive about Christian tradition is not its emphasis on the moral qualities of Israel's God per se, but rather the fact that Jesus plays an essential role in enabling the faithful to participate in the divine life and likeness. Particularly in the thought of Augustine, the goal of the Christian life is neither virtue for its own sake nor "becoming divine," but instead the emulation of divine love in particular through fellowship with God.[15] How, then, according to the church fathers, might one resemble God? Above all, it is in practical demonstrations of Godlike—Christlike—humility, patience, charity, compassion, and forgiveness, as we have already seen in Tertullian's treatment of divine forbearance, or as is expressed in John Chrysostom's comment on James 1:27: "It is this by which we are able to be like God: in being merciful and compassionate." Thus what Joseph models for Judaism, Jesus not only models but also makes possible for the church: the transformation of the human character according to the

[12]Quoted from Frederic H. Chase Jr., trans., *Saint John of Damascus: Writings* (FC 37; New York: Fathers of the Church, 1958), 235.
[13]Wilken, *The Spirit of Early Christian Thought*, 275.
[14]Ibid., 281.
[15]Ibid., 286.

character of God. If Jesus is the "human face" of God, Jesus' followers are enabled to reflect the same image and likeness in their own conduct. Much after the manner of Joseph in Egypt, they demonstrate these qualities to one another because this is how God in Christ has dealt with them. Recalling the language of Isaiah and Matthew, even as Jesus is "God with us" (Mt 1:23; cf. Is 7:14), so, through Jesus, his followers reflect the continued presence and character of God in their midst. Still, those who attempt to imitate God are profoundly aware of how far short of this ideal they fall, a realization that causes them to flee in prayer, worship, and devotion to precisely those divine characteristics that they have failed to emulate fully. Paradoxically, for those whose own piety and conduct cannot meet the standards set by Joseph and Jesus, the character of God provides a source not of condemnation, but rather of consolation, encouragement, and hope, for here too they are bidden to call upon the whole name and nature of Yahweh.

## Calling upon the Lord

In her compelling spiritual autobiography, *Girl Meets God*, Lauren Winner succinctly describes the way in which recitation of the thirteen attributes—the divine qualities enumerated in Exodus 34:6-7—represents one of the cornerstones of traditional Jewish piety. As we saw in chapter 2, they are especially prominent in the devotional practices that characterize the High Holy Days:

> As part of the work of repentance, Jews say special penitentiary prayers called *slichot*. The *slichot* start at midnight the Saturday before Rosh Hashanah [Jewish New Year], because the rabbis knew that the heavens are most open to prayers at midnight. Among the *slichot* prayers is one you will say again on Rosh Hashanah, and on all the days between Rosh Hashanah and Yom Kippur [the Day of Atonement], and again on Yom Kippur, when God is making His final judgments about who will live and who will die, whom He will forgive and whom He will punish: *Adonai, Adonai, el rachum v'chanun, erech apayim, vrav chesed v'emet, notzer chesed lalafim, nosey avon vafesha v'chatahah v'hakeh.* "The Lord, the Lord, of compassion, Who offers grace and is slow to anger, Who is full of loving-kindness and trustworthiness, Who assures love for a

thousand generations, Who forgives iniquity, transgression, and misdeed, and Who grants pardon." It is a list, culled from the thirty-fourth chapter of Exodus, of God's thirteen merciful attributes, attributes that, according to the rabbis, shine most brightly during the season of repentance.

The prayer, a reminder to God not of our merit but of his capacity to overlook sin, is sung to a particularly haunting melody, my favorite from the entire cantorial literature. It is minor, and repetitive, and dirge-like, and some people say that Jews wailed its tune as they walked to the gas chambers in Treblinka and Sobibor.[16]

The practice of reciting the divine attributes is said to have originated with Moses, who repeated back to God an abbreviated version of the formula from Exodus 34, praying, "Forgive the *iniquity* of this people according to the greatness of your *steadfast love*, just as you have *pardoned* this people, from Egypt even until now." Although certain conditions were attached (such as having to wander in the wilderness for another forty years), the prayer proved successful: "Then the LORD said, 'I do forgive, just as you have asked'" (Num 14:20). Accordingly, Moses' prayer traditionally forms part of the penitential liturgy recited between New Year's Day and the Day of Atonement, which the congregation repeats in trust and expectation that their own petitions will be as efficacious as those of Moses.[17]

We have seen how King David (in the psalms attributed to him); King Manasseh; the prophets Micah, Habakkuk, and Daniel; Ezra the Scribe (in both canonical and deuterocanonical portrayals); Ben Sirach; and even the high priest on the Day of Atonement all take their cue from Moses, reciting in God's presence the divine attributes on which they and their people depend. Likewise, the Qumran sectarians frequently express their devotional zeal in terms of the qualities revealed to Moses. Two further examples, one again re-

---

[16]Lauren F. Winner, *Girl Meets God: On the Path to a Spiritual Life* (Chapel Hill, NC: Algonquin Books, 2002), 16-17.

[17]So Abraham E. Millgram, *Jewish Worship* (2nd ed.; Philadelphia: Jewish Publication Society of America, 1975), 229-30; see also *y. Ber.* 4:1. Many of the relevant texts are collated in Shmuel Yosef Agnon, *Days of Awe: A Treasury of Traditions, Legends, and Learned Commentaries Concerning Rosh Ha-Shanah, Yom Kippur and the Days Between* (New York: Schocken, 1965), 141-47.

calling the life of Joseph in Egypt and the other forming part of a summary of biblical history, also originate in the period prior to the destruction of Jerusalem. What they demonstrate is that already around the time of Jesus, prayer to and recitation of the divine character is a devotional staple, part of how—in addition to the more formal avenues provided by temple and synagogue—the faithful seek to approach their God.

### *Joseph and Aseneth*

Joseph is only thirty years of age when, having successfully interpreted Pharaoh's dreams, he not only is released from prison but also is granted authority over the land of Egypt second only to that of the monarch himself. In addition to wearing Pharaoh's signet ring, fine clothing, and a golden necklace, Joseph is given a new name—and an Egyptian wife: "Pharaoh gave Joseph the name Zaphenath-paneah; and he gave him Aseneth daughter of Potiphera, priest of On, as his wife" (Gen 41:45).[18] As with the problematic issue of King Manasseh's long reign, pious interpreters wondered how the faithful Joseph—"one in whom is the spirit of God" (Gen 41:38)—could possibly consent to marry a foreign woman, and the daughter of a pagan priest at that! At some point between about 100 BCE and 100 CE or slightly later, a Greek-speaking writer set out to resolve this difficulty, producing a moralistic novella some twenty-nine chapters in length commonly known as *Joseph and Aseneth*.[19]

Although the plot is somewhat complicated, it begins simply enough. Aseneth is eighteen years old and beautiful, while her father is cast as an exceedingly wealthy nobleman and priest. So attractive is she that even Pharaoh's firstborn son keeps pleading with his own father to arrange a marriage between them. Aseneth, however, scorns his attentions, together with those of a host of other suitors, preferring to spend her time either sacrificing to her many idols or keeping company with her seven equally beautiful servant girls. Joseph, beginning to make the

[18]Aseneth bears him two sons, Ephraim and Manasseh (Gen 41:50; 46:20), but the latter is not to be confused with the later king of the same name.

[19]See Randall D. Chesnutt, "Joseph and Aseneth," *ABD* 3:969-71. The translation cited here is by C. Burchard, "Joseph and Aseneth," *OTP* 2:177-247.

rounds of the land in search of surplus grain, announces a planned visit. Hearing the news, Potiphera makes plans of his own: he wants his daughter to marry the newly rehabilitated and virtuous Joseph. But Aseneth is livid: "plenty of red sweat poured over her face, and she became furious with great anger." It turns out, in true romantic fashion, that Aseneth is smitten at the very sight of the noble and handsome foreigner. Now it is Joseph's turn to be aloof, as he refuses to consort with an idolatress. He does, however, condescend to pray for Aseneth's conversion, departing with a promise to return in a week's time. Joseph's prayers are answered in remarkable fashion: Aseneth fasts in sackcloth and ashes, throws much of her wealth (literally) out the window, and grinds her idols into dust.

On the morning of the eighth day, Aseneth utters three extended soliloquies, first considering the basis on which such a sinner as herself might approach a holy God, then crying out for mercy to the One whom Joseph worships. For a committed pagan, Aseneth possesses uncannily accurate information about Joseph's God:

> I have heard many saying that the God of the Hebrews is a true God,
> and a living God, and a merciful God,
> and compassionate and long-suffering and pitiful and gentle,
> and does not count the sin of a humble person. . . .
> Therefore I will take courage too and turn to him. . . .
> Who knows, (maybe) he will see my humiliation and have mercy on me.
> Perhaps he will see this desolation of mine and have compassion on me. (*Jos. Asen.* 11:10-12)

While this exploration of the divine character represents the theological heart of her first soliloquy, the second contemplates the risks of uttering the "terrible holy name" of Israel's God—a chance she takes, presumably, because she already knows that God's holiness is tempered by mercy and grace. Likewise, her third address comes to a climax with a prayer of repentance that is remarkable for its tenderness and intimacy, recalling both the filial piety of Jesus and, once again, the revelation accorded Moses:

For (just) as a little child who is afraid flees to his father,
and the father, stretching out his hands, snatches him off the ground,
and puts his arms around him by his breast,
and the child clasps his hands around his father's neck,
and regains his breath after his fear, and rests at his father's breast,
the father, however, smiles at the confusion of his childish mind,
likewise you too, Lord, stretch out your hands upon me as a child-
    loving father,
and snatch me off the earth. . . .
What father is sweet as you, Lord,
And who as quick in mercy as you, Lord,
and who long-suffering towards our sins as you, Lord? (*Jos. Asen.* 12:8, 15)

Aseneth at once receives a visit from God's chief angel, converts, marries Joseph, and lives happily until, some years later, Pharaoh's eldest son makes a second, murderous play for her hand in marriage. For our purposes, however, the most remarkable feature of this account is its description of God's character. Apparently taking priority even over the express name of Israel's God, the descriptive terms with which we have become so familiar provide the basis for Aseneth's prayer and her penitent approach to God. Scholars have debated whether the story's pious propaganda is intended for Gentiles or for Jews, but whichever the case, Aseneth proves to be the ideal convert. By praying in this manner, Aseneth provides the perfect model of orthodox devotion. Jew and Gentile alike learn from her example that addressing the God of Israel depends less on the condition or qualities of the petitioner than on the character of the One to whom their prayers are addressed.

### *Biblical Antiquities*

Just as vocabulary derived ultimately from Exodus 34:6-7 provides a recognizable theological focus for popular legends about the life of Joseph, so it undergirds the prayers of Moses (especially as his own death approaches) in a summary of salvation history from the same era entitled *Biblical Antiquities*. An otherwise anonymous interpreter, known as Pseudo-Philo, apparently compiled this brief history of Israel from Adam to David at some point soon after the turn of the common era.[20] In relating the episode of the golden calf and its aftermath, Pseudo-Philo makes only fleeting reference to the formula of the divine name. He depicts Moses praying for God's rebellious people: "If you do not *have mercy* on your vine, all things, Lord, have been done in vain, and you will not have anyone to glorify you"; and God replies, "Behold *I have been made merciful* according to your words. Therefore cut two stone tablets for yourself from the same place where you cut the former ones, and rewrite on them the commandments that were on the first ones" (*L.A.B.* 12:9-10 [italics added]). The response clearly indicates that God is "made" merciful precisely because Moses has appealed to the quality of divine mercy. No explanation is offered because none is necessary; readers evidently know that Moses' prayer calls forth the divine qualities on which they themselves have come to depend. Given that Pseudo-Philo is ostensibly summarizing the biblical narrative, his omissions are telling: rather than pausing to expound the divine name itself, or even to relate the circumstances of its revelation, he need only point to the consequences of appealing to God's character in order to make his point.

Deuteronomy 34 records Moses' last act as that of surveying the promised land from the top of Mount Nebo in the land of Moab, at which point God says to him, "I have let you see it with your eyes, but you shall not cross over there" (Deut 34:4). Moses dies shortly thereafter. But according to Pseudo-Philo, Moses' last conversation with God includes an extensive prayer for the people whom he has led since the Exodus from Egypt:

> Behold I have completed my lifetime; I have completed 120 years. And now I ask, May your *mercy* with your people and your *pity* [or "compassion"] with your heritage, Lord, be established; and may your *long-suffering* in your place be upon the chosen race because you have loved them before all others. . . . And unless your *patience* abides, how would your heritage be established, if you were not *merciful* to them? Or who

[20]This work is often referred to by its Latin title, *Liber antiquitatum biblicarum* (abbreviated as *L.A.B.*). For discussion of dating and other introductory questions, see D. J. Harrington, "Pseudo-Philo," *OTP* 2:297-303 ("A date around the time of Jesus seems most likely" [ibid., 299]). Quotations here of *Liber antiquitatum biblicarum* are from Harrington's translation.

> will yet be born without sin? Now you will correct them for a time, but not in *anger*." (*L.A.B.* 19:8-9 [italics added])

In this version of events God shows Moses not only the physical extent of the promised land, but also the future history of Israel and even "the paths of paradise" (*L.A.B.* 19:10). Knowing everything that is yet to be, Moses realizes the extent of the people's future sin, which leads him to pray as he does, appealing to God's mercy, compassion, and long-suffering. Here too Pseudo-Philo seems to assume familiarity with the "thirteen measures of love" on the part of his readers, for he never actually describes God's revelation of them to Moses.

This passage and the previously quoted sections of *Joseph and Aseneth* together provide the clearest indication yet of how the practice of basing prayer on the qualities of God's character was already widespread around the time of Jesus. Its presence in these texts suggests that it was a staple feature of popular piety and devotion. The Talmud refers to this custom in the context of synagogue worship and public liturgy, although the earliest authority cited dates from at least a century later. But in addition to being demonstrably ancient, the liturgical tradition to which Lauren Winner introduced us also provided a topic for learned debate amongst the rabbis.

### *The Order of Prayer*

Previous chapters have briefly surveyed the rich rabbinic tradition encouraging recitation of various attributes as a reminder both to God and to the penitent of the divine qualities that make prayer—and forgiveness—possible. The Talmud directly addresses the role of such recitation in public worship:

> *And the Lord passed by him and proclaimed.* . . . R. Joḥanan [d. 279 CE] said: Were it not written in the text, it would be impossible for us to say such a thing; this verse teaches us that the Holy One, blessed be He, drew his robe round Him like the reader of a congregation and showed Moses the order of prayer. He said to him: Whenever Israel sin, let them carry out this service before Me, and I will forgive them. (*b. Roš. Haš.* 17b)[21]

[21]See also *Midrash Tanḥuma* Genesis 18:17ff., Parashah 4.9, Part IV (John T. Townsend, trans., *Midrash Tanhuma: Translated into English with Introduction, Indices, and Notes [S. Buber Recen-*

The congregation is thus invited to read the biblical text relating the divine attributes as a public liturgy, an "order of prayer" or "rite of forgiveness." As the same Talmudic passage goes on to explain, "Rab Judah [d. 299 CE] said: A covenant has been made with the thirteen attributes that they will not be turned away empty-handed [i.e., when the people pray in this manner], as it says, *Behold I make a covenant* [Ex 34:10]."[22] Accordingly, the passage from Exodus 34 is traditionally recited not only on the Day of Atonement, but also on festivals and holy days in preparation for the Torah reading, and during the Torah reading on fast days.[23] Along the same lines, we recall from chapter two the saying of Simeon ben Yoḥai, according to whom the divine attributes govern not only the content of prayer, but also its method and conduct:

> R. Simeon said: . . . When you pray, do not regard your prayer as an appointed routine but as an appeal for mercy and favor before the Omnipresent, for it is said: "For he is gracious and full of mercy, slow to anger and abundant in loving-kindness, and relenting of the evil decree." (*m. ʾAbot* 2:13)[24]

Jewish literature provides many more examples of how this kind of prayer works in actual practice. According to the biblical text, Moses responds to the revelation of the divine name by falling down before Yahweh: "And Moses quickly bowed his head toward the earth and worshiped" (Ex 34:8). This leads to an important question:

> R. Simon taught: In the Torah are mentioned thirteen attributes of God through every one of which the Holy One, blessed be He, may grant mercy to the children of Israel. . . . Which one of these attributes was

*sion]*, vol. 1, *Genesis* [Hoboken, NJ: Ktav, 1989], 97).

22"This talmudic conception explains how the Thirteen Attributes became the nucleus of all prayers for atonement, so that they serve to this day as a refrain constantly repeated in all the *seliḥot* [prayers for forgiveness]. And since the verse 'The Lord, the Lord, merciful and compassionate God' could not be recited by itself, an introduction was provided for it explaining the talmudic thought behind the use of the Thirteen Attributes" (Ismar Elbogen, *Jewish Liturgy: A Comprehensive History*, trans. Raymond P. Scheindlin [Philadelphia: Jewish Publication Society, 1993], 178).

23Nahum M. Sarna, *Exodus: The Traditional Hebrew Text with the New JPS Translation* (JSPTC; Philadelphia: Jewish Publication Society, 1991), 216.

24Simeon's reference to "appointed routine" in association with the vocabulary of Exodus 34:6-7 may imply liturgical use of the latter, which occasions his warning against rote repetition.

> Moses thinking of when he prostrated himself in prayer? Rab said: The attribute of His being *abundant in goodness*, for it is said, *And Moses made haste and bowed his head toward the earth, and worshiped* (Ex. 34:8). R. Eliezer ben Jacob said: The attribute of His being *long-suffering*. The Rabbis said: The attribute of *mercy*. (*Midr. Ps.* 93 §8)[25]

What impelled him to bow down so suddenly? Was it the mention of the divine name itself, the promise of "mercy," or perhaps the overwhelming force of so many compelling graces all enumerated at once? Whichever the case, Moses' response is, precisely, one of worship and not prayer alone. Thus the revelation of the divine character is not simply a means of obtaining a favorable answer from God. It was to avoid such a conclusion that God responded to Moses' original demand with the intentionally evasive name "YHWH." On the contrary, as biblical texts and rabbinic commentary indicate, the proper human response to such a revelation is heartfelt devotion and holy awe.

But this is not the only possible response, according to the early medieval *Seder Eliyahu Zuta*. In this retelling of the encounter on Mount Sinai, when Moses asks God, "Show me your ways" (Ex 33:13), God reveals to him the future generations of Israel and the sages through whom his plan for creation and the world to come will one day be revealed. Thereupon Moses prays more specifically, "Show me your glory" (Ex 33:18):

> The Holy One replied, Moses, you cannot fathom My ways. But I will show you some of My ways. . . . And God went on: *I will make all My goodness . . . pass before thee* (Exod. 33:19)—*"My goodness,"* as specified by its thirteen attributes . . . (Exod. 34:6-7). Had God said, "My goodness," and not *all My goodness*, I might have supposed that the days of the Messiah were not included. . . . But since He said, *all My goodness*, He meant to include the days of the Messiah. And God went on to say, *I will proclaim the name of the Lord . . . before thee*. . . . When Moses saw God's way to be one of loving-kindness and of compassion, he enfolded

[25]Quoted from William G. Braude, trans., *The Midrash on Psalms* (2 vols.; YJS 13; New Haven: Yale University Press, 1959), 2:129. The rabbis cited here flourished from the mid-second to third centuries CE. A parallel passage in *b. Sanhedrin* 111a attributes the reference to "long-suffering" to Ḥanina ben Gamla, who lived at the end of the first and into the early second century CE.

himself [in a prayer shawl] and stood up in prayer before the Holy One, as is said, *If now I have found grace in Thy sight, O Lord, let the Lord, I pray Thee, go in the midst of us* (Exod. 34:8). (*S. Eli. Zut.* 6 [183])[26]

This interpretation offers a number of interesting twists and turns on earlier versions, expanding significantly on the account given in Exodus. Here it is Moses, not God, who wraps himself in a prayer shawl. God returns to the original subject of the divine "ways" and appears to ignore the question of "glory" altogether. Even then the answer is intentionally incomplete. There is an intriguing reference to the Messiah, whose advent seems to be an extension of the thirteen divine attributes.[27] The "days of the Messiah," like the divine character itself, are said to express God's "goodness" in its entirety. But perhaps most significant for our purposes is the assertion that rather than falling down, Moses stands to pray of behalf of the nation, claiming their identity as the chosen people. Far from humbling or overwhelming him, the revelation of divine glory emboldens him to act. At this moment Moses not only discovers who God is; he also discovers his own identity as a leader and intercessor, and he claims the identity of Israel as those whom God will favor. A more fitting illustration of the full consequences of knowing God would be difficult to find; rather than eliminating any role for the beholder, knowing the fullness of the divine identity calls forth and affirms human identity in turn.

How, then, may mere humans approach a majestic God? Not, surely, because of who they are, but rather because of who God is. This, as with so many other texts, is the view of God found in the anthology known as *Pesiqta Rabbati*, although following its logic proves to be something of an adventure.[28] In this work the fourth-century Rabbi

---

[26]Quoted from William G. Braude and Israel J. Kapstein, trans., *Tanna Debe Eliyyahu: The Lore of the School of Elijah* (Philadelphia: Jewish Publication Society, 1981), 431; see also *Pirqe R. El.* 5 [42] (ibid., 516). *Seder Eliyahu Rabbah* (cited in chapter 2 above) and *Seder Eliyahu Zuta* are the first and second parts of the work known collectively as *Tanna Debe Eliyahu* or, more simply, *Seder Eliyahu.* A similar passage in *Tanḥuma* Vayera 46a is attributed to rabbis of the fourth century CE (quoted in C. G. Montefiore and H. Loewe, *A Rabbinic Anthology, Selected and Arranged with Comments and Introductions* [London: Macmillan, 1938], 324-25).

[27]On the association of the Messiah with mercy, see *b. Sanhedrin* 97b, on Isaiah 30:18.

[28]As with *Seder Eliyahu Zuta*, estimates regarding the date of composition for *Pesiqta Rabbati* range from the fourth or fifth to seventh centuries CE or later. See H. L. Strack and G. Stem-

Yehudah bar Simon avers that upon completion of the tabernacle, the place where atonement for sin would be made (Num 7:1), Moses was unsure whether God was still angry over the sin of the golden calf. "Is it possible," asked Moses, "that there is still something against Israel in the heart of the Holy One, blessed be He?" The answer to Moses' concern, says Yehudah, is suggested by Psalm 85:8: "Let me hear what God [*ʾēl*] the LORD [*yhwh*] will speak, for he will speak peace to his people, to his faithful, to those who turn to him in their hearts." In this verse an initial reference to "El" is followed by a second reference to "Yahweh." Since the first of these divine names traditionally is associated with the attribute of justice while the second denotes the attribute of mercy, and since it is the latter in particular who "will speak peace to his people," this verse must refer to divine mercy predominating over justice and judgment! Just so, said Rabbi Yehudah, with Exodus 34:6-7 as well:

> Were the text to speak only of God, it would imply His intention to continue in just wrath against the children of Israel. But the text goes on to speak of God as Lord, as "The Lord, the Lord, God, merciful and gracious," clearly implying the possibility that He may comport Himself toward them in His aspect of mercy. Hence, the Holy One, blessed be He, at once reassured Moses that there was nothing against Israel in His heart, as it is written, And the Lord passed by before him, and proclaimed: The Lord, the Lord, God, merciful and gracious. (*Pesiq. Rab.* 5.11)[29]

Here in the answer to his question lies the assurance that Moses seeks, which is that the relationship between Yahweh and Israel is henceforth established on the basis of what was first revealed on Sinai: the Holy One is indeed merciful, as his sacred name implies. Hence the ensuing comment, which again depends on the equivalence of Yahweh with mercy:

> In connection with this verse, R. Simon said: Why does the text say twice, *The Lord, the Lord* [Ex 34:6]? It must be that the Lord was reas-

berger, *Introduction to the Talmud and Midrash*, trans. Markus Bockmuehl (Edinburgh: T & T Clark, 1991), 325-29; William G. Braude, trans., *Pesikta Rabbati: Discourses for Feasts, Fasts, and Special Sabbaths* (2 vols.; YJS 18; New Haven: Yale University Press, 1968), 1:2-6.

[29]Quoted from Braude, *Pesikta Rabbati*, 1:113-14. See also A. T. Hanson, *The New Testament Interpretation of Scripture* (London: SPCK, 1980), 107-8.

> suring Moses, saying to him: Moses, in days gone by, before they did that deed of theirs [i.e., making and worshiping the golden calf], I dealt with them by the measure of mercy, and so even now, I deal with them by the measure of mercy. (*Pesiq. Rab.* 5.11)

The Babylonian Talmud likewise observes that Israel's relationship with God is predicated on the unvarying predictability of the divine character: "'*The Lord, the Lord*': I am He before a man sins and I am He after a man sins and repents" (*b. Roš. Haš.* 17b).[30] Here the reiteration of the name "Yahweh" is taken as an indication that the attribute of mercy ultimately predominates, regardless of fidelity or infidelity on the part of God's people. How then, asked one rabbi, can the final phrase of Exodus 34:6 declare Yahweh to be abundant both "in goodness [or, 'steadfast love']" and also "in truth"? Might the order in which these attributes are listed suggest that "truth," implying divine righteousness and justice, is what prevails at the moment of judgment? On the contrary, say the rabbis: "At first, '*truth*,' and at the end, '*abundant in goodness*'" (*b. Roš. Haš.* 17b). In this case, rabbinic interpretation determines that the relative importance and priority of these attributes is opposite to the literal order of their occurrence in Scripture; ultimately, it is the divine character that determines the meaning of the biblical text, and not the other way around. Thus not prayer alone, but also worship, providence, the Messiah, the identity of God's people, and their hope in the face of holy judgment—all these hinge on the nature and character of the one who is revealed as Yahweh, Israel's Lord.

## The Character of God in Christian Devotion

If the thirteen attributes are of profound and enduring significance both within the biblical text and for Jewish devotion, as well as having influenced Islamic devotional practices, why are they not more prominent throughout the full range of Christian tradition? To be sure, various Christian theologians comment on individual attributes, even as various aspects of the divine character come to the fore in particular New Tes-

[30]Following the literal sense indicated in the footnote to this passage in the Soncino edition.

tament texts. But whereas Jewish devotion has consistently focused on the character of Yahweh, just as Islamic tradition enumerates the "names" of God, Christian devotion has directed its gaze to Jesus and to the devotional outlook that he exemplifies. Christian spirituality is predicated on the claim that Jesus of Nazareth embodies the full reality of God and that mystical union with Christ itself constitutes communion with God. "Whoever has seen me," Jesus tells his followers in John 14:9, "has seen the Father." Jesus' mediation is essential to the disciples' experience of God: "No one," he insists, "comes to the Father but by me" (Jn 14:6). Thus participation in the life of Jesus is the means by which believers encounter the One whom he calls "Father," as Jesus invites his followers to participate in his own experience of God. So Jesus prays immediately prior to betrayal and crucifixion, "As you, Father, are in me and I am in you, may they also be in us" (Jn 17:21). From the Synoptic Gospels comes Jesus' declaration "No one knows the Father except the Son and anyone to whom the Son chooses to reveal him" (Mt 11:27 // Lk 10:22). Best known of all Jesus' teaching is his instruction that the disciples pray to God as "our Father" (Mt 6:9 [cf. Lk 11:2]). The determinative influence of Jesus' spirituality is likewise evident in the way that Paul opens his letters, as he addresses the congregations at Colossae and Corinth in the name of "God our Father" and "the God and Father of our Lord Jesus Christ" (2 Cor 1:2-3; Col 1:2-3).[31] For Paul the most basic Christian prayer is the cry "Abba! Father!" (Rom 8:15; Gal 4:6), as those who place their trust in Jesus are adopted or incorporated into the "sonship" of the Messiah. Here too the experience of the One is extended to the many. As Larry Hurtado explains,

> To pray in Jesus' name and through him means that we enter into Jesus' status in God's favor, and invoke Jesus' standing with God. . . . Christians properly call God "Father" . . . because we enter in *Jesus'* relationship to God as Father. We are to consider ourselves enfranchised into Jesus' sonship with God.[32]

---

[31]See, similarly, Romans 1:7; 1 Corinthians 1:3; Galatians 1:3-4; Ephesians 1:2; Philippians 1:2; 1 Thessalonians 1:3; 2 Thessalonians 1:1-2; Philemon 3.

[32]Larry W. Hurtado, *At the Origins of Christian Worship: The Context and Character of Earliest Christian Devotion* (Grand Rapids: Eerdmans, 2000), 107-8, citing the fuller treatment by James B. Torrance, *Worship, Community, and the Triune God of Grace* (Downers Grove, IL: InterVarsity Press, 1997), esp. 13-41.

Christians appear not to have made more thoroughgoing use of Exodus 34:6-7 (and subsequent texts), first, because communion with Jesus himself provides a "personalized" and relational vision of God and, second, because Jesus opens the way for them to encounter One whom he called "Father." That is, by bidding his followers relate to God as "Father," Jesus invokes a relational category that, at its best, encapsulates the qualities earlier enumerated in the revelation to Moses.

Not only can Jesus' relationship with the Father be read in light of Moses' knowledge of the divine name, but also Exodus 34:6-7 has itself been read in light of the church's convictions about Jesus. Accordingly (much as with Augustine's view of God's "posterior" [*Trin.* 2.17.32]), Cyril (ca. 315-386), archbishop of Jerusalem, goes so far as to claim that what Moses beheld on the mountaintop was not simply a series of divine qualities, but Christ himself! This, for Cyril, is demonstrated by Exodus 33:19, where God says to Moses, "I will make all my goodness pass before you, and will proclaim before you the name, 'The LORD.'" "Being himself the Lord," asked Cyril, "what Lord does he proclaim?" Cyril thereupon cites the full text of Exodus 34:6-7 as an exposition not just of God's character, but of Christ's as well (*Catechetical Lecture* 10.8 [*APNF*² 7.59]). Likewise the ancient "Liturgy of St. James," one form of which Cyril apparently knew, offers the following prayer not just to God the Father (to whom it more properly applies), but to all three persons of the Holy Trinity:

> Compassionate and merciful,
> long-suffering,
> most merciful and true Lord,
> look down from your holy dwelling-place,
> hearken to us, your suppliants,
> and deliver us from every trial and temptation,
> both diabolic and human.[33]

The liturgy, still used by Christians of Syriac tradition, contains many further references to the mercy and compassion manifested in Jesus, as do many other Orthodox rites.

---

[33]Translation from www.anastasis.org.uk/lit-james.htm. See also *ANF* 7:538.

What, then, do Christians stand to gain from meditating on the thirteen attributes, in common with Jewish believers and, to some extent, the pious within Islam? Most profoundly, reappropriating this tradition offers the possibility of knowing the ways of God, after the manner both of Moses and of Jesus. Exodus 34:6-7 describes the God with whom Jesus continually invites us to share a deeper intimacy and communion. Contemplation of the divine character recalls for us the foundations on which the life of faith is ultimately based, setting forth the ultimate goal for which discipleship aims, the ideal against which any progress may be measured, the true source of grace for spiritual transformation, and the means of consolation in the face of inevitable failure. Faith (in the sense of calling on God), faithfulness (attempting to imitate God), and unfaithfulness (failing to be Godlike) are the three basic elements of an ongoing spiritual dynamic of life in the presence of God. This alone is more than sufficient justification for us to reappropriate such a rich exegetical and devotional tradition. But in addition to all this, reflection on the legacy of Exodus 34:6-7 may lead to a deeper understanding of a common theological heritage—a common vision of God—that invites Jew, Christian, and Muslim into conversation with each other despite otherwise insurmountable divisions and difficulties.

## God

### *A Working Knowledge*

It is unfortunately the case that Abrahamic faith and religious intolerance go frequently hand in hand. The paradox, however, is that zeal for the God of Abraham (whether exercised by Jew, Christian, or Muslim) can easily amount to a betrayal of Abraham's God. For in cases of specifically religious intolerance among these three groups, the greater the zeal, and the more absolute the adherents' dedication to a certain kind of obedience, the more profound is likely to be their divergence from an authentically biblical imitation of God's character and purpose.

Long-standing historical conflicts between Muslim and Jew, Jew and Christian, Sunni and Shiite, Catholic and Protestant, and so on, in an ever-expanding multitude of combinations, are in every case predicated on the conviction that the other party is apostate, heretical, or otherwise deserving of divine (and therefore also human) condemnation. Yet Israel's encounter with God leads to just the opposite conclusion. Precisely on the grounds that one's religious opponents have willfully excluded themselves from God's covenant, we are bound, not to condemn them, but to exercise compassion, mercy, and forgiveness, for the simple yet compelling reason that this is God's own way of acting. Followers of Jesus may note that it was for failure to observe this principle that he rebuked his disciples when they wanted to call down heavenly fire on an unwelcoming village of heretics (in this case, Samaritans [Lk 9:52-55]). If it is truly the case that the God of Abraham and Moses is unfailingly merciful, slow to anger, and ever ready to forgive, then surely these, more than anything else, are the characteristics required of all who call upon this God. It may well be that from one's own point of view the "other" is truly in error, in need of correction or conversion. But especially if we believe this to be the case, we are constrained by the conviction that God "makes his sun rise on the evil and the good, and sends rain on the righteous and the unrighteous alike" (Mt 5:45). If nothing else, this means that God does not enforce on us the rigors of religious or sectarian allegiance that we so grimly enforce on one another. That alone should give the pious pause for thought.

The point may be suitably illustrated with a story whose curious literary pedigree indicates its relevance to Jews, Christians, and Muslims alike (possibly Zoroastrians also). In 1647 the Anglican cleric Jeremy Taylor (1613-1667) published an appeal for religious toleration to which he had given the rather cumbersome title *A Discourse of the Liberty of Prophesying: Shewing the Unreasonableness of Prescribing to Other Men's Faith, and the Iniquity of Persecuting Differing Opinions*. He then revised the work for republication in a 1657 volume entitled *Symbolon Ethiko-Polemikon, or, A Collection of Polemical and Moral Discourses*. One revision was the addition of a concluding story about Abraham's lack of hospitality toward an old man, a wayfarer who happened along one night. Taylor comments vaguely that the story had come from a Jewish book, by which he probably meant the introduction to a 1651 Latin translation, published in Amsterdam, of *Shevet Yehuda*, or *The Sceptre of Judah*, a chronicle of Jewish suffering from 1553 by Solomon Ibn Verga (1460-1554). Although this was likely Taylor's immediate source, the tale that he relates in fact originates some four hundred years earlier, in a poem of ethical instruction, the *Bustan* (or "Fragrant Garden"), written about 1257 by the Muslim poet Saadi (ca. 1200-1292), one of the greatest poets of classical Persian literature.[34] The story in question is set in the Holy Land and, at least in Saadi's version, refers to Abraham by the all-important title of "Friend of God" (as in 2 Chron 20:7; Is 41:8; Jas 2:23). The tale of Abraham and his unexpected guest, cited in different forms by adherents of all three religions, is quoted here as it appears, complete with antiquated spelling and odd punctuation, in the 1657 edition of Taylor's *Collection of Polemical and Moral Discourses*:

> When *Abraham* sat at his Tent-door, according to his custome, waiting to entertain strangers; he espied an old man stopping and leaning on his staffe, weary with age and travell coming towards him, who was an hundred years of age; he received him kindely, washed his feet, provided supper, caused him to sit down; but observing that the old man eat and prayed not, nor begged for a blessing on his meat, asked him Why he did not worship the God of heaven? The old man told him, that he worshiped the fire only, and acknowledged no other God: At which answer, *Abraham* grew so zealously angry, that he thrust the old man out of his tent, and exposed him to all the evils of the night, and an unguarded condition: When the old man was gone, God called to *Abraham* and asked him where the stranger was? he replied, I thrust him away because he did not worship thee; God answered him, I have suffered him these hundred years, although he dishonoured me, and couldest not thou endure him one night, when he gave thee no trouble? Upon this, saith the story, *Abraham* fetcht him back again, and gave him

[34]For the text in question, see G. M. Wickens, trans., *Morals Pointed and Tales Adorned: The Būstān of Saʿdī* (Persian Heritage Series 17; Toronto: University of Toronto Press, 1974), 71-72 (lines 1184-1205).

> hospitable entertainment and wise instruction: *Go thou and do likewise*, and thy Charity will be rewarded by the God of *Abraham*.[35]

Implicit here is a recognition that Abraham himself was not circumcised, and in this sense not a true "friend of God," until he was fully ninety-nine years of age (Gen 17:1, 24), a fact that at least one rabbinic source cites as an example of divine forbearance (*Mek. Nezikin* 18). The point of the story, then, is that Abraham should have demonstrated the same patience toward his wayward guest that God had shown him for nearly as many years.

To claim that we ourselves are sons, daughters, or "friends" of the God of Abraham must, surely, entail responsibility for bearing a recognizable resemblance to that God, as described by Scripture. Here the fuller context of Jesus' statement is instructive: "Love your enemies and pray for those who persecute you," he insists, "*so that* you may be children of your Father in heaven; for he makes his sun rise on the evil and on the good" (Mt 5:44-45). As we saw in an earlier discussion, the implications are even plainer in the Lukan formulation of this saying:

> Love your enemies, do good, and lend, expecting nothing in return. Your reward will be great, and [by implication: then and only then] you will be children of the Most High; for he is kind to the ungrateful and the wicked. Be merciful, just as your Father is merciful. (Lk 6:35-36)

Unfortunately, the converse is also true, and plainly so when we act with prejudice, intolerance, or violence: the conduct of religious people is an unmistakable indicator of how they understand their God. As Stanley Hauerwas and William Willimon, commenting on the Christian church in particular, observe,

---

[35]Jeremy Taylor, *Symbolon Ethiko-Polemikon, or, A Collection of Polemical and Moral Discourses* (London: R. Royston, 1657), 606 (§22). As an interesting historical footnote to this account, Benjamin Franklin was so taken with the tale that he apparently proposed adopting it as the fifty-first chapter of Genesis! In Franklin's version the man is an idolater rather than a fire worshiper: "And the man answered and said, I do not worship thy God, neither do I call upon his name; for I have made to myself a god, which abideth always in mine house, and provideth me with all things." See Prudence L. Steiner, "Benjamin Franklin's Biblical Hoaxes," *Proceedings of the American Philosophical Society* 131, no. 2 (1987): 183-85.

> The biggest problem facing Christian theology is not translation but enactment. . . . No clever theological moves can be substituted for the necessity of the church being a community of people who embody our language about God, where talk about God is used without apology because our life together does not mock our words. The church is the visible, political enactment of our language of God.[36]

## "Welcome One Another"

This is not to suggest that adherents of the three Abrahamic faiths should be any less zealous, committed, or convinced. On the contrary, deeper conviction would serve us infinitely better. The problem, rather, as our conduct too often proclaims, is that we are insufficiently convinced of God's character—above all, God's mercy, compassion, forbearance, and forgiveness. We are amply convinced that God will condemn and destroy various heretics, apostates, and unbelievers, on the grounds that they do not see things our way. Nor can it be denied that Hebrew, Christian, and Islamic Scriptures each provide certain evidence to this end. Yet the prevailing conviction of the texts that we have reviewed is that God stubbornly errs on the side of magnanimity and forbearance, precisely in order that the violent and vengeful (especially those who are so by reason of religion) might come to resemble more closely the One whom they serve. Therefore, because of who and what God is (and because we ourselves are not God), we need to be cautious, in the words of the apostle Paul, not to "pronounce judgment before the time" (1 Cor 4:5 [cf. Rom 12:19, citing Deut 32:25: "Vengeance is mine, says the Lord, I will repay"]). Just so, Paul has blunt advice for the quarreling and divided members of at least one Christian congregation: "Welcome one another," he insists, "just as Christ has welcomed you, for the glory of God" (Rom 15:7). His reasoning is compellingly theological: they are to treat one another as God in Christ has treated them.

All three Abrahamic faiths (and their various offshoots) are revealed faiths, faiths that claim not to have been invented by, or to be ultimately

---

[36]Stanley Hauerwas and William Willimon, *Resident Aliens: Life in the Christian Colony* (Nashville: Abingdon, 1989), 171.

dependent upon, their adherents. In all three of them divine initiative takes precedence over the response that it evokes. We are who we are as people of faith not by virtue of our responses to God, or our arguments about which response is most adequate, but rather by virtue of who God is, and God's making us who we are. If Abrahamic faiths are indeed divinely initiated, then they must be defined primarily in terms of their objective and not their subjective poles. Of course, Jews, Christians, and Muslims insist that the distinctive features of their respective faiths are in each case an extension and expression of primary divine initiative. These competing claims will continue to divide us, and necessarily so. Precisely because of such irreconcilable differences, attention to the character and characteristics of God reminds us that it is we who are in God's hands and that God is not in ours. Precisely in the sense that God refuses to be controlled by the revelation of his name, refuses to give Moses a "handle" by which to manipulate him, so the God of Moses must continue to elude our attempts at ownership and control, even as we yield ourselves to the grasp of God. This is not to suggest that God cannot be known, but simply that God can be neither co-opted nor constrained. It is to argue for the priority of compassion, humility, forbearance, and charity, on the sole grounds that this is how the God of Moses acts and commands us to act in turn.

To some extent, the resolution of our mutual intolerance lies beyond time, for only in seeing God fully will we be fully conformed to God (1 Jn 3:2). As Paul insists, for the time being we see and know God only in part: only "then" will we see "face to face" (1 Cor 13:12). But that—to follow Paul's reasoning to its intended conclusion—is why "faith, hope, and love" must suffice in the meantime. Faith is the will to trust in a divine reality as yet experienced only in part; hope is the anticipation of fuller experience yet to come. But of the three—faith, hope, and love—"love is the greatest of these," as Paul insists (1 Cor 13:13), because it is the one human quality that most fully reflects and participates in the divine character. This is not love according to some vague romantic or socially current definition; it is divine love as specified in the reiterated biblical descriptions of generous covenant fidelity with which we have been occupied throughout this book.

## Beholding the Face of God

Many years ago, as I was contemplating the prospect of ordination, a pastor whose ministry seemed to me quite successful offered a helpful word of advice. He drew my attention to the difference between poring over the geographical outlines recorded on a contour map and actually slogging through valleys, laboring up hillsides, and stumbling down the other side of each successive slope. His point was that maps, directions, and general instructions are of limited value because the lay of the land looks entirely different when one is physically confronted by it. All that I thought I knew about pastoral ministry and all the "surface" features of his ministry that I so admired, he assured me, would look altogether different when I came to attempting something similar of my own.

Addressing the practical dimensions of topography is altogether appropriate in relation to a revelation received on a mountain top, for the descriptions of God's mercy, steadfast love, fidelity, and forgiveness with which we have been occupied here are only that—descriptions. Insofar as they describe God's way of actually relating to people in the context of covenant, they are meant to be much more than concepts or ideas alone. Possessing a map is helpful only to the extent that one makes use of it to begin, to resume, or to continue a particular journey, especially so if one feels the need to move in a different direction.[37] Thus the character of God is most relevant to those who seek to live by it, in the sense of testing such characteristics in personal experience, consciously depending upon the divine nature, and seeking to imitate God's ways by modeling their own conduct accordingly.

Each of the many Jewish, Christian, and Islamic texts that we have reviewed in the course of this study records, with varying degrees of authority, the human encounter with God. As such, each of them represents an invitation for readers to share a similar experience, not simply by reading the passages in question, but by moving beyond the texts

[37]As Harry Emerson Fosdick once observed, "Knowledge is a map of the unvisited land of God's care; prayer is actually travelling the country. The tragedy of the Church is to be found in the thousands who fondle their credal maps, on which are marked the roadways of God's friendship, but who do not travel" (*The Meaning of Prayer* [London: Student Christian Movement, 1915], 53. I wish to thank Robert Mancini for bringing this quotation to my attention.

themselves to encounter the God of whom they speak. As we have also seen, some of these writings provide specific instructions to assist the reader toward such an encounter. If, then, the ultimate purpose of this study is as much pragmatic and devotional as informative or conceptual, what practical instructions do Christian Scriptures provide regarding the encounter with God?

One text in particular points both to Jesus and to the experience of Moses on Sinai.[38] In a passage common to Matthew and Luke, Jesus tells his disciples, "All things have been handed over to me by my Father; and no one knows the Son except the Father, and no one knows the Father except the Son and anyone to whom the Son chooses to reveal him" (Mt 11:27 // Lk 10:22). As we saw earlier, Jesus explains that knowledge of God is a matter of being invited to participate in his own intimacy with the Father. This particular saying, however, directly echoes Exodus 33:12-13, in which the relationship between Moses and God is likewise predicated on mutual knowledge:

> Moses said to the LORD, "See, you have said to me, 'Bring up this people'; but you have not let me know whom you will send with me. Yet you have said, '*I know you by name*, and you have also found favor in my sight.' Now if I have found favor in your sight, show me your ways, *so that I may know you* and find favor in your sight."

The ensuing narrative affirms that Moses' prayer is fully answered, to the lasting benefit of subsequent generations. According to Deuteronomy 34:10, only Moses comes to such a relationship directly: "Never since has there arisen a prophet in Israel like Moses, whom the LORD knew face to face" (cf. Num 12:8). Yet this reciprocal familiarity between God and his favored one is precisely what Jesus claims for himself: he, even more than Moses, so fully knows God's will, purpose, and identity as to be able to reveal them to all who will learn from him. Accordingly, Jesus directly invites his hearers, and his readers, to enter into the rest that God once promised Moses (Ex 33:14: "My presence will go

[38]For a fuller discussion, see W. D. Davies and Dale C. Allison Jr., *The Gospel According to Saint Matthew* (3 vols.; ICC; Edinburgh: T & T Clark, 1988-1997), 2:272, 283-87, which provides the basis for the treatment offered here.

with you, and I will give you rest" [NRSV] or "[I] will lighten your burden" [NJPS]) by learning from his own gentleness and humility:

> Come to me, all you that are weary and are carrying heavy burdens, and I will give you rest. Take my yoke upon you, and learn from me; for I am gentle and humble in heart, and you will find rest for your souls. For my yoke is easy, and my burden is light. (Mt 11:28-30)

How, according to Jesus, might one see God "face to face"? Jesus drew to himself those who were least likely to claim knowledge of God, many of them social outcasts and sinners whose manner of life betrayed a scandalous absence of piety. Perhaps, then, failure to find God or a prior refusal to walk in God's ways is the first qualification for answering his invitation. But if this is so, surely it is in Jesus' own persistent graciousness with the confessedly wayward, heterodox, and lost that we glimpse the face of God. Jesus, in short, offers to take us personally where we cannot or will not go by ourselves—into God's presence—and generations of his followers confess that this is still where he leads.

Paul was one such disciple, a man whose intense zeal for God led to complicity in murder and, as he himself later viewed it, substantial misunderstanding of God's ways. Years later, Paul also recalls Exodus 33 to explain the manner in which Christ continually works to transform him and those to whom he writes. The first such reference, from his first letter to the Corinthians, comes in a passage that we have already noted briefly:

> For now we see in a mirror, dimly, but then we will see face to face. Now I know only in part; then I will know fully, even as I have been fully known (1 Cor 13:12).

Here Paul contends that full knowledge of God after the manner of Moses lies yet in the future, beyond the limitations of this world. Fortunately, however, that is not his last word on the subject, for in his second letter to the same congregation, the apostle all but contradicts himself:

> And all of us, with unveiled faces, seeing the glory of the Lord as though reflected in a mirror, are being transformed into the same image from

> one degree of glory to another; for this comes from the Lord, the Spirit. (2 Cor 3:18)

Here the reference to Moses is more explicit, as Paul develops an extended contrast between the glory that shone in Moses' face and the glory that transforms those who are filled with the Spirit of God. As with the passage from 1 Corinthians 13, here too Paul acknowledges that the glory that we behold is only glory "as though reflected in a mirror." In similar fashion, members of the Qumran community were said to reflect divine glory: "They have made you holy among your people, like a luminary [which lights up] the world with knowledge, and shines on the face of the Many" (1Q28b 5:27).[39] But for Paul, it is the exalted Jesus who most fully mirrors God's glory, and Jesus himself whom believers in turn reflect:

> For we do not proclaim ourselves; we proclaim Jesus Christ as Lord and ourselves as your slaves for Jesus' sake. For it is the God who said, "Let light shine out of darkness," who has shone in our hearts to give the light of the knowledge of the glory of God in the face of Jesus Christ. (2 Cor 4:5-6)

The purpose of Christian proclamation and teaching, says the apostle, is to present the One in whose face God's glory shines most brightly. As a result, those who behold such reflected glory are themselves "transformed" little by little through the agency of the indwelling Spirit that is the gift of the risen Christ.[40] Perhaps, therefore, Christian believers do not see God "face to face" as Moses is said to have done and as Jesus undoubtedly did. Nor do they reflect the full reality of God. Nevertheless, they are able to see Jesus, in whom God's glory, generosity, and goodness are made visible, and that sight alone is enough to change them (cf. Heb 2:9). Finding that the God of Jesus treats them with the very grace and compassion, forbearance and faithfulness, love and forgiveness that they most need is enough to inspire both devotion and imitation.

---

[39]Translation from García Martínez, *Dead Sea Scrolls*, 433.

[40]This motif is more fully discussed in Margaret E. Thrall, *A Critical and Exegetical Commentary on the Second Epistle to the Corinthians*, vol. 1, *Introduction and Commentary on II Corinthians I-VII* (ICC; Edinburgh: T & T Clark, 1994), 282-90.

This being the case, God's people may reflect heavenly glory not in shining faces only, but also in the deeper transformation of their lives according to the divine nature. This, surely, is the point that Paul wants to make: reflecting the reality of God is not a matter of outward appearance, but rather of deeper, inward change. The fact that such change occurs at all, and that God's character becomes visible, however partially and imperfectly, in flawed human beings is itself testimony to the reality of grace. It is, in the end, evidence that God is indeed "compassionate and gracious, slow to anger, and abounding in steadfast love and faithfulness, keeping steadfast love for thousands, forgiving iniquity and transgression and sin." To encounter this reality is to behold the face of God; to be transformed by it is the first step of our journey toward the full knowledge and presence of this God.

God of burning compassion,
look again upon the work of your hands,
that we might once more bear your image and reflect your likeness;
God of grace and mercy,
grant us favor in the eyes of those who hate us,
that we might be gracious in the same measure as you have shown us grace;
God of forbearance and long-suffering,
delay your judgment one more day,
that we might yet repent and make amends;
God of abundant, steadfast love,
keep covenant for another thousand generations,
that we might learn to imitate your acts of loving-kindness;
God of faithfulness and truth,
enable us to trust in your fidelity,
that we might be both faithful and trustworthy in your sight;
God of forgiveness,
absolve our iniquity, transgression, and sin,
that we might forgive others in the same measure as you have forgiven us;
God of righteousness and justice,
deliver others from the wrongs that we have done them,

that we in turn might forgo vengeance and find deliverance
from our suffering.
God of Abraham and Sarah, of Moses, and of all who turn to
you,
we bow down low in worship,
to celebrate your holy and life-giving Name.
If we have now found favor in your sight,
take us for your inheritance,
that we may reflect your glory and your grace,
through Jesus Christ, your well-beloved Son. *Amen.*

## Name and Subject Index

## Scripture Index